P9-ARJ-189

The Prodigal South Returns to Power

HARRY S. DENT

A WILEY-INTERSCIENCE PUBLICATION

JOHN WILEY & SONS, New York • Chichester • Brisbane • Toronto

Library of Congress Cataloging in Publication Data

Dent, Harry S   1930-
   The prodigal South returns to power.

   "A Wiley-Interscience publication."
   Includes index.
   1.   Political parties—Southern States. 2. Southern States—Politics and government—1951-
I. Title.

JK2295.AI3D46   329'.00975   77-25249
ISBN 0-471-03913-6

Printed in the United States of America

10 9 8 7 6 5 4 3 2

To my late Mother
Sallie
who inspired me always to try to do my best
and to my Wife
Betty
who is always exhorting me to be my best

Foreword

The author of this book is one of America's foremost political strategists and a highly respected expert on southern politics of recent vintage.

Harry Dent understands politics as well as anyone I know, and he is one of the finest practitioners of the political arts in the country today.

Harry made a major contribution to my candidacy, both in the nominating process and in the general election of 1976. I shall always appreciate the way he went the extra mile for me, as he has sought to do in all his efforts to establish a competitive two-party system in the South and to maintain a viable competitive political system nationally.

Harry's contributions to the political process go far beyond any single campaign. He also played key roles in the presidential campaigns of 1964, 1968, and 1972. Perhaps his greatest contribution to the country has been in working with other leaders to bring the South into the mainstream of modern American politics—an accomplishment the entire nation can welcome.

This book tells his inside story of many interesting and important events in the recent emergence of southern politics on the national political scene. Harry gives his own candid eyewitness accounts, observations, and opinions regarding these events, some of which are certain to generate debate and discussion. His eyewitness reports and personal views should prove to be very valuable to students of American government and politics in evaluating, debating, and writing the history of the exciting times of the 1960s and 1970s.

Not having witnessed all these events myself, I am not in a position to endorse Harry's version of the various happenings. However, I am certainly in general agreement with his recommendations for broadening the base of the Republican party. We Republicans must be more practical about the issues and challenges of the day. We must advocate and implement effective solutions to basic needs and desires of the people we seek to serve and lead within the framework of our conservative and compassionate philosophy designed to maintain freedom, justice, and equality before the law for all our people in a world dedicated to peaceful resolution of international problems.

GERALD R. FORD

August 1977

Acknowledgments

Permission to reprint the following material is gratefully acknowledged.

Quotation, pp. 37–40: from David Keene, in *The Alternative*, November 1976.

Quotation, pp. 85–86: from Rowland Evans, in *Evans-Novak*, July 28, 1976.

Quotation, pp. 87–88: from Lewis Chester, Godfrey Hodgson, and Bruce Page, *An American Melodrama: The Presidential Campaign of 1968*, Viking Press, New York, 1969, pp. 454–455. Copyright © 1969 by Times Newspapers Ltd. Reprinted by permission of the Viking Press.

Quotation, pp. 111–112: from *The Charlotte Observer*, September 13, 1968.

Quotation, p. 115–116: from Hugh Gibson, in *The Charleston News & Courier*, November 7, 1968.

Quotation, p. 175–176: from Patrick Buchanan, *Conservative Votes, Liberal Victories*, Quadrangle Books, New York, 1975, pp. 49–50.

Quotation, pp. 180: from *The Washington Post*, October 23, 1971.

Quotation, pp. 181: from Don Bacon, in *The Washington Evening Star*, May 17, 1971.

Quotation, p. 214–215: from *The Washington Evening Star*, May 23, 1973.

Quotation, p. 221–222, from William Safire, *Before the Fall: An Inside View of the Pre-Watergate White House*, Doubleday, New York, 1975, p. 203.

Quotation, p.233–235: from Stewart Alsop, in *Newsweek*, April 9, 1974. © 1974 by Newsweek, Inc. All rights reserved. Reprinted by permission.

Quotation, p. 236; from Theodore White, *Breach of Faith,* Atheneum
    Publishers/Readers Digest Press, ©1975 Theodore H. White, pp. 87,
    88, reprinted by permission.

Quotation, pp. 247-250: from *The National Journal,* April 22, 1972.

Quotation, p. 298-299: from Jerry terHorst, in *The Detroit News,* 1976.

Quotation, pp. 291-293: from Everett Carll Ladd, Jr., "The Democrats
    Have Their Own Two-Party System," *Fortune,* October 1977.

The author is grateful to many friends for advice, contributions, and other
assistance in making this book possible. Among those are Dr. Richard Brannon, LaRose Smith, Alex McCullough, Robert King, John Calhoun, Essie
Baker, Ben Hammet, Dr. Charles Dunn, my faithful secretary, Lynn Dillard,
and Rev. Wallace Henley whose papers on the work of the Cabinet Committee on Education (Chapter 6) were very valuable. My thanks go also to the
South Carolina Republican Party, Senator Strom Thurmond, President
Nixon, and President Ford for providing tremendous opportunities and experiences in the fascinating game of politics, which I have enjoyed and now
leave to others to carry on.

H. S. D.

Contents

battle for Mississippi's votes. The struggle over Mississippi caused Reagan to make his controversial vice-presidential selection in advance, and the Mississippi convention actions were the most crucial breaks for Ford at the closely contested convention.

The story of how the South's new Republican party came into being and made its way to kingmaker role in 1968.

Much like Carter in 1976, the southern GOP came up with a plan to make the difference in the 1968 Republican convention and the general election. The story of the evolution and successful implementation of this plan is related in this chapter—how Reagan was stopped to nominate Nixon and how the Wallace tide was rolled back to elect Nixon.

It fell to Nixon to desegregate the South. The story of how he peaceably accomplished this feat and gained southern support is one of the most overlooked but interesting stories of the Nixon presidency.

During Nixon's first term he was working to win both the Wallace vote and the black vote for 1972. Strangely, the author, while giving his prime attention to the Wallace vote and to Wallace himself, was also assisting with the black vote efforts in modifying the southern strategy to be all-inclusive in seeking both black and white votes in Dixie. This chapter tells the story of how the Nixon team worked both sides of the race question in trying to put together its New Majority for the future.

Chapter 8   Nixon Delivers on Busing, Textiles, the Court, and Vietnam

Nixon had a deliberate plan to please the South. It was political and ideological, with a feeling of a special kinship. The author tells how and why this plan worked and also the impact it had on key decisions affecting the Nixon presidency.

Chapter 9   CREEP—From Perfection to Disaster

The 1972 Nixon campaign was the best planned and executed presidential campaign in history except for one item—Watergate. The disastrous excesses of the Committee to Re-elect the President, derisively called CREEP, are all that is remembered about CREEP. Yet, otherwise, it was a masterful performance by the CREEP leaders and planners. The author was a planner and leader and gives the inside story of the successful side of CREEP. He also gives his assessment of the other side and its victims.

Chapter 10   Plans for a Successor

Nixon had a plan for continuing his policies with the man who most impressed him in his Administration. This is the story of that plan and how it was thwarted at the last minute. This all revolves around Agnew, Connally, and Ford and Nixon's relationship with each. The author played a part in the plan for Nixon's successor, as it was concerned with the southern strategy.

Chapter 11   W(h)ither GOP?

The author candidly discusses the problems and pluses of the Grand Old Party and offers his suggestions for a more realistic and flexible party for the future.

Name Index

The
Prodigal South
Returns to Power

Introduction

I n 1924 Senator Coleman L. Blease, Democrat of South Carolina, was alarmed to learn that Calvin Coolidge had won 1123 of 50,131 votes cast in South Carolina in the presidential race.

"I do not know where he got them," Blease supposedly said. "I was astonished to know they were cast and shocked to know they were counted."

The Republican party in the South and also Jimmy Carter's party have both come a long way in a short period of time. GOP votes are being counted in Dixie, and Republicans are actually winning political contests. And a "good ole southern boy" is installed at 1600 Pennsylvania Avenue as the "head knocker."

This book tells the unusual and interesting story of the return of the old Confederate States of America from the role of prodigal son to favorite son in American presidential politics.

Long a sleeping giant and the political and economic stepchild of the nation, the South has now become the balance of power in presidential politics and is well on the way to becoming the new political, economic, and population power base of the nation. Kirkpatrick Sale, a liberal Yankee professor, has recorded the shifting of power from the once strong Northeast to the rising new forces in the Southeast and Southwest in his 1975 book, *Power Shift*. Sale refers to the "Southern Rim" of states stretching from southern California to Virginia, closely paralleling what conservative author and columnist Kevin Phillips called the "Sunshine Belt" in his 1969 book, *The Emerging Republican Majority*.

The late President Lyndon B. Johnson, in part a Southerner and also a Westerner, opined in his memoirs that a Southerner could not lead the nation in unity because of inherent bias against southern manners and mores. In his book, *Vantage Point*, Johnson wrote: "I was not thinking just of the derisive articles about my style, my clothes, my manner, my accent and my family . . . I was also thinking of a more deep-seated and far-reaching attitude—a disdain for the South that seems to be woven into the fabric of Northern experience."

British historian Denis Brogan called this the "damnosa hereditas" of the South—a curse for what southern historian George B. Tindall describes as "the burden of Southern history: the poverty, the habits of defeat and failure, the guilt of racial oppression that bound white and black in a common tragedy."

What is it that has brought the South back to national prominence, prestige, and power after more than a century of stepchild status? The prime answer is political: the reintroduction of two-party competition in southern politics and the peaceful and honorable resolution of the South's age-old bugaboo, its racial problem.

3

From my various positions inside the southern political wars from 1964-1976, I have been able to reach back into many rich and exciting experiences to relate from the Republican side the fascinating story of the rerising of Dixie as a political power.

Strangely enough, two of America's most enigmatic presidents, the thirty-seventh, Richard Nixon; and the thirty-ninth, Jimmy Carter, are the leading contributors to the dramatic change in American politics. On the Republican side I worked with many people in key supporting roles, including Mississippi GOP leader Clarke Reed. On the Democratic side, the most effective helpers have been Carter's inner-circle brain trust of Charles Kirbo, Hamilton Jordan, and Jody Powell. After all, they have pulled off the southern miracle of modern times.

The "Republican Southern Strategy" is more responsible, however, for the South's political resurgence because it preceded the Carter strategy and, in fact, laid the groundwork for Carter's eventual acceptance as a southern candidate for president.

Two-party competitive politics was spurred by the Thurmond defection to the Republican party in 1964 and the vital part played by southern Republicans in providing the necessary margin for Nixon's 1968 nomination and election. We stopped the southern bandwagon for Governor George Wallace's 1968 presidential try and elected a man destined to handle the sensitive desegregation of the South with the velvet-glove approach required to avert bayonets, bullets, and bloodshed.

Former President Nixon, in one of his crowning achievements, brought the South through the throes of desegregation in the manner that enabled it to face up to its duty with relative honor. Simultaneously, Nixon initiated a desegregation program for the rest of the country. The peaceable desegregation of the South changed Dixie's national image and then cast other parts of the United States as being more segregated, or less honorable, than the prodigal Dixie had proved to be in facing its responsibilities. I sensed this change when I was speaking to GOP groups over the country as Nixon's southern adviser during 1971 and 1972. In 1969 and 1970, there was concern whether I would be a political liability speaking above the Mason-Dixon line because of my southern background and accent. All that changed with the evolution of the South's new image and national acceptance.

Thus we Republicans made Dixie politics competitive again, and the president we nominated and elected in 1968 changed the South's national image with his approach to desegregation.

All of this made it easier for a Deep-South governor to embark on a successful mission to seek and win the Democratic nomination for president, and eventually, the general election—the first time a southern son had been elected president in 128 years.

The "Democratic Southern Strategy" was thrust upon the party and accepted only reluctantly. Yet it was probably the only way the Democrats could successfully reconstitute the old Roosevelt coalition of the 1930s and win over an incumbent Republican president, Gerald R. Ford, running on an appealing record of peace, prosperity, and public trust. The new Republican frontier in the South was beginning to compensate for sagging Republican fortunes in previous Midwest and Northeast strongholds. The only realistic answer to the new GOP inroads in Dixie was to trump the GOP's ace with a royal flush—like nominating a "good ole southern boy" to top the Democratic ticket in 1976. It could not have been better if it had been planned by the Democratic party chiefs in Washington. Indeed, it was planned; but against their will. The plan was devised by the brash Carter and his small core of what was assumed to be "Georgia crackers." And with the dissipation of most bias against the South elsewhere in the country, shrewd planning by Carter, and a little luck a la Hubert Humphrey's 1976 indecision, the Democratic Southern Strategy was born and blossomed into an important national victory for the Democratic party.

So now a Southerner is in the White House. Again, the vital difference in the close election was made in the South.

It is ironic that two competing southern strategies, the Republican and Democratic versions, should become the center-stage attraction in national politics. They are die-hard competitors and are bottomed on different political philosophies. The GOP strategy is dedicated to the conservative approach of less government through more southern influence in national affairs.

The Democratic strategy is dedicated to the opposite end: the liberal approach of more government through the influence on national politics of what is called "New South" politics. Thus both seek to magnify the political power of the South—and they have—but to differing ends. These opposing approaches reflect the different constituencies of the two competing strategies.

In these pages, I have sought to reveal from an insider's view the evolution of the Republican strategy from the early 1960s through its successes to its defeat in the 1976 presidential election. I began plotting a GOP southern strategy while working as administrative assistant to then- Democratic Senator Strom Thurmond in 1964. Plotting with me was another Thurmond staffer,

J. Fred Buzhardt Jr., later to become general counsel of the Defense Department and counsel to President Nixon.

In the summer of 1964 Buzhardt and I helped convince Thurmond to switch parties and fight for Goldwater. Then there I was running a special southern operation for the Goldwater campaign. The next time I was commanding another southern operation—this time for Nixon. And then, I was suddenly sitting in the White House with the lofty title of Special Counsel to the President of the United States of America. My job was to serve as political liaison between the president and all Republican organizations in the country. In addition, I was Nixon's adviser on any matter affecting the South. They called me the southern strategist, or as *Time* magazine reported, "the Southern-fried Rasputin" in "Uncle Strom's Cabin."

When I arrived at 1600 Pennsylvania Avenue on January 20, 1969, I was the stepchild appointment of the Nixon Administration, because I possessed all the southern accouterments: a full-bred southern white boy, replete with accent, birthplace (in John C. Calhoun County), a political godfather named Thurmond and a Dixie-style plan for saving America for the cause of freedom.

As a 38-year-old father of four, I was convinced that what was good for the South was good for the cause of freedom, a wilting Republican party, and the new president who had honored me with such a nice title. This was the basis on which, as South Carolina GOP chairman, I had sold a "southern strategy" to citizen Nixon in 1966 while he was campaigning for congressional candidates in Columbia, South Carolina.

As can be discerned in these pages, I advocated the continuation of this plan during the years 1969-1972 from my perch in the Nixon White House. In part, the strategy contributed to historic results in two respects—the largest presidential election margin ever and a GOP victory in every southern state for the first time, and by a 70 percent margin, an achievement which may never be repeated.

Supposedly, Joseph Alsop, one of America's most distinguished journalists, coined the term "southern strategy." As William Safire explains in his book, *The New Language of Politics,* Alsop applied the term to the presidential campaign of Senator Barry Goldwater in 1964 when the conservative candidate won in the South and lost overwhelmingly in the nation.

It is fitting that the term "southern strategy" should have been coined in the Goldwater campaign of 1964 because that campaign planted the seed for a radical new direction in national politics, leading to a conversion of Democratic Dixie into a new Republican heartland for presidential elections. For almost a century the Old South had been taken for granted by the Democrats and ignored by the Republicans. The reason for the treatment stemmed from Reconstruction and the foul taste the Radical Republicans of the 1860s left in southern pallets for generations.

Finally in 1964, the Republican party nominated a presidential candidate who stood more with the South than the rest of the country. Ironically, a Southerner, President Lyndon B. Johnson of Texas, was the nominee of the Democratic party. However, LBJ was perceived by Southerners as being anti-South, as was his party—even more so than the 1948 campaign of the late President Harry S. Truman.

The South's unofficial slogan, "Don't Tread on Me," was being violated by the "party of our fathers." However, the "party of reconstruction" was now giving southern voters "a choice, not an echo."

From the ashes of the 1964 defeat, there emerged what the late Napoleon Hill of South Carolina calls "the seed of benefit." Hill, the author of many books on human motivation, taught his theory that from every tragedy there is the "seed of benefit" when one searched properly for it.

The "seed of benefit" in the 1964 Goldwater debacle was sought for by us southern Republicans. It was found in the rise and development of a competitive two-party system in the South. Suddenly, Republicans started springing up and covering Dixie like the dew. From the new political system in the South came fresh hope and victories for a national Republican party that was heading the way of the old Whig party elsewhere in the country.

Down South, we new Republicans were first concerned about saving America from the leftward gallop of the Democratic donkey. The national Republican party was seen as the best vehicle.

Second, we Goldwater Southerners wanted a "new day" for Dixie and the South's battered image up North. As President Franklin D. Roosevelt proclaimed in 1937, "The South is the nation's No. 1 economic problem." The only time any president had come South was seemingly to purge or punish any southern legislator who voted too southernish or too much against New Deal court packing and other FDR legislative programs.

We wanted to see the Yankee candidates come down South and at least curtsey during election time by visiting Dixieland and wooing southern folks.

Southern strategy made all this possible. National political leaders now crisscross Dixie and speak in eloquent terms of states' rights (as did Vice President Nelson Rockefeller in 1975). Instead of a never-never land politically, the South became a national political battle ground.

Following the unprecedented victory in 1972, the South's hero, Richard Nixon, became engulfed in the biggest and most publicized political scandal in American history. This book touches on this tragic story and some of its characters and victims. All of these events had their impact on the Grand Old Party's fortunes nationally, including independent Dixie.

This book tells the story of the wooing and winning of the old confederate states from the early 1960s through the 1976 presidential campaign as seen through my eyes as a southern boy who wanted to help the South rise again in national politics.

My southern thinking came naturally. I was the last of five sons born to a middle-class family in the rural southern town of St. Matthews, with a population of 2500, mostly black and almost totally Democratic when I was growing up there from 1930 to 1947, the year I finished St. Matthews High School.

A great-uncle, John the Baptist Prickett, editor of the local weekly newspaper, once kayoed a fellow townsman for calling him a "Republican S.O.B." When the protestor recovered consciousness, he asked puzzlingly: "John, why did you get so mad about just being called an S.O.B.?" Prickett angrily snapped, "But you called me a *Republican* S.O.B.!"

Such was the odious nature of the term "Republican" in small town Deep-South circles, especially in the black belt.

Yet as I grew into young manhood, the term came to mean something different from Reconstruction. Like Thurmond and Buzhardt, I came to understand that national Republicans stood more in line with our political thinking—for individual freedom versus government coercion, for free enterprise versus the trend toward socialism, for a strong national defense, and in opposition to the principal enemy of all these— communism.

We saw all this first in the Citizens for Eisenhower movement in South Carolina in 1952; and then in the U.S. Senate in 1955 when Thurmond became a U.S. senator, and Buzhardt and I became his top aides from the mid-1950s to the mid-1960s.

The Southern strategy we envisioned was designed to fashion the ends of southern power in the executive councils of the national government to compensate for the diminishing southern power on Capitol Hill. Old-time southern leaders had learned long ago that any minority must stand together and use every ounce of available power to just keep minority heads above water. The blacks have become masters of this tactic today.

The aim of southern strategy was not rule or ruin, but to have the South treated just like any other section of the USA—not to be looked up to, only to be seen on a par; not to impose the southern will, but to have it considered without regard to preconceived notions about the southern states and their people.

In a sense, the plan was to get non-Southerners to understand what Wilbur Cash called in his classic work on southern politics, *The Mind of the South.*

Nixon came to understand the southern mind during his law school days at Duke University in Durham, North Carolina. It was much the same as he had felt in his own life—not too handsome, coming out of poverty, and feeling put upon by those in authority.

By understanding the southern mind and how to approach southern problems, Nixon created a political base in the region that even today, with his problems, gives him a residual base of sympathy and understanding.

In 1976 a man who also understood the southern mind from his 25 years of service in the U.S. House of Representatives miscued initially in handling the southern Republicans when he became president and almost lost his party's nomination at their hands while sitting in the Oval Office. President Ford later lost the general election to the newer Southern Strategy of Jimmy Carter.

I became intimately involved in the Ford campaign from May 1976 through the election. As with Nixon, I was tabbed as this president's southern strategist. However, this time I fought against many of my old southern GOP allies, including Thurmond, in the 1976 Ford-Reagan nomination struggle. My job was to corral all the vital uncommitted southern delegate votes possible at the Kansas City GOP convention to again stave off a Reagan threat the same as in 1968 at that year's Miami convention. In the end, these votes were important to the nomination outcome.

From Kansas City, it was back to South Carolina and helping President Ford try to close the mammoth gap of favorite son Carter all across the South. We did make remarkable progress, but not enough to overcome the new monolithic black voting strength and the Carter regional appeal. As the South went, so went the election, and for the moment, the GOP's southern strategy as well.

This is the story of the GOP's southern strategy—from whence it came in the explosive 1960s to where it may go from here forward as affected by the Carter presidency and the ideological battle for the future heart of the Grand Old Party.

Included in this story are my candid views on the problems plaguing the Republican party, especially in the South. Also, I have added my concerns about politics in general based on my up-close observations at all levels— local, state, and national. Again, I am candid, not with the idea of creating a cynical view of politics, but rather with a better insight for those outside politics who wonder if this area is as bad as the public suspects.

I hope you find the material interesting and worthwhile. You may not agree with all of my views, but I assure you the events and anecdotes are as I perceived and believed them to be.

1
Swing High, Swing Low

The Southern Strategy of Harry Dent was shot full of holes." This was the exultant cry of Russ Marane, Jimmy Carter's campaign manager in South Carolina, on the day following the 1976 presidential election.

Southern Democratic leaders had reason to crow loud with the southern roosters as the sun was rising on the morning of November 3, 1976. A small margin of 56 votes in conservative Mississippi, a state that had not voted Democratic in a presidential election since 1956, was putting the Democratic presidential nominee over the top in the electoral vote count.

NBC News flashed the magic number on the TV screen at 4 A.M., showing Jimmy Carter to be the next president. Southern Democrats felt a huge sense of relief. Not only had they put a Democrat back in the White House, but they believed they had finally stiff-armed the GOP's specter of southern strategy, which had embarrassed southern Democrats at the polls rather consistently since 1964. And the squeeze was not only being felt in the presidential contests, but had been moving down to the local level, at the heart of the southern Democratic power base—the courthouses. The new Democratic Southern Strategy fashioned by Jimmy Carter had come through in the nick of time.

While my arch rivals were celebrating many southern Republicans were crying. Oh how sweet it had been—a decade of steady progress in developing our two-party beachhead in the South!

I thought back to our moment of greatest triumph just four years earlier.

This was on the morning of November 8, 1972. Richard Nixon and his inner circle awoke to headlines proclaiming the biggest presidential election victory in American history—more votes than even "Landslide" Lyndon Johnson had garnered in his massive triumph over Senator Barry Goldwater in 1964. While Nixon, H.R. Haldeman, John Ehrlichman, and company gloated over the national results, I was pointing out to all who would listen in the White House a more significant result of the 1972 presidential election. The Solid South had voted solidly for the first time in history for the Republican nominee for president and by an average vote of 70 percent. In all the White House celebration this vital point of history was being overlooked.

Initially, only President Nixon and I, of all the others present at the time, seemed to appreciate the point. We had concentrated the most on achieving a Solid South through our southern strategy. However, the work of the southern coup spread rapidly around the inner councils, and even the in-house skeptics of southern strategy were now rejoicing over the historic feat, as well as over the national scorecard.

With this electoral coup, we South Carolina Republicans in Columbia had control from the top to the bottom. We had the presidency, the senior

U.S. senator, the congressman from our district, the county council, the school board, and a good chunk of our state legislative delegation. In 1974 we were to top it all off with the election of our first Republican governor since Reconstruction.

Realistically, however, on November 3, 1976, we had to face the new facts of life. This was another election, and we had been clobbered nationally and locally.

In sweeping the South except for Virginia, Carter had left us southern Republicans pondering the question of whether all we had worked for might be gone. We had figured we would never be able to equal the Nixon 70 percent score on 1972. Now we wondered whether even 50.1 percent would be possible?

The Democrats had finally come up with a southern strategy of their own, even though reluctantly. The national Democratic leaders had tried as best they could to scuttle the Carter dream of a reunited Democratic South putting him in the White House as the first Southerner since President Zachary Taylor in 1848.

In unseating incumbent President Ford in the closest Electoral College battle since 1916, Carter won only because he reclaimed many southern states, which had not voted Democratic for president in 20 or more years.

While Republicans had been winning southern states in recent years with substantial white votes, the Democrats prevailed in the South with a nigh-solid black vote, coupled with an increased minority of white votes, primarily from the lower socio-economic stratum. What made a key difference for the Carter-Mondale ticket was the record turnout of black voters in Dixie. They saved Carter in the South, and the South won the election for Carter.

The *Washington Post* reported on November 4, 1976, that voting was down in the 1976 general election, as had been projected by the pollsters. However, 14 states showed an increase. Ten of these were in the South, where voting records were set in some states, such as South Carolina. There approximately 800,000 of 1.1 million registered voters, 72 percent, participated. This topped the 1972 record by 100,000, as recorded in the *State*, November 4.

Carter's own state of Georgia showed a big increase with a turnout of 43 percent of the adult voting age population, compared to 30.3 percent in 1960. Louisiana had the largest increase of all states with 51.7 percent in 1976, compared to 44.3 percent in 1972.

The upsurge in black voting can be attributed to the Voting Rights Act of 1964 and the black preference not only for the Democratic nominee, but especially for a southern Democratic nominee.

During my time in the Nixon White House I was requested numerous times to speak to black audiences. In honoring these requests, I learned from various blacks that they trust southern whites more than they did even their professing allies among northern whites.

Three other ingredients in the black voting record were the voter registration and turnout efforts by organized labor and the Democratic party, the President Ford Committee assumption that no more or less than 10 percent of black votes could be had, and the last-minute effort by a controversial black minister to integrate Carter's family church in Plains, Georgia. The church incident spurred black Carter support by the belief that the effort was a Republican "dirty trick." It gave Carter the opportunity to explain again how he and his family had tried to desegregate their Baptist church in the mid-1960s.

The Ford Committee strategists, pinched by campaign fund limitations, gave their black vote effort a much lower priority than did Nixon in 1972 when he captured more than twice the black vote Ford received.

Strangely, two voices speaking loudest on the Ford Steering Committee in favor of a stronger black vote effort were Robert J. (Bob) Brown and me. Brown was Nixon's key black in the White House. He and I worked together on black voter efforts during Nixon's first term. Both of us are Southerners, he from High Point, North Carolina; and I from Columbia, South Carolina. We formed the White House Prayer Breakfast group together. In addition, we made many joint appearances before black groups, at the instigation of Brown. Together we worked to place many blacks in Nixon Administration positions.

Initially, Brown and I were the only two Deep-South members of the president's general election steering committee. In every meeting we advocated a better black voter program. The comments were echoed by others on the committee. However, the limited program was miniscule compared to Brown's efforts prior to and during the 1972 Nixon campaign.

I particularly proposed letting black leader Arthur Fletcher from the White House staff head up a black speakers' program. There is no more effective, entertaining, or inspiring speaker, black or white, than Fletcher. I also suggested Brown be put in command of the black voter division. In 1972 black leaders from all over the country had overflowed the mammoth Washington Hilton ballroom in a sickle cell anemia fund- raising dinner in honor of Brown. His influence with black leaders in America was truly amazing for a black Republican.

The pleas were made in the presence of campaign chiefs Rogers Morton, Jim Baker, Stu Spencer, and the president himself.

After a White House dinner for the steering committee, Baker, the campaign chairman, revealed the black vote strategy to me when he confided from one white to another that "the black vote would be 10 percent, regardless."

This conclusion was one of the few mistakes made by the Ford strategists in the general election.

The vital black vote also illustrated the expertise of the southern Democratic parties in training black voters to pull the master lever for straight party voting at the expense of GOP local candidates. In fact, the blacks have become the shock troops who keep the Democratic officeholders in command of the southern courthouses and legislatures.

The Washington-based black political study group, the Joint Center for Political Studies (JCPS), calculates that 70 percent of the registered black voters cast ballots and that 94 percent of them voted for Carter. JCPS estimated there were 9.5 million blacks registered in 1976 and that 6.6 million of them voted. The increase in voter registration for 1976 represented 750,000 more than in 1972 as reported in the *Washington Post,* November 5, 1976.

JCPS figures showed a 58 percent black turnout in 1972, with 87 percent voting for Senator George McGovern, the 1972 Democratic nominee for president.

The percentage of black votes for Carter varied little in the southern states. In South Carolina, the estimate was 98 percent. This is illustrated in Richland County (Columbia, South Carolina) voting precincts. In Ward 9 and Greenview precincts, which are 98 percent black in registration, Carter and local Democratic candidates won 98 percent of Greenview and 97 percent in Ward 9. In low-state Orangeburg County, the Democrats garnered 98 percent in Suburban Ward 1, where black registration was 98 percent.

The blacks thus made the difference in many states, including all of the southern states, except Virginia, the only one to vote for Ford.

A postelection analysis by Kevin Phillips in his February 4, 1977, issue of *The American Political Report* credits "poor" whites with the key role in putting Carter over the top. Here is Phillips' analysis:

State	Most-shifting County	1972 GOP %	1976 GOP %	Shift	Intrastate Geographic-Demographic Description
N.J.	Cumberland	59%	42%	−17	South Jersey rural-smalltown*
Pa.	Greene	57	38	−19	SW Pa. Appalachian WASP*
Md.	Dorchester	76	51	−25	Chesapeake Bay smalltown rural*
W. Va.	Wyoming	64	32	−32	Southern poor white coal area*
Va.	Franklin	67	35	−32	Rural Appalachian-Southside*
N.C.	Columbus	72	23	−49	SE coastal poor white*
Ky.	Marshall	60	27	−33	SW "Little Dixie"*
Tenn.	Lake	68	23	−45	West Tennessee rural white
Ala.	Lawrence	76	18	−48	Tennessee Valley white rural*
Miss.	Tippah	88	31	−57	Poor white NE foothills*
Fla.	Holmes	93	37	−56	NW Panhandle "Cracker" Country*
Texas	Delta	62	21	−41	East Texas-Sulphur River Delta
Okla.	Atoka	74	25	−49	SE farm-coal area (poor white)*
Mo.	Dunklin	68	32	−36	SE "Boot" rural area*
Ill.	Massac	70	45	−25	"Little Egypt" poor white*
Ind.	Owen	70	48	−22	Southern Indiana rural WASP*
Ohio	Meigs	71	48	−23	Ohio River- Appalachian*
Iowa	Ringgold	69	46	−23	South Iowa WASP (poor farms)*

* This was also state's general region of *worst* GOP decline.

In the case of Jimmy Carter's narrow victory, group after group claims to have provided the critical margin—labor, Chicanos, blacks, fundamentalists, Southerners. Different yardsticks will yield different results, of course . . . in raw percentages, blacks did best by Carter. But in terms of 1972 electoral group shifts, by far the biggest came among Southern and Border state poor whites. By contrast, affluent suburbanites and upper-middle-income professionals in many areas did almost as well by Ford as by Nixon in 1972. Catholics were probably only 5-10 percentage points less supportive. Ford's black percentage was only a few points lower than Nixon's. Overall, black turnout ballots—either via slightly increased turnout or 1972-76 party shifting—were only a minor factor in the Republican presidential vote plummet from 61% in 1972 to 48% in 1976. *The real key lay in the working-class and lower-middle-class constituencies—perhaps 15% of the national electorate — routinely ignored by Gerald Ford-type Establishment Republicanism.* Using *unofficial* 1976 figures, APR has checked key states and calculated the county in each with the heaviest 1972–76 GOP vote fall-off . . . they are *all* rural or smalltown WASP areas.

The Carter pull at the top of the ticket caused some erosion of GOP officeholding across the South.

The Republicans dropped from 3 to 2 governors in the old confederate states, from 6 to 5 U.S. Senate seats, and held even at 27 seats in the U.S. House. The GOP losses were heavier in local offices.

In effect, the Democratic Southern Strategy stymied the progress the GOP Southern Strategy had compiled at the national, state, and local level since 1964. Carter had, indeed, "shot full of holes" the GOP's southern strategy so far as the White House was concerned. Under the delegate apportionment formula for the 1980 Republican National Convention, the southern Republicans will move from the highest to the lowest number of delegates since the area suffered officeholder losses and only carried one state for president.

The Democratic Southern Strategy victory of 1976 contrasted sharply with the southern GOP triumphs of 1968 and 1972. Southern Republicans were credited with key roles in Nixon's two presidential wins. Thus where there were joyful sounds on the Republican side election nights in 1968 and 1972, there was gloom in 1976.

2
Reagan
versus
Ford

J erry Ford should not feel too kindly toward the South. Southern Republicans almost denied the incumbent president his party's nomination. In the general election, it was the electoral votes of southern states, almost solid, that destined Ford to be recorded in history as the only unelected president.

Yet Ford was a friend to the South in his service as a congressman from far-off Grand Rapids, Michigan, as vice-president, and as president. He never displayed an anti-South bias, and his voting record in Congress was decidedly conservative, to the South's liking.

The nomination for an incumbent president, even an unelected one, should not have been so difficult. For Ford, however, there were two problems: Ronald Reagan's frustrated desires left over from his abortive 1968 nomination try and Ford's political advisers who seemingly refused to understand the Reagan threat and the difference between a primary season and the general election.

The essence of the Ford problem was the failure to see the Republican party realistically as the conservative party it is. Two former defense secretaries, Melvin Laird and Donald Rumsfeld, perceived the party as being more centrist, in accord with their desires.

While in the Nixon White House, I was the president's political liaison to all Republican organizations, including the various state parties. I spoke in almost every state to GOP groups. What amazed me most was the basic conservatism I found everywhere I appeared. Even in liberal Connecticut I found myself defending U.S. Senator Lowell Weicker for his liberal voting record against Nixon Administration proposals. I was meeting with 300 leaders of the state Republican party and wincing all through my defense of Weicker.

I also found in speaking to Republican audiences that the more I turned up my southern accent and invoked the name of my former boss, Senator Thurmond, the better was my reception. The same was true regarding conservative rhetoric. Previously, I had assumed the conservative Republicans were located primarily in the South. My speaking tours in 1971 and 1972 convinced me conservatives predominated at the organizational level in the great majority of the states.

Give a Republican a choice of Goldwater or Reagan versus almost any other Republican, and the purist yearning in his heart is difficult to suppress.

Ford mistake No. 1 to the conservatives was his early decision as president to select the nemesis of most conservative Republicans as vice-president: former Governor Nelson Rockefeller of New York.

The John Birch Society maintains that the descending order of evils confronting America and the cause of freedom are (1) the Council on Foreign

Relations (CFR), (2) the Rockefeller family; and (3) the Communist party. Supposedly, the CFR and the Rockefellers are manipulating the Communist party for their own selfish ends. Thus the ultraconservatives had to challenge Ford for this the original of his political sins as president.

Next, came the unpopular decision to grant amnesty to Vietnam War resisters on a case-by-case basis. Many conservatives saw this as unpatriotic until they heard Carter advocate blanket pardons for all draft resisters without any hearings.

The third big Ford act, and most unpopular, the pardoning of Nixon, hardly affected his standing with the conservatives. If anything, this was a plus with conservative Republicans.

Another point of consternation to conservative, and especially southern Republicans, was Ford's announced intention to sign into law a compromise bill permitting common situs picketing by labor unions. This was later ameliorated when the president reversed his stance under Reagan cajoling, and his secretary of labor resigned in protest over the veto that finally came. Reagan cited this effectively with conservatives even after Ford switched positions.

A constant irritant to Republican conservatives was Kissinger and his very high profile in Africa, especially against South Africa's white government policies. I urged several times that Kissinger's statements and actions be muffled. Even though the Ford operatives, particularly Cheney, seemed to understand, Ford evidently did not slow Kissinger down until convention time—almost too late for political purposes.

I later learned from my contacts with Ford that he felt strongly about the timeliness of the Kissinger statements and actions regarding black Africa, which he favored.

Contributing to the conservative dismay with Ford were the key administration appointments being credited chiefly to recommendations of Ford chief of staff, Don Rumsfeld. The appointments, coming from the Chicago area, were dubbed the "Chicago Mafia."

These appointees were considered to be on the liberal and/or nonpolitical side, such as Attorney General Edward Levi. Rumsfeld had been most remembered as head of Nixon's Office of Economic Opportunity. Instead of working to dismantle OEO, the government program most despised by Republican conservatives, Rumsfeld had seemingly run counter to Nixon's wishes in fighting on Capitol Hill to keep the program going.

Thus the appearance was created that Rumsfeld was running the domestic side for Ford, while Kissinger was in charge on foreign affairs.

The next major action disconcerting to conservatives was the firing of Defense Secretary James Schlesinger, a brilliant hardliner, in favor of Rumsfeld in what was considered a Kissinger coup. Rumsfeld soon proved to be Kissinger's nemesis and a more effective hard-line defense secretary. However, his move to the Pentagon did little to change fixed conservative concerns about the Rumsfeld desire to become Ford's vice- president, and eventually the 1980 presidential nominee.

In spring 1975, Rumsfeld invited me to visit with him. I welcomed the opportunity because all my earlier admonitions to White House aides of lesser importance regarding the growing conservative move to replace Ford with Reagan had not penetrated upward to Rumsfeld and Ford.

When I walked into the old Haldeman office, Rumsfeld was very hospitable. I had assumed he wanted my advice about the president's political strategy. Instead, I soon realized I was there to be politicked in favor of Rumsfeld's vice-presidential hopes. The idea I perceived was that I might be the link to southern GOP conservatives to pave the way for acceptance of Rumsfeld as Rockefeller's replacement.

Rumsfeld told me how close he had come to being selected by Ford as vice-president. He said the choice was down to Rockefeller, George Bush, and Rumsfeld. All three names were submitted to the FBI. However, Bush and Rumsfeld raised slight questions because of an ill- informed effort to connect them to the 1970 secret White House fund for GOP U.S. Senate candidates. Several of Nixon's top White House aides had some contact with the fund program, then being investigated by the special prosecutor; and Bush had received some of the "Operation Townhouse" funds.

Rumsfeld left me with the impression he was Ford's choice; but "Operation Townhouse" questions had caused him to be passed by, and also Bush, the man who had been my first choice.

Even though Rumsfeld was not on the conservatives' most admired list, his selection, and especially, that of Bush, probably would have defused the Reagan challenge. Only Rockefeller could have catalyzed the conservatives to fuel the Reagan drive to the point of finally being launched.

Ironically, had the conservatives been more tolerant of Rockefeller, hindsight now indicates his presence on the Ford ticket might have made the vital difference on November 2, particularly regarding New York's crucial 41 electoral votes.

Rumsfeld did consider one of my suggestions for trying to head off the Reagan challenge. He hired my friend and former preacher, Richard Brannon, in part to be a liaison with southern Republicans. I explained that the

Republican leaders were accustomed to having a political liaison service in the White House, as I had provided for Nixon. This was especially true for the Southerners.

However, Ford's White House operatives never did get an effective liaison operation going. Brannon was even discouraged from making the contacts needed to win the favor of southern GOP leaders. This ignoring of the political liaison necessities contributed to the Reagan momentum.

The selection of Howard "Bo" Callaway as the President Ford Committee chairman had little impact on the conservative Republicans. Callaway's purpose seemed to have been twofold: Hold the right wing in line and move Rockefeller out of the vice-presidency for Rumsfeld or whomever and also as a pacifier for the conservatives. However, Callaway was not the man to accomplish the first task. He had an abrupt manner in handling his friends. By December 1975, when the southern Republicans were gathering for their biennial conference, it was apparent Callaway was not scoring because of his ineffective politicking manners. He was perceived as a "sop" for the South. What they wanted was a southern boy running the White House operation, not handling the nonsubstantive job of campaign manager.

Not only was Rumsfeld credited by Rockefeller confidants with forcing Rockefeller off the ticket for 1976, but Rumsfeld's vice-presidential motives also came into question by friends of John Connally. His close associates wrongly believe Rumsfeld to have dictated the ultimate decision to prosecute Connally, in order to destroy his hopes for the number two position on the 1976 ticket. Friends of Bush feel he was selected to be head of the Central Intelligence Agency so he would have to pledge to the Senate—as he later did—not to be political in 1976.

It is doubtful Rumsfeld had such motives or took any such actions. However, the Connally and Rockefeller enmity toward him made it impossible for Rumsfeld to be considered a vice-presidential candidate in 1976. I personally delivered one of the Connally threats never to support a Ford-Rumsfeld ticket.

Rumsfeld's transfer from the chief of staff position at the White House to secretary of defense was thought to be designed to prepare Rumsfeld for the vice-presidency. It gave him the opportunity to improve his philosophical image with conservatives and, indeed, had this effect because of his pro-military stands and effective service at the helm in the Pentagon.

In December 1975 at the southern Republican conference in Houston, Texas, the Reagan forces were better represented. Not only did the president not appear, but his advisers only produced one Ford Cabinet member, albeit the best speaker of the conference, Agriculture Secretary Earle Butz.

Reagan and John Connally of Texas both made speaking appearances. However, Reagan almost bombed out with his standard speech presented in an untypically poor Reagan style. Nevertheless, Reagan and his forces had shown the Southerners more attention with his personal appearance, plus many Reagan operatives.

Then the Ford people permitted Vice president Rockefeller to talk to the southern chairmen while making a visit to another group in Houston. In this closed door session, Rockefeller clashed with the chairmen over his frustration at being run off the proposed 1976 ticket by Ford efforts to appease the party's conservative wing. After being asked to raise funds at southern party functions by Georgia chairman Mack Mattingly, Rockefeller retorted: "You SOBs have lotsa nerve. You get me off the ticket and now you want my help! OK, I'll do it anyway."

Seemingly, every time the Ford people would step up to bat on a key political question—either in liaison with the party or on a matter of administration policy—the outcome was more likely to be a minus for the president. They were seen as being politically hapless. With a recession upon the country, a poor political liaison operation, and in conservative eyes, a series of policy miscues, the Reagan candidacy was officially launched in November 1975.

The president hired Stuart Spencer and other experienced political professionals for the prospect of an early wipeout of the Reagan drive. Until the primary campaign hit a typical southern state—Florida excluded—the president seemed to be on the way to squeaking Reagan out of the contest with close victories in New Hampshire, Florida, Illinois, Vermont, and a good margin, as expected, in Massachusetts.

Then came North Carolina and a crucial Reagan upset over Ford. Ordinarily, Reagan should have been the favorite, but the Ford momentum and unexpected victories in New Hampshire and Florida seemed to indicate that the incumbency was too much for Reagan to overcome.

John Sears, the Reagan manager, had erred in setting Reagan as the potential winner in the early primaries. Now, the Ford leaders had made the same mistake in permitting the president to have the top-dog role in North Carolina. It was assumed Governor James Holshouser, who supposedly had control of the North Carolina GOP, could handle the right-wing challenge of Reagan, especially with the early Ford momentum of consecutive primary victories.

What was overlooked here was the lack of Holshouser popularity in the state and the backlash of strong-arm tactics by his key political operatives in the party. Also, the grass-roots influence of Senator Jesse Helms was not properly calculated.

Holshouser worked hard on wooing the party leaders. However, the Ford problem of having the party leaders, but less of the grass-roots workers, came to the fore in the North Carolina primary.

Senator Thurmond's help in ending the Ford-Reagan battle in North Carolina was sought by Spencer and me. In talking with the senator, I had sensed a concern that the continuation of the Reagan challenge would only worsen the prospects for November and that Ford was apparently stronger than Reagan had expected.

Spencer, Brannon of the White House staff, and I took the senator and his young wife, Nancy, out to dinner at the Joshua Tree in McLean, Virginia, ten days before the North Carolina primary. Our suggestion was to have the senator call on Reagan to withdraw and if Reagan did not withdraw, then have the senator assist the Ford campaign in North Carolina. Thurmond had taken a neutral stance since he had indicated to Reagan in 1971 he would support him in 1976 for the presidential nomination. The senator had not taken into account the possibility there might be an incumbent in the White House seeking the nomination. Thus at my suggestion he had informed Ford and Reagan in January 1976 he would have to be neutral in the nomination contest.

We proposed to the senator that in the interest of party-victory prospects he needed to use his key position to avert the fruitless bloodletting that would ensue with Reagan trying to go all the way to the Kansas City convention.

When the three of us left the senator and his wife that evening I was requested by him to draw up the appropriate language for a statement by Thurmond to accomplish the end we sought. Two days later the senator dropped the idea.

The closeness of the North Carolina outcome, 52 percent to 46 percent, convinced me Thurmond's intervention there could have made the difference. In my view, the Reagan challenge up to that point had been good for Ford. It had pulled him further right and had caused him to sharpen his political operation. He had become a winner and thus had more claim to the presidency than just a Nixon appointment. And even more important, the South would have provided the two keys, the final victories in Florida and North Carolina and, also, the intervention of the 1968 kingmaker, Thurmond. I still believe the Ford campaign would have been in better position to win the presidency had the Republican forces been able to unite in advance of the North Carolina primary or with a Ford victory there.

Following North Carolina came the Kissinger black Africa decision and speech, and Ford's political blood was spilled consecutively in Texas, Georgia, Alabama, Indiana, and Nebraska. Reagan took the delegate vote lead, and Ford's candidacy was weakened more and more until Rockefeller restored Ford to a slim margin by dropping Rockefeller's favorite son candidacy in New York and the Northeast.

The South had pushed President Ford right where Rockefeller wanted him—into the arms of the northern GOP. Sitting back in South Carolina in a position of occasionally advising the Ford campaign, the southern strategy I was witnessing seemed based on emotional abandon. To my mind, we were heading toward a disaster at Kansas City and in the general election with the southern GOP leading the way.

3
Fighting for the Uncommitteds; 1976

I nitially, Jim Baker's appointment as Ford's Chief recruiter of the uncommitted delegates seemed to be another Ford campaign boo-boo. Subsequently, he became the general election campaign chairman and won high marks for his performances before and after the convention.

In April 1976 Baker began seeking my participation as southern recruiter. I declined because of my concern that my bout with the special prosecutor might be injurious to the president. Instead, I suggested J. Drake Edens, Jr., of Columbia, South Carolina, a former top leader of the Republican National Committee (RNC) under Ray Bliss when he was Republican National Committee chairman. Baker tried Edens, but he declined. Thus on May 23 while at Sea Island, Georgia, to address the South Carolina Textile Manufacturers Association, Baker reached me by phone. He reiterated his request that I serve. Again, I declined, thinking Baker was nice but naive. Then Stu Spencer came on the line and said, "Dammit, Harry, don't you want to help us?" I explained my problem again. Spencer responded emphatically, "Don't you worry about that. We don't see any problem. Besides, we're willing to risk it. Now will you help us?"

Put that way, I answered affirmatively, but with the understanding that the task would not take long. I had not realized then that the key to the uncommitted contest would turn on the battle of Mississippi, one of the nine states assigned to me. Mississippi was to account for most of my waking hours for the next three months, through the end of the GOP convention on August 19.

At the same time I was volunteering to help Baker's delegate hunt operation, the Ford Committee's southern primary campaign was being closed down for financial reasons. This had been under the direction of Governor Holshouser. One of the campaign aides deposed by the financial cutback was a 29-year-old former schoolteacher from Mississippi named John Davis. He had worked earlier in the year in the gubernatorial campaign of Gil Carmichael. The moderate Carmichael was the Mississippi GOP's candidate who barely lost an exciting race for governor.

Carmichael's campaign attracted many young Mississippians of a more moderate stripe than most Mississippi GOP leaders. Afterward, most of the new recruits joined the ranks of the party. Davis was one of these.

Learning of my appointment, Davis called and asked that I get him hired to assist me. Baker ruled out any paid help for me because of the financial squeeze. When I gave Davis the bad news, he volunteered to help without pay.

"Harry, I want to see this campaign through," Davis pleaded. "This is my first presidential campaign, and if you'll just feed me and give me a place to sleep I'll help you for nothing.

"There's gold to be mined in that Mississippi delegation," he went on. "I think we can turn the Reagan tide in Mississippi around and win all 30 votes under Clarke Reed's unit rule."

Davis then explained about the younger alternate delegates in the Mississippi contingent and how every vote—of full and alternate delegates—counted the same, one-half vote each, and that a majority of 31 half votes of the 60 half votes in the delegation would control the total unit vote of 30 full delegate votes.

I told Davis to come on down—that he could stay at my home. Once there he was added to our family roster as our fifth child.

Meanwhile, I began communicating with my old southern strategy collaborator, Clarke Reed, Mississippi chairman and chairman of the southern Republican chairmen. Reed had tried to be for Ford in the early days. However, that was before the Ford forces awakened to the political realities of 1976. Thus Reed had been undercut with his conservative friends. He was particularly embarrassed by Ford's amnesty program and his initial talk of signing a common situs picketing bill. He was taunted by conservative friends at political meetings.

Now Reed was professing neutrality between Ford and Reagan. However, his delegation was loaded to fire for Reagan; and that's how Reagan and the national news media had Mississippi figured as 30-0 for Reagan, yet officially uncommitted.

Reed is a staunch conservative, but he understands the importance of winning. Ultraconservatives and/or purist conservatives do not care for this brand of politics, but I do.

Knowing Reed's political disposition, I went to work on rewinning him to the Ford side. I realized his support would give the president a strong psychological boost nationally and could tip the balance to the president under Mississippi's unit rule. Thus Reed became the most wooed delegate in the GOP once I convinced Dick Cheney of the Reed potential and this impact on the ultimate outcome of the delegate hunt and thus the nomination vote in Kansas City. The Ford Committee leaders were not impressed with the Mississippi possibilities because of their previous disastrous results everywhere in Dixie except Florida. Also, they did not understand Reed and had little confidence in Davis's judgment.

The first opportunity for exploring the Mississippi potential came at the meeting of southern GOP chairmen at Atlantic Beach, North Carolina, June

11-13, 1976. Governor Holshouser had been entertaining the southern chairmen each summer since 1974.

Cheney and Spencer represented the Ford campaign. David Keene, a friend of mine from the old Agnew staff, was Reagan's spokesman. Getting prime attention at the conference were Reed and his newly elected successor as Mississippi chairman, state Senator Charles Pickering. I learned that Reed had decided against running for reelection as chairman because he realized he had served long enough—more than a decade—as state chairman and southern chairman. However, in moving to national committeeman, Reed retained the power as state chairman through the national convention. He wanted to play to the fullest the game of being the most wooed man prior to and at the convention. He did, only later to regret the bed of thorny roses he had made for himself in trying to be the center of attention at what everyone knew would be one of the most hotly contested convention fights in Republican history.

After talking with about everyone at the conference, including long sessions with Reed and Pickering separately, I thought we might win both. Pickering was even more encouraging. He indicated we might get the unit rule dropped so we could at least get our votes out of the delegation. Anything from Mississippi would be better than zero.

The conference also gave me an opportunity to talk extensively with Cheney and Spencer about Mississippi and the overall potential of winning the majority of the South's uncommitted delegates. I advocated presidential wooing in the Oval Office and even boat rides down the Potomac. They agreed to give full cooperation.

Paula Unruh of Oklahoma, Reed's successor as southern chairman, mentioned the idea of persuading the president to open the vice-presidential nomination to a convention floor battle. This appealed to me for two reasons: It would undercut the Reagan sentiment for top spot in the South, and it would insure the nomination of Reagan, or if he refused, then Connally.

Thus when the chairmen met with Cheney and Spencer, Unruh and I proposed the idea with almost everyone in support except Reed.

According to an article by Keene in the November 1976 issue of *The Alternative: An American Spectator,* a very conservative philosophical journal, Keene and Reagan had a commitment from Reed early in the campaign. This must have been the reason Reed was so staunchly opposed to the idea of an open convention on the vice-presidential nomination.

In the article, Keene gave his version of the Reed commitment:

> Early in the campaign, Reed had personally indicated that he was
> with us, but refused to endorse Reagan publicly or deliver his
> delegation to us before the convention. I had urged him to do both
> in the spring while we were still ahead in most of the public
> delegate counts, but he told me then that if he tried, a few Ford
> supporters on the delegation might get upset and break the unit
> rule. Therefore, if he was to try to bring out his delegates he might
> only be able to deliver 25 or 26 and that, he assured us, would be
> viewed in the press as a victory for Ford, not Reagan. He was right,
> of course, since most people were assuming that we would receive
> all 30 of Mississippi's votes.
>
> "Let me do it my way," he said, "and I'll get you at least 28 and
> possibly all 30." That very afternoon, I took the matter to cam-
> paign manager John Sears and outlined our options. We could ask
> the Mississippian to commit as many as possible right away (which I
> was afraid he might not be willing or able to do regardless of what
> he was saying) or we could trust him to handle things his own way.
>
> My assurances were good enough for Sears. He told me to get
> back to Reed and tell him that we would be counting on him and
> that he could handle things his own way. I did just that, but added
> that we were both on the line. He because he had given his word
> and me because I had backed him up. He told me that he
> understood and that I had nothing to worry about.

Reed kept professing to me, Cheney, the president, and others that he was
truly uncommitted. In fact, on occasion I would accuse him of being committed to Reagan, and he would fire back: "That's a lie!"

At Atlantic Beach, I first began painting for Reed the picture of him and
his Mississippi delegates playing the "catbird" role at the 1976 convention, as
we had done in 1968. He relished the idea.

I finally turned the persuasive point into a playacting joke. I would get
Reed in front of Spencer, Cheney, and others and needle him with what I
called my "updated version of the parable of the talents":

> Just imagine after Ford's won this nomination, and we're sitting up
> there at the big table, carving up the pie. There's Rosy Rosenbaum

(Richard Rosenbaum, the New York state chairman) sitting up there at the head of the table, where he belongs. Boy, he's really been delivering and holding every time he delivers.

The President's going to turn to Rosy and say, "Well done, thy good and faithful servant. Thou hast five talents, and thou hast increased them fivefold. Therefore thou hast 25 votes at this table.

And Clarke, he's gonna look at me sitting down there at the other end at the foot of the table. And he's gonna say, "Well done, thy good and faithful servant, Harry Dent. Thou wast instrusted with one talent and thou increased it onefold. Therefore thou hast one vote at this table.

There we are. Old Rosy Rosenbaum, the new king of the Republican party. The new northeastern strategy of the Republican party. There's gonna be ole Harry. Strom Thurmond (for Reagan) ain't gonna be there; Clarke Reed ain't gonna be there.

But Clarke, baby, you got 30 pieces of silver you can walk in there and throw on that table. Thirty pieces of silver in a timely fashion would cover those 25 talents that Rosy had on the table. Then the president could.say:

"Well done thy good and faithful servant, Clarke." And he could put you at the head of the table and put Rosy at the foot of the table. And the southern strategy would prevail again. Long live the king!

Reed and all present would laugh. Yet to me it was not funny—I was dead serious, and I knew as much as my joke was coming across to Reed, so was my point. I knew Reed's Achilles' heel—his desire to be the kingmaker. And in his interest and that of the South—and ultimate victory at the convention—I wanted Reed to be that kingmaker, not Rosenbaum and the Northeast.

However, Reed proclaimed no desire to be the kingmaker. So, I began referring to him jokingly as the "reluctant kingmaker." He kept telling me Mississippi could not be won as John Davis had told me—and especially not without his leadership.

Reed's biggest obstacle seemed to be his friendship with Billy Mounger, the powerful state finance chairman and then almost a brother to Reed. Mounger kept the pressure on Reed to resist all my entreaties.

I have since learned why. Reed and Mounger visited the Reagan headquarters in Washington early in the campaign; evidently, when the Keene commitment was supposedly made, they came away with Mounger as the Reagan chairman for Mississippi.

After the North Carolina conference, I next saw Reed and Pickering at a meeting of the Republican National Committee in Washington. I continued to wheedle and needle Reed.

The president was entertaining RNC members at the White House on Friday evening, June 25, 1976. He opened up the Lincoln bedroom and every room on the third floor of the White House except his own bedroom. Before going to the reception, I called Cheney and suggested he and the president work on Pickering, as he sounded more amenable to helping us than Reed.

When we got into the East Room, the military aide announced, "Ladies and Gentlemen, the President of the United States!" Walking in with the president was Pickering. When Reed saw this he was astonished, and his startled reaction showed. Reed needed to know we might win Mississippi without him. Now he saw that potential for the first time.

Later at the reception Pickering sought me out to suggest Reed be taken in for an Oval Office session following the reception lest he be alienated by the superior attention given Pickering. I agreed and relayed the suggestion to Cheney. I was instructed to escort Reed to the Oval Office at the conclusion of the reception.

When we arrived at the president's office from the Rose Garden entrance, the president and Cheney were waiting for the important visitor from Mississippi. Reed playfully resisted all the way to the Oval Office. As with anyone else, once inside he enjoyed every minute of the hour-long visit.

We asked him to air his many gripes about the Ford Administration. And he did, just as I had heard them over and over again: He did not trust the Ford people; they had missed the opportunity to get the Voting Rights Act extension sidelined or at least applied to the entire nation, so all states had to submit voting law changes to the Justice Department for approval; he questioned whether the president believed in the "Grand Design," meaning the gathering of all conservatives under one tent; he deplored the Rockefeller appointment and the Vietnam amnesty program.

The president and I stressed his voting record in Congress as proof he was as conservative as the realities of the presidency would permit.

Asked about his choice for vice-president, Reed was silent, saying he would leave that to the president. However, he did not want any ticket balancing, his strongest point.

The only request Reed made was that the president come to Mississippi and woo his delegates. Ford indicated he would.

When we departed the Oval Office, I felt more than ever we had a chance to win Reed and Pickering and thus, all of Missisippi's 30 votes under its unit rule.

What I did not know then was that Reed, Mounger, and Pickering had planned to have fun with their supposedly uncommitted bloc of 30 votes, expecting the race to end before Kansas City. This strategy gave Reed the flexibility to play both sides without the concern of finally having to choose or get caught.

Phone lines buzzed back and forth between Reed and me. The cumulative effect of these calls was a growing concern Reed would never come over to our side. All the persuasion at my command could not move him, although I knew I was connecting with the pragmatic side of Reed. Thus I became convinced he was committed to Reagan or scared of Mounger—and I told him so.

Then I suggested to Cheney and Davis it was time to work around Reed and go directly through to his delegates. I told Reed I wanted to meet with his delegates. He said okay, but it would not do any good.

Meanwhile, the battle for Mississippi's 30 votes, the largest outstanding bloc, was taking on increasing importance. The Reagan forces were becoming concerned that I might be able to get to Reed's pragmatic side. In his memoir on the subject, Keene gave this picture from his side:

The resources of the White House could prove unbearable in such a contest and the President's people knew it. They began inviting delegates to the White House to see their President, to talk to Cabinet officers about pet projects and to impress upon them the majesty of the Office they were being asked to support. And they were beginning, by mid-July, to pull some of our own people as well as a number of the uncommitted. For the first time since March, we were on the defense.

Clarke Reed realized about this time that if we didn't do something soon, we were going to lose—making him neither comfortable nor happy. We knew this and so did Clarke's old friend Harry Dent, a former Nixon operative from South Carolina, now working virtually full time in the South for the President. Dent spent a good deal of time during this period badgering Reed about how it felt to be backing a loser. It didn't feel very good and Reed began to show it—publicly. He knew he couldn't just break his private commitment to us—at least not without a good reason—but he began to move as far away from us as possible. He started telling reporters that our count was no good, that although he was leaning our way he fully expected Ford to win and, worse, that he wouldn't be at all surprised if his own delegation went for Ford.

This was devastating stuff. Harry Dent was already running around the South saying that Mississippi's 30 votes were going to end up with Ford and now Clarke Reed who everyone thought was a Reagan man was saying that Harry might well be right.

One has to know Clarke Reed pretty well to understand him most of the time, but the message coming across didn't need much interpretation—Reagan was slipping badly in the South.

While Harry Dent travelled the South, other Ford operatives were directing the attention of soft Northern delegates to Mississippi. "Better stick with the President," they were saying, "because Reagan isn't even going to be able to hold his base." They had a point.

In the South Dent was playing one weakness off against another. He would tell Reed that Reagan was slipping in South Carolina and Louisiana and that Ford was on the verge of picking up the votes he would need to lock up the nomination. His message was clear—join us now while you can still make a difference. Or get used to the fact that your 30 votes aren't going to matter and that there won't be any more invitations to State Dinners or informal calls from the Oval Office. Reed didn't want to get used to anything like that.

As soon as he finished one of his calls to Reed, Dent would call delegates in other Southern states with the corollary: Reed is about to jump so you'd better move first before it's all over and your vote doesn't matter.

The tactic hadn't worked by early July, but there were signs that our support was getting softer by the day. And delegates we were talking to in other parts of the country began to use Clarke Reed and our weakness in the South as an excuse to stay away from us.

According to Keene, the Reagan concern over the Reed erosion was the catalyst that led to the astounding decision to select Senator Richard Schweiker as the Reagan running mate. He reported further:

Thus it was that on Saturday, July 17, Andy Carter, the crusty, conservative former Goldwater hand who was serving as our Director of Field Operations, and I sat in John Sears' office nodding agreements as John ran through the situation with us and asked if we could think of any way out of our predicament. We couldn't.

□ □ □

Sears agreed with our assessment of the situation, but insisted that we still had one card left to play: the Vice Presidency. He said he believed that if Reagan were to announce his choice for that office he could pressure Ford to do the same and thereby fracture the rather shaky regional coalition the President's people had managed to put together for him.

Sears had a point. Ford's Northeastern liberal supporters were scared to death of John Connally and they were afraid the President just might pick him. Many of them had already attended a "stop Connally" meeting hosted by Nelson Rockefeller in Maine and they had received assurances, both implicit and explicit, that they had nothing to worry about. But they were still worried.

They had reason to be. In the South Ford operatives were assuring delegates that they didn't have a worry either: Ford would pick someone they would like rather than someone who might appeal to the Nelson Rockefellers of the world. And those who wanted something a bit more explicit were told that it would probably be either Reagan (if he would take it) or good old John Connally. But they were worried too, because they suspected that they were being told something different than the Northeasterners.

Sears' theory, therefore, was that if we picked our man right away we could get a good number of Ford's people to start demanding that he do the same—if only to allay their fears. And if we picked the right man we might just crack his support. At the very least we would be off the defensive and that would in itself be worthwhile.

□   □   □

Eventually—and by a process of elimination—Sears began to focus attention on Pennsylvania and Richard Schweiker. This approach incidentally was typical of John's usual way of talking people into doing things willingly that they would ordinarily have no part of. He was good at it.

By the time we finally got around to Senator Schweiker, we were just about ready to buy anyone. But none of us seemed to know very much about the man. I had worked on Capitol Hill for two years, but had to confess that I wouldn't recognize the Senator if he walked into the room. I did, however, know that he was a liberal.

Thus Reagan's southern coordinator credits or blames our efforts to fetch Reed to our side for the panicky Schweiker decision. Keene had told me this story at Kansas City in the midst of our battle for the soul of Reed.

In his 1976 campaign book, *Marathon,* Jules Witcover relates a similar version of the motivation to select Schweiker (page 458). He reported:

The White House was really playing its advantage now, and it was hurting. Then came word of cracks in the South Carolina and Mississippi delegations, and the possibilities in Louisiana and Virginia. Clarke Reed was saying himself that Reagan was in trouble—and that kind of talk didn't help—in the North or South. Sears' optimism turned around; the nomination was slipping away from Reagan unless something could be done at once.

The only real feeler I ever had from a top Reagan operative was a telephone call from my old White House friend John Sears. He called me in early 1976 to ask my advice on the Reagan campaign. I indicated what I then expected at that time—I would not become actively involved in the 1976 campaign.

I gave one specific bit of advice: Don't let Reagan go the far right way of Goldwater. I told Sears I had come to realize a far left or far right campaign could not win in America, as per 1972 and 1964. He assured me Reagan would move left after the nomination and would balance the ticket. I did not realize what a subsequent role I would play in criticizing Reagan for his

Schweiker ploy and how crucial that would be in turning around the Mississippi delegation and some other southern delegates.

Ironically, I had campaigned with Schweiker in Pennsylvania in 1972 when Nixon and Schweiker were running for reelection. As the late Senator Everett Dirksen, Republican of Illinois, used to say, "Such are the vagaries of politics."

As Keene mentioned in his article, I was particularly driving home the point that Ford would probably pick Reagan or Connally for veep. This was effective because many of the Reagan-inclined delegates were also susceptible to the argument that Reagan, like Goldwater in 1964, would not be able to win in the general election because he was too far right. So if they could get a Ford-Reagan ticket, that was good enough for almost all except the ultraconservatives. And they liked Connally almost as much as Reagan.

For me, all this was easy to talk about because I believed my argument and preferred a Ford-Reagan, or Ford-Connally ticket if Reagan insisted on continuing to reject the idea of the vice-presidential nomination.

What the Reagan people did not know was the problem I was encountering with the Ford Committee leaders over our Mississippi strategy. They had written off Mississippi. And they were afraid that if we got caught reaching for it and losing we would have our delegate search momentum checked, maybe irreparably. Also, they were short of funds; and anything spent on Mississippi was a "foolish waste," as one Fordite explained to me.

However, I had convinced Cheney and the president of the Mississippi potential. So I had already won out in our political supreme court.

Nevertheless, when Reed set up a delegation meeting in Jackson, Mississippi, for Sunday, July 25, 1976, I had to wrestle with the Ford people to get Cheney to make the trip with me. They were certain we would be rebuffed, and Cheney was too close to the president to absorb that rebuff.

Reed called the meeting specifically to rebuff us. Early in that week, Davis and I, with Cheney's approval, had launched a campaign to enlist telegrams of support for the president to convince the Ford leaders the president would not be embarrassed if he would visit the Mississippi delegation on their own turf. I was convinced a presidential visit to Mississippi, the stepchild state, would be the key to winning part or all of Mississippi's votes. As it turned out, this was true, although more crises occurred between the time of the president's visit on July 30 and the final convention vote on August 19.

Reed had suggested we poll the Mississippi delegation to show the Ford people there was good sentiment for a presidential visit. We decided to go one step further and ask for their current intention of support of the president. When Reed and Pickering discovered the telegrams could be used as claims of support in the game of psychological warfare being conducted between the Ford and Reagan camps, they moved to stop the participation just as we were nearing a majority. They were particularly angered over comments Carmichael was making to some delegates. Reed claimed Carmichael was talking to delegates leading each to believe his or her telegram would be the crucial one and that Reagan would take the number two spot.

The Carmichael calls and our telegram drive forced Reagan to get on the telephone himself, denying Carmichael's suggestions. This was one of many times Reagan had to personally defend his ground in Mississippi. No doubt, we had him tied down in his own backyard while the president and his campaign team were working the rest of the country.

Directing operations for us in Mississippi was a young, forceful city commissioner named Doug Shanks of Jackson. Shanks was also irritating Reed, Pickering, and Mounger with his threats to bolt the unit rule to vote for the president.

All this tension set the stage for a blowup in the key delegation. So Reed pulled to Jackson a large entourage of reporters, with national attention focused on Reed's delegation and state—exactly what Reed wanted.

Finally deciding to go over Ford Committee objections, Cheney and I were given time on the program as was Keene for the Reagan side. The delegates were impressed that the president cared enough to send his chief of staff. Cheney and I made strong pitches, while Keene gave the impression he was there just to tend to his flock of sheep. What we did not know was that Keene had dropped a bombshell on Reed before the meeting—the Schweiker selection. However, it evidently did not sink in on Reed that day as it did the next day when on arriving in South Carolina I learned of the Reagan announcement and immediately called Reed to agitate him about the "Reagan betrayal" and "ticket balancing act." I knew that besides the Voting Rights Act, the other unforgiveable act to Reed was balancing the ticket with a liberal and a conservative. This had been Reed's big concern as we were working to nominate Nixon over Reagan in 1968—the fear Nixon would betray us with a "balancing act," as Reed called it.

My call to Reed initiated a three-day struggle to get Reed to declare for the president on the basis of the "Reagan betrayal." Reed indicated he would be coming with us. Cheney called him also and was likewise encouraged. However, he got no clear-cut time either.

Then Reed called back to say he would be coming later, not sooner. I could tell the Reagan counterpressure was on.

Then Cheney called to urge me to get Reed over the line immediately. "We need the psychological impact while the tempers are hot over the Schweiker ploy," he barked.

I called Reed several more times and got others, like Mack Mattingly, the Georgia chairman to call him. Every time Reed would say he needed "more time, more time, more time." With every call Reed's anger over Schweiker cooled a little more.

So on Tuesday morning, I called Cheney and gave him the solution to the Reed reluctance: "You've got to play the big card—get the president on the phone to tell Clarke to come and come now, today. Tell the president not to be his nice self—to push for a certain time and not to hang up till he gets it. Clarke won't back up on his word to the president."

Cheney told me he had Connally in the office. I said, "Use him, too. But there's no substitute for the president and a definite time."

So on Wednesday morning the president made his call to Reed. Every time previously when I took a delegate or delegates in to see the president he had not asked them directly for their vote. However, this call was different. He pressed for a Reed commitment and got it. Then he insisted Reed come over that day—Wednesday. And, again, Reed agreed.

Cheney had told me Wednesday was the key deadline for Reed. The next day the Pennsylvania delegation, which Schweiker was now trying to crack, was coming to visit the president. It would be important for them to know a switch to Reagan would be futile since his southern base was crumbling over the Schweiker deal. Reed would be the best possible proof.

So I phoned Reed many times that day trying to get the commitment executed in the form of a Reed statement. I asked him, "Where's the statement, Clarke?" Want me to write it for you? What can I do to help?"

While I was pushing on our side, Keene, Mounger, Haley Barbour (the party's executive director), and even Reagan himself were all calling Reed at his office in Greenville, Mississippi, to try to hold the line.

Finally, Reed read me the statement about 5 P.M. He said he was calling it to Barbour to be released through state headquarters. I was anxious to get the announcement on the network news that evening—under strong pressure from Cheney. However, I ran into difficulty with Barbour, who was for Reagan and knew what I did not: His boss was breaking a Reagan commitment.

Finally, at 8 P.M., Barbour reluctantly released the statement after much badgering from me. However, we knew it was coming on two of the three networks before Barbour finally turned it loose.

The Reed story had the desired impact. Pennsylvania held, and the South appeared to be cracking. Reagan was beginning to appear to be coming unraveled as a candidate.

However, while we were working to exploit the Reagan desperation gamble, the Reagan leaders were on the phone lines explaining, rationalizing; and begging their delegates to hold on for 24 to 48 hours. This was the line they were giving Reed as he had kept asking for "just 24 hours—I've got to, I've got to!"

With the Reed breakthrough, Cheney then signaled that the president would indeed be flying into Jackson on Friday to meet with the Mississippi delegates. Again, there was opposition from the Ford Committee, but the president and Cheney decided to go anyway.

The visit was most impressive for the president. He stood for more than two hours talking to and answering tough questions from the Reaganites. He won rounds of applause on every answer.

Of particular interest was the president's answer to the first question and the strong ovation he received from the Mississippi delegates. This question, concerning the free hand being given to Kissinger on Africa, was one of 20-odd Birch-type questions.

Ford forthrightly stood by his support of his secretary of state. He pointed out that the Kissinger acts had his approval as strategic moves to thwart Soviet efforts to win the dark continent through use of racial agitation.

I sat down after the meeting, assured there would be no more problems with Mississippi. Then it was confirmed that Reagan and Schweiker would be coming into Jackson the following Wednesday.

This caused me to make another trip to Jackson. It was determined we should take no chances on a Reagan revival because the anger was subsiding. The defections were stopping. The fire was out in many Reagan bellies, but they were not giving up. A surprising number of the most conservative types had finally swallowed the ploy as a necessary means to accomplish a vital end, the nomination and election of Ronald Reagan.

The Reagan-Schweiker visit did not come off well. Schweiker's explanation of how he could all of a sudden switch from a very liberal Republican senator to a very conservative Reagan-running mate fell flat. One delegate told him: "Look, senator, you Yankees think we southern boys are stupid, but we ain't that stupid!" Had Mrs. Schweiker not been present, the senator would have been subjected to more such delegates' jibes.

Again, I called Cheney to assure him we were over the hump in Mississippi. However, we again underestimated the Reagan determination. Back in California, Reagan called delegate after delegate urging them to hold on. Mounger rededicated himself and effectively rallied his troops while we were assuming all was well. Also, we were still trying to recruit a new leader to replace Carmichael and Shanks, both of whom realized they had lost their effectiveness under unrelenting attacks from Reed and Mounger. We were concentrating on Tommy Giordano, party secretary, but we could not get a full commitment until we got to Kansas City.

Meanwhile, Reed had been so chastised by Reagan, Keene, and Mounger until he had pledged himself to assist them on key procedural votes at the convention and to do nothing for Ford beyond the earlier Ford endorsement. So when I got to Kansas City a week in advance of the convention I was tipped off by a South Carolina delegate that Reed was working against us. I would encounter this problem over and over again in Kansas City.

Reed was Mississippi's representative on the important Rules Committee, where the key floor fight would develop over the addition of Rule 16(c). This was John Sear's strategy for forcing Ford to suffer the same tribulations as Reagan by naming his proposed running mate in advance. The rule would require the selection of vice-presidential candidates before the vote for president. Sears calculated the vote on 16(c) would determine the nomination struggle. Some Ford delegates who were required by law to vote for Ford's nomination could help Reagan by casting a Reagan vote on 16(c). Reed fell into that category, and a Reagan vote by him on 16(c) might have caused the same psychological effect for Reagan that his earlier Ford endorsement had caused for Ford.

So the tug-of-war between Keene and me over Reed's political soul began again. Cheney said: "Harry, we've got to keep Clarke honest on 16(c). This will be the key vote of the convention."

On Saturday morning, August 14, I hauled Reed in to see top conservative Ford operatives such as Governor Holshouser, Bryce Harlow, Bill Timmons, and Dean Burch. I bore down on Reed before this group he so respected. Then I took him upstairs to meet with Cheney. We again explained the importance of the 16(c) vote. Reed agreed to vote as planned and that if he did anything adverse it might be to cast a throwaway vote on 16(c) if we did not need his vote. So far as the Mississippi delegation was concerned, it would be substantially in our corner.

We felt much better until Sunday afternoon when I got a beeper call to find Reed and get him back on track on 16(c). Cheney had just heard him tell Mike Wallace of CBS-TV that he would lead Mississippi to support a move to adopt Rule 16(c) at the first convention session Monday morning when the customary motion is made to adopt the old rules as the temporary rules until the new rules can be considered Tuesday evening when the only key vote, preceding the nomination would be taken—that being on 16(c).

When my beeper message came through, I raced from the South Carolina delegation's bitter credentials fight to Ramada Inn East, where the Mississippi delegation was headquartered and housed.

Upon arriving I finally found Reed after a three-hour search. I told him about the Mike Wallace TV report on his surprise 16(c) plan to be executed at Monday's opening convention session. He collapsed on the motel bed in Doug Shank's room, looking physically and mentally exhausted.

"How could I do that?" he cried.

I shouted back: "That's what I want to know. Clarke, you've promised us and promised us, and you've collapsed on every promise. Man, you just can't do that way. When you get on one side you're supposed to stick there and fight with all you've got."

Reed turned over on his back and said, as he had before: "I'll get it straight. I'll take care of it in the meeting (delegation meeting set to begin at that time, 6 P.M. Sunday.)"

True to his word, he did. Meanwhile, the word had spread among reporters that Mississippi was about to break open for Reagan on 16(c). A crowd of reporters thus had assembled at the Ramada Inn East awaiting the outcome of the meeting. Also present were a few Reagan operatives, including my good friend, former Kentucky Governor Louie Nunn. I believe Nunn had convinced Reed on the 16(c) ploy.

As reporters gathered around me, I told them of the 16(c) maneuver and how it had been quashed, even before the delegation meeting had ended. Nunn eavesdropped on the talk, and his face showed dismay as I revealed the unraveling of what was to be the key Reagan coup of the convention. Again, I felt secure about Mississippi—until next morning when the gavel sounded for the opening of the first session.

Doug Shanks and Tommy Giordano were frantically seeking me on the convention floor. "Clarke's done it again," Shanks yelled. "Now he's gonna' take our delegation to Reagan 30-0 on 16(c) Tuesday evening."

Shanks, Giordano, and I grabbed Reed and Pickering and began berating them for pulling another "Reed flip flop." The words turned heated. Billy Mounger yelled at me: "Harry, what're you doing in this delegation? You ain't from Mississippi!"

"No need to get upset, Billy, all we want is a vote." I responded. "We got the votes, and you ain't!" I yelled full of bluff.

"Well, I don't want to vote even though I might have the votes, anyway!" Mounger hollered back.

"Quit selling your snake oil, Harry," Pickering shouted at me. "You're gonna' get hurt if you force this thing!"

By this time reporters were hovering around. They sensed the first fight—maybe even physically—was underway on the floor.

Barbour grabbed the five of us and started pushing us off the floor with his hefty frame, all the while calling out numbers and names to make it impossible for the reporters to hear the epithets and verbal threats flying back and forth. Finally, he had shoved us to the rear of the floor. Seeing a curtained space under a temporary stairway, I pulled all five of us under the steps and behind the blue curtains where we continued fussing and finger pointing and jabbing.

Meanwhile, Tom Brokaw of NBC-TV News stuck a camera under the curtain to get a live view for NBC-TV watchers; however, the light was too dim. Jabbing into every side of the closet-sized space were several microphones.

We Fordites were asking for a 50-50 split of the delegation vote on 16(c) and the nomination roll call. Also, we wanted an immediate caucus to vote on the proposed split vote idea. Cheney had told me 15 of the 30 votes was all we needed and that the sooner we got them the better for psychological reasons. Thus a Mississippi compromise vote Monday would be a coup for Ford.

The morning sessions ended before we could conclude our war of words under the stairs. Shanks, Giordano, and I left threatening to charge publicly that Reed and Pickering, the two leaders, would not give us a delegation meeting, even though we had the necessary votes to override Reed's refusal. The only agreement we reached was to let Pickering try to arrange a later time for a delegation meeting and check back with me. For us, it was meet and vote Monday or else we would expose the undemocratic leadership tactics and get a meeting of our own with 31 of the 60 delegates and alternates and take all 30 Mississippi votes for 16(c) and the nomination roll call.

In the meantime, I had scheduled a 1:30 P.M. meeting with some key Mississippi delegates and the president. I had invited Reed to be present.

Our blowup on the floor delayed my arrival as I missed my ride from the convention arena and had to walk and hitchhike back to the Crown Center Hotel. There Ford had a presidential office almost as plush and impressive as the Oval Office. It made a good massage parlor for working over delegates, especially from Mississippi.

When I arrived, Cheney was already meeting with the dozen Mississippians and Reed. They were talking compromise; Reed was complaining about my strong pressures. He was trying to use his complaints to win Reagan favor and get me called off by Cheney.

Cheney gave me the picture outside the room. I volunteered I would back off despite my conviction we were now in a position to win all Mississippi's votes on 16(c) and the nomination vote. Cheney indicated a compromise would be good enough.

So when we went in to see the president, Reed again pledged his support on 16(c) and the nomination. The others variously indicated we would get at least one-half or more of the Mississippi votes if we called off the pressures. Joining Reed in pledging to help us on 16(c) was Mrs. Lillian Todd, the national committeewoman and other Rules Committee member from Mississippi. With pledges from Reed and Todd, we seemed safe again in Mississippi.

Then on the floor Monday night, the Mississippi panic button was pushed again, just as I was relaxing in the plush sky suite overlooking the convention floor. This was the Ford floor massage parlor. I had my shoes off and my tie loose as Shanks and Giordano beeped me to urgently report to the Mississippi delegation. We had relaxed again, only to now discover we had been undermined again.

This time the Reaganites had used Pat Boone and Reagan to switch or soften a few key delegates, including two of our black delegates. One was a preacher who had lionized the president with a brief emotional love sermon when the president was visiting the delegation in Jackson. I told Shanks, "My goodness, if they can take the preacher from under us, who is immune from the Boone-Reagan charisma?"

Shanks and Giordano insisted I get the affected delegates to a meeting with the president Tuesday morning following the Mississippi delegation's appearance on NBC-TV's "Today Show."

Governor Holshouser and I scheduled breakfast together the next morning to plan how to cope with the new Reagan success. We had about worn out our presidential welcome on Mississippi crises.

Just as we were eating, Shanks and Giordano knocked on Holshouser's door. They had the affected delegates downstairs with their spouses and had told them they would shortly be escorted in to see the president. Holshouser and I were flabbergasted. I explained that presidential visits could not be arranged "just like that."

"Well," Shanks reacted, "just find us somebody big to see 'em—how 'bout Cheney, Baker, or somebody?"

I quickly climbed the stairs to the seventeenth floor where key Ford operatives had their offices. I ran into Stu Spencer, Bryce Harlow, and Jim Baker. They agreed to see the delegates. Meanwhile, Baker said he would try to convince Cheney that a quick presidential session was vital.

I called Shanks to get the delegates and their spouses up to the seventeenth floor right away. Just as they were poured coffee, Baker appeared and announced, "The President will see you now."

When I saw the startled looks on their faces, I knew we were well on the way to trumping the Boone-Reagan aces with a royal flush. The Ford meeting had the desired effect, including all the magic of the presidential suite and flashbulbs flashing all over the room.

Again, I relaxed, feeling secure once more.

Then, later Tuesday morning Shanks informed me he and Giordano had another group who had been penetrated by Reagan visits and/or calls. They had to see the president before the important 2:30 P.M. meeting in which the Mississippi delegation would take its first and key vote on Rule 16(c). Reagan was going to have the final visit with the delegation at Ramada Inn East right before the vote.

So I went back to Cheney one more time with a brassy request. The president's schedule had already been rearranged for the morning meeting with problem Mississippians. Now it would have to be changed again. As Cheney told me, "You know, Harry, we've got some other key delegates other than just in Mississippi." However, Cheney had come to love the "Battle of Mississippi" as much as I, and he realized its importance. So he said, "Have 'em here by 1 P.M. sharp!"

We had a dozen in, with the same impressive show of flashbulbs popping by White House photographer Dave Kennerly and his assistants. Also, the usual big glass of iced tea, brewed especially for southern tastes, was served.

As in previous delegate meetings, the president performed magnificently by being his genuine self. He would begin by talking about the presidency and key policy concerns. Then he would answer questions. The Mississippi delegates always wanted to know if he would campaign in their state and the South and what type vice-presidential candidate he had in mind. I was always quick to point out that if Rule 16(c) should be adopted there would be no chance to consider Reagan.

The president most impressed the delegates with his "good guy" personality and his sincerity. He made no attempts to win them with promises. He flattered them by asking for their individual choices for veep and for any other suggestions they had. The meetings would run to one and one-half hours or more so that each delegate and spouse would have the opportunity to speak up with questions or suggestions.

When they would leave, Terry O'Donnell, the president's appointments secretary and personal aide would give me numerous presidential trinkets to distribute. Shanks and Giordano always wanted more of the fountain pens, tie clips, cuff links, and ladies' pins. Mississippi won far more than its share of the valuable keepsakes.

I had learned from my White House days that the presidential trinkets worked more magic than anything except the small presidential meetings.

The Ford operatives had not understood the value of the trinkets in earlier campaigns. Initially, I would take delegates in to see the president and would have to go back and demand the trinkets. By convention time, the Fordites were much wiser in the art of plying delegate votes with trinkets. They had not recalled the trinket value to early American traders in dealing with the American Indians. The name of the game was the same—winning favor and ultimately the contest for control of America.

When the presidential meeting was finished I was chauffered by the Ford motor pool to the Ramada Inn East just in time to arrive for the preliminary meeting of Ford delegates prior to the key delegation vote on 16(c). The Ford delegates were assembled in Giordano's room. The crowd was overflowing. Giordano was in charge. Prior to the convention, we had difficulty getting him to take charge. Now he was the leader so much so that he commanded me wisely to cease pushing for a 30-0 vote on 16(c) because they were the delegates and had determined prior to my arrival to "shoot for the earlier Dent proposal to split the delegate votes 50-50." Although embarassed outwardly, I smiled inside knowing I no longer would be forced to provide the leadership for the Ford forces in the Mississippi delegation from the outside.

What concerned me was that after the 50-50 compromise was struck the Reagan forces would challenge the illegal unit-rule system and disallow the alternate votes so that only full delegate votes would count. This way it was possible we could lose 20-10 or 18-12. At that point I wanted nothing less than total victory—or at least a 16-14 margin for the president.

Holshouser and I comforted each other after the delegates departed for the big vote.

Then, "Big John" Connally arrived—too late to make a Ford pitch to the entire delegation to offset the final Reagan plea, which we later learned was subpar for the charismatic conservative.

I wanted Connally to talk to the delegates, so we sent in a message he was available and wanted to talk to the delegates. Barbour came out to warn against a last-minute Ford plea, even by Connally. Since Barbour was against, I was for the Connally appearance, as I knew Barbour to be a strong Reaganite. We sent Barbour back in to get a feeling from the delegates whether they wanted to hear from him. When Barbour returned with the message that only one raised hand favored a Connally talk, I told the persuasive Texan: "Don't be affronted governor. That means our folks believe they've got the votes."

And when they were preparing to adjourn 45 minutes later, Barbour came in to tell Connally the delegates were now ready to hear him. He added, "Ya'll won."

"How much?" I asked. "It was 31-28," he responded. I said, "You mean we got 'em all?"

"That's right—30-0," he said.

Holshouser and I let loose a few rebel yells and ran outside to await the arrival of our Mississippi heroes.

What we had not realized was that while our folks did not want to risk "shooting the moon," the Reagan delegates were under orders from John Sears to "go for broke." They had to have all 30 votes to win. We needed only half to be sure of victory.

Joe Coors, the Coors beer magnate and Reagan supporter, was just placing the beer and ice chests around the pool for the expected Reagan victory celebration when Holshouser and I came out announcing the vote while the Mississippi delegates were listening to "Big John."

After congratulating our Ford delegates, Holshouser and I took his limousine back to Crown Center to inform Cheney and the president. En route, we reflected on the fact that our old friend Reed had been defeated in his own delegation, and Pickering, too. In other words, our alternates had whipped the whole Mississippi leadership—Reed, Pickering, and Mounger. Reed had awaited the vote, then cast his lot with the Reagan side, making it 31-28. One of our delegates did not show up.

At the Crown Center's eighteenth floor, we were quickly escorted down to the Cheney suite, where Cheney, his wife, and Stu Spencer were beginning the celebration. I had got through to Cheney before leaving Ramada Inn East.

While in Cheney's suite, NBC-TV's early evening news announced the "stunning Ford victory" in the Mississippi delegation. We all roared our approval.

As we were leaving, Terry O'Donnell came running down the hall calling for me. I went back and O'Donnell informed me the president had just returned to his office and wanted to see me. I tried to catch Holshouser and John Davis, but they had vanished.

Back in the president's office, I was received most graciously by our candidate. This time I received the flashbulb treatment. The president told me: "Harry, I can never thank you enough for all you've done for me. Just know I'll be eternally grateful because I know what it cost you to do what you've done."

I told the president the effort would never have succeeded had it not been for the understanding and cooperation of Cheney and himself. I reflected back that it would not have been possible with Nixon and Haldeman because there would not have been the access and cooperation exhibited by Ford and Cheney. To me, it all went back to the North Carolina beach weekend with the southern chairmen when I had sold Cheney on the prospects in Mississippi, thanks to John Davis's sales job on me.

I left the president's office on cloud nine, thinking all my crises were over. Then as soon as I kicked off my suffocating patent leather shoes and loosened my tie in the sky suite, in rushed Jim Baker with a new crisis. It was a copy of the *Birmingham News* with a big headline reading: "Ford Would Write Off Cotton South?" Just what we did not need. And who was circulating the copies but Clarke Reed. Again, I was off my rear on the floor trying to explain. I grabbed a nearby pay phone and got through to Cheney with an urgent message to have the president call Reed and Pickering and disavow the story.

The quote had come from Rogers Morton, the Ford chairman who had made similar statements previously—all at great consternation to the president, Cheney, and me. This Morton gaffe, more than any other, cost him the chairmanship in the general election.

Cheney was furious. Morton's face in the sky suite showed his personal pain, especially as he was confronted by Senator John Tower with the article. Morton had not said the Cotton States would be written off, but the implication was there in his comments.

Reed, Mounger, Pickering, and other Reaganites were using the article to try to reverse the 30-0 vote scheduled for 16(c). Keene and Sears were on the Mississippi delegation phone line urging the Reagan delegates to call a caucus and reverse the earlier close vote on 16(c).

Our job was to keep our delegates and alternatives in their seats, since the only place to caucus would be outside the arena in one of the trailers. While I was keeping our alternates in their seats in their alternate area above the arena, Pickering found me and asked that we get Cheney on the phone together. We used a pay phone in the corridor. Pickering pleaded for the old Dent 50-50 split. Cheney told him the decision would be mine to make. I got on the line and told Cheney we could hold the line—that we should agree to no compromise. He agreed, although his TV set was giving the impression Reed had now switched and that Mississippi was changing from 30-0 against Rule 16(c).

Pickering was sorely disappointed. I took him back to the Mississippi alternate section where the Ford alternates let him know they felt the move to call a caucus was "low" and "dirty."

Meanwhile, Reed and Mounger took a group of delegates out to find a caucus room. They wound up in the CBS trailer with less than a majority of delegates. Some had forgot to bring their convention credentials and thus could not get back on the floor. This tactical error further doomed the last-minute Reagan effort to turn around the Mississippi delegation and thus the crucial vote on 16(c).

This had all reminded me of the 1968 battle we Nixon delegates had with the Reagan and Rockefeller efforts to panic our delegates against Nixon. We had held the line then. However, this time my 1968 co-worker Reed seemed to be the one who panicked; and my old mentor, Thurmond, was on the other side, too.

When the roll was called. Keene convinced Reed, with Mounger's assistance, to pass for Mississippi on the first ballot—much to my disappointment—so that Florida provided the deciding vote right ahead of Mississippi on the call of the roll for delegations that had passed on the first ballot.

However, the Mississippi caucus vote Tuesday afternoon had been the real deciding factor. Its early release had provided the psychological impact of victory needed by the Ford campaign. Baker had told me prior to the Mississippi caucus we could count exactly the 1130 votes required to win without Mississippi. He said any miscount on our part would be fatal, so every Mississippi vote was vital for insurance of victory on 16(c). Of course, without winning on 16(c), no one expected Ford would be nominated Wednesday night.

When Reed cast Mississippi's vote 30-0, the final tally hit 1180 against 16(c), 50 more votes than necessary.

This time I relaxed in the knowledge we could not lose the next night, especially since the Reagan floor maneuver had even angered some delegates who had voted for 16(c) in the Tuesday caucus. In a discussion with Cheney later Tuesday night, we concluded our victory margin would be such Wednesday night that we should urge our delegates to retain the one-half vote each and then count the Mississippi vote on a proportional basis. At the next caucus on Wednesday the delegates voted 32-28, dividing the delegate vote 16-14 for the nomination ballot.

On Wednesday night the expected happened, and Ford was nominated by a vote of 1187 to 1070. The victory parties went late into the evening. For Ford, however, the selection of a vice-presidential running mate was the next order of priority.

I was in the first group to visit with the president at 3 A.M. There were approximately 30 in the group. Most were members of the committee to notify the president of his nomination. Clarke Reed was not in the group, but Rosenbaum and I were. Unfortunately, my voice was not as strong as Rosenbaum's because he had Rockefeller in the room backing him, and I had no support when I proposed an open convention on the vice-presidency. Everyone knew this was the answer to Reagan's professed reluctance to accept the number two nomination.

I told the president the Reagan delegates had fire in their eyes on the convention floor—that he could only get a conservative through the convention. I said: "If the choice is left to the convention Reagan would be first choice. If he refused, then the Reagan delegates would have been substantially mollified though disappointed. Yet the disappointment would be with their hero, not the president. Also, the anti-Reagan people couldn't complain with an open convention—the choice would be that of the convention's not the president's, whether it's Reagan or someone else if he should decline."

However, I hardly got the proposal out of my mouth when the anti-Reagan voices sounded off. First came Rosenbaum, then Kent McGough of Ohio, then Paul Haerle of California, and finally the strong opposition of Rockefeller himself. No one seconded my suggestion, and it died aborning.

The president then spoke and acknowledged the very conservative nature of the convention. This is when I knew only a conservative would be proposed to the convention. However, I never believed it would be Senator Robert Dole. His name was never mentioned in the first meeting. It surfaced in the final meeting later in the morning.

It may have been better to select a more moderate nominee for winning purposes, especially considering the South's failure for winning the GOP ticket and the better potential elsewhere. However, the conservative convention would not have voted for anyone to the left of Dole.

Reagan now says he might have accepted the vice-presidency if asked. However, he not only repeatedly rejected the idea; but he ruled out the possibility of the offer when he said he would meet with Ford after the nomination vote Wednesday night only with the understanding he would not be offered the number two spot. So it is unfair to say after the election that he would have accepted had the offer been made or that he would have won had he been at the top of the ticket. He would have scored better than Goldwater in 1964, but he would not have fared as well as Ford. Reagan's vote would have been no better in the South. Yes, Reagan was more popular with southern Republican delegate types, but not necessarily beyond that circle and certainly not beyond the GOP ranks. In 1964 and 1972 the American people demonstrated that they would not approve a very conservative or very liberal presidential candidate. The Reaganites and McGovernites will never accept this proved political proposition. But this lack of reality, which surrounds zealots of left and right, is the reason they seldom prevail and why they can prevent their side from winning.

The American Political Report of November 11, 1977, reports that "Unpublished Louis Harris poll data presented to Democratic congressmen on 9/27 said if RR had opposed Carter in 1976, 'he would have lost by at least 57-43.' " The Harris poll is proof of the pudding.

Had there never been a Reagan candidacy in 1976, or had it all ended in North Carolina, Ford would have been elected in 1976—in my opinion. Reagan more than anyone was responsible for Jimmy Carter's success at a crucial juncture—the Florida primary.

When Reagan became a candidate, George Wallace was abandoned by the John Birch Society. This, more than the 1972 wound, caused the demise of Wallace and the consequent loss to Carter in the big southern primary stakes between the two southern Democratic hopefuls, Wallace and Carter. True, organized labor and other liberal groups helped Carter pull the key upset that enabled him to catapult on the national scene. However, without the Birchers forming the base of his support, as they had in 1968 and were doing in 1972, Wallace could not make it. While the Birchers liked Wallace, he was not the idealist conservative that Reagan was. Wallace was too much of a populist. Reagan was not everything, but he was almost the ideal. And give the Birchers a chance to wreck the GOP over the Democratic party, they'll take on the GOP fight every time. This, unfortunately, is the bane of the Grand Old Party's existence, as I tried to explain to Secretary of State Henry Kissinger while flying back to Washington when the convention was concluded. I was on the plane carrying White House staffers and Kissinger to Washington. In flight Kissinger caught my attention and asked me to sit down for a conversation about the convention. I could tell he was perplexed about the fact that he was kept out of sight at the convention until the nomination battle was completed. Also, he had been forced to accept an unpalatable platform amendment by Senator Jesse Helms of North Carolina. The Helms amendment in effect was blatantly critical of and counter to key parts of Kissinger's foreign policy.

"What is it, Harry, with these southern kooks?" he inquired of me. "Why don't they like me?"

I could feel his agony by the question and the exasperated look on his face.

I explained that the Reagan-type conservative is very hard-lined on foreign policy and national security and that for the Birch types, Kissinger was in the same category as the late President Dwight Eisenhower. I reminded Kissinger that Robert Welch had labeled Eisenhower a Communist. I also explained that the Birch Society lists the Council on Foreign Relations and the Rockefeller family as being greater dangers than the Communist party itself.

"But, Harry," he intoned with his thick German accent, "I always go for the hard-line option—everytime. Ask Senator Thurmond. I don't understand what they can be thinking."

I concluded by assuring Kissinger that frankly the Birchers and other unrealistic ultras baffle me as well, even though I have been with them in the trenches in so many political skirmishes.

4
The
Origin
of
Southern
Strategy

The use of a political strategy designed to win the South had its clearest beginning in 1960 when Senator John F. Kennedy took three significant actions that resulted in his carrying the South over Richard M. Nixon in the general election and winning the presidency with one of the slimmest margins in history.

What were Kennedy's three actions? He selected Senator Lyndon B. Johnson of Texas as his running mate, promised to protect the southern textile industry from low-cost imports, and made a sympathy call to Martin Luther King Jr. during the civil rights leader's imprisonment in an Atlanta jail.

While these three moves may not have been a part of a grand southern strategy, they were deliberate actions taken by JFK in the full knowledge of their importance in his race to carry the South and thereby win the presidency. For Kennedy selecting Lyndon B. Johnson as his running mate was of profound significance because Johnson had most southern senators and many congressmen neatly tucked away in his hip pocket. These legislators would use their credibility with southern voters to assure them that LBJ was a "good ole boy" who had been of invaluable assistance to them in maintaining the filibuster rule and otherwise helping them where he could "under the table" in their states' rights battles.

Furthermore, as the Senate majority leader, Lyndon Johnson had done legions of favors for his southern legislative buddies; and as the vice-presidential candidate he could demand loyalty despite the general distrust and dislike of the standard-bearer.

In numerous instances, LBJ knew the secrets of the southern politician—his desires, needs, and misdeeds—and such knowledge has a way of bringing many a public figure into line.

While on Capitol Hill, I watched Johnson and Bobby Baker, the senator's chief floor assistant, operate in the Senate Democratic cloakroom. It was the beginning of an enlightening lesson in pragmatic, winning politics.

The sharpest ever as Senate majority leader, Johnson seldom lost with his flashing displays of legislative legerdemain.

Baker, from South Carolina, was invaluable to his boss in the execution of political victories. When a new senator (Democrat or Republican) came to town, Baker met him at the plane, train, or car and began the process of politically lathering him up from head to toe.

In these initial meetings, Baker found the new senator's Achilles' heel: What aspect of personal greed or personal interest most motivated the new senator? This knowledge enabled Baker and LBJ to go straight to the man's vulnerability in getting what LBJ needed for winning Senate votes.

Often, for example, it was necessary to get a senator—Republican or Democrat—to pair his vote (neutralize his vote by withholding his vote and announcing for or against the pending issue). Johnson won many legislative squeakers by this and other methods. After all, he was usually dealing with a slim partisan majority, but one subject to upheaval by volatile, ideological issues. These issues could push Democrats Strom Thurmond of South Carolina and Harry F. Bryd Sr. of Virginia to vote with the Republicans, while Republicans Jacob Javits of New York and Clifford Case of New Jersey could swing to the Democratic side.

Lyndon and Bobby specialized in doing little favors for senators, and they always expected repayment later when a key vote was facing the Senate majority leader.

The considerable power of naming committee and subcommittee chairmen, as well as committee members, rolled up hundreds of credits for the Senate majority leader, which he called upon during his 1960 and 1964 national races.

Maintaining the general unity of the southern senators was paramount for Johnson as Senate majority leader. Kennedy called him to exercise this same skill in keeping the South solid for the Democratic ticket in 1960. Johnson was an expert at playing a hand designed to keep the Southerners in his corner.

After all, the late Senator Richard Russell of Georgia and his southern colleagues had installed Johnson in his leadership position after Russell had turned it down.

Thurmond, the king of states' rights, was one senator whom LBJ had trouble keeping under control. Even as Thurmond was a thorn in LBJ's flesh from the right, the late Senator Wayne Morse of Oregon was a thorn from the left. Both Thurmond and Morse changed parties—Morse became a Democrat and Thurmond a Republican. Both switched parties for ideological reasons and won reelection under their new labels.

LBJ and Thurmond became strongly antagonistic in the Senate, especially after Thurmond set a new filibuster record of 24 hours and 18 minutes in 1957 against Johnson's wishes. However, Johnson was not to be denied his finding a way to influence Thurmond, the 1948 states' rights presidential candidate. After failing in about every other effort to saddle Thurmond, Johnson finally broke the crust of distrust in January 1960.

Thurmond is the classic southern gentleman. He has profound respect for womanhood in general and has been devoted to the two younger women in his life—his present wife, Nancy Moore Thurmond; and his first wife, Jean Crouch Thurmond, who died in January 1960 of a brain tumor.

Despite their ideological differences, Johnson and Baker led a delegation of senators from Washington to the funeral of Jean Thurmond in Aiken, South Carolina, on January 8, 1960.

I was standing next to Thurmond when LBJ came through the line to express his sympathy. When he reached Thurmond, the grief stricken South Carolinian said: "I hope you're the next president of the United States!" That's all he could get out before he broke down and cried.

LBJ and Baker returned to Washington with what I believe must have been a conviction that they had finally penetrated "ole Strom's" hard shell, but they were to discover ultimately that they had not.

Thurmond went to his last national convention as a Democrat in 1960, favoring Johnson over Kennedy as the presidential nominee. Thurmond's leadership undercut the influence with the South Carolina delegation of the state's young governor and now U.S. Senator Ernest F. "Fritz" Hollings, who was firmly planted in Kennedy's corner.

Thurmond was later to discover his mistake in supporting LBJ at the 1960 convention, for when Johnson became president following JFK's death, he out "Kennedied" Kennedy with an unprecedented flow of costly social legislation called the Great Society. LBJ as president showed himself to be a political opportunist. Thurmond viewed this as a betrayal of earlier trust.

Kennedy won the nomination in 1960; and against the advice of most of his advisers, he selected LBJ as his running mate. Thus the Kennedy Southern Strategy was underway. It was designed to win the old Solid South through the effective influence of "lovable" Lyndon, "the Southwesterner" (South was played up, western played down), as Johnson described himself.

The Kennedy strategy received kid-glove treatment by the national press, which was captivated by the Kennedy personality. By contrast, Kennedy's southern strategy was never kicked around by the press generally as was Nixon's.

Using Johnson to hold the South for Kennedy proved to be a productive strategy because the difference in the general election was made in Dixie.

The second thrust of Kennedy's southern strategy involved one of the region's principal employers, the textile industry.

Candidate Kennedy agreed to support a policy of protecting textile jobs by stemming low-wage cotton textile imports from Japan. Opponent Richard M. Nixon declined to support textile protection. This position cost Nixon at least two southern states—South Carolina and North Carolina—by very slim margins in the closing days of the campaign. It was a bitter lesson for Nixon— one he was not going to forget.

Kennedy's third action that played a major role in winning the South in the 1960 presidential race was his dealings with Martin Luther King Jr. By the 1960 election, King's name had become a household word throughout the nation. Daily, King and his supporters were receiving nationwide publicity for their activities in the South. When King and some of his associates were jailed in Atlanta for civil disobedience, Kennedy called the civil rights leader in jail to express his sympathy. The call received immense publicity, and it resulted in solidifying the southern black vote for Kennedy.

According to many black southern Republicans, prior to that telephone call, many southern blacks had planned to support Republican Nixon.

Kennedy's move did, however, hurt him with white voters; but the damage was not enough to break the Democrats' armlock on southern white voters. It was not until the 1964 presidential race that the growing erosion of the national Democratic party among Southerners was evident. Thus the result of the Kennedy call to King was to keep what the Democrats had previously—white voters—and add black voters.

Kennedy's southern strategy worked. The senator carried the South and won, however slim the vote.

For almost a century, the South had been ignored by both major political parties. Because of Reconstruction scars, the Democrats had the South "in the bag," and the Republicans knew better than to try to change this. But situations change.

The 1960 presidential race demonstrated the importance of the South in winning nationally. But as Senator Barry Goldwater was to find in the next election, the South is an essential base, yet by itself, the South is not enough to carry a presidential election.

Southerners liked Senator Barry Goldwater of Arizona, but unfortunately, the senator was nominated to run on the Republican ticket at a time when it was practically impossible for him to win. First, he was running against Johnson, the incumbent president who was finishing the incompleted term of the assassinated Kennedy. The nation, still emotionally caught up in the tragic occurrence in Dallas, was in no mood to vote on substantive issues. Thus it was to be an emotional election, and Johnson had the tides of emotion running strong in his favor.

Second, because of this emotional factor, Goldwater's attempts to address himself to issues fell upon deaf ears most of the time. In some cases, Goldwater's opposition distorted his views; in others, Goldwater ineffectively presented his views. The final analysis: The incumbent had the upper hand. He told the voters what they wanted to hear, whether he intended to keep his promises or not. As it turns out, Goldwater was considerably more honest than his opponent, but that straight-from-the-heart approach just was not the vogue when LBJ rode Texas style across the national scene.

While Goldwater failed miserably on the national scale, he was a raging success in Dixie. In 1964 Goldwater carried five Deep-South states and his native state of Arizona and scared the Democrats in the rest of the South. But this was all.

However, the important happening in 1964 where this writer is concerned is that the Goldwater fever which enveloped the Southland in 1964 set the stage for the rise and development of a truly competitive two-party political system.

Across Dixie, Republican candidates were swept into office, riding the Goldwater popularity. In Alabama, four Republicans were elected to Congress. Three are still there, and in 1962 the GOP barely missed ousting long-time Democrat Lister Hill from the U.S. Senate.

A friend living in Birmingham tells of one fellow whom he had never heard of, a perpetual runner for elective office as a Republican and a perpetual loser. This fellow had got his name in the race for a minor office in Alabama; he had not campaigned and did not expect to come close to winning. But with Goldwater leading the national ticket, the perpetual loser was swept unwittingly into office. On the night of the election returns when Goldwater went under, the perpetual loser, now a winner for the first time, was interviewed on local television. The only words he could say were, "I'm amazed! I'm amazed!"

But then, election night 1964 was amazing for many reasons. It was an amazing loss for Goldwater. It was an amazing victory for the Democrats nationally, and it was an amazing day for the Republican party in the South.

The key to Goldwater's southern success was another U.S. Senator, Strom Thurmond of South Carolina. Not only did Thurmond help persuade Governor George Wallace to forego his presidential ambitions in 1964, but he came to be Goldwater's staunchest campaigner—and the most effective.

Thurmond was becoming more and more restless on the Democratic side of the aisle in the Senate, especially with the flood of New Frontier programs being advanced by the liberal Kennedy Administration, and following Kennedy, the Great Society proposals of the Johnson Administration.

During those years, J. Fred Buzhardt Jr., counsel to President Nixon from 1973 to 1974, and I worked for Thurmond at the Senate. We talked frequently with the senator about the upcoming 1964 presidential election picture. Goldwater and Thurmond had fought side by side on many battles in the Senate: Together they fought against repeal of the right to work authority, "no-win" foreign policy when conflicts arose, and the civil rights bill of 1964. And together they fought for a strong program of national defense and a diffusion of national power in favor of more states' rights.

Goldwater and Thurmond were like the golddust twins. Back in 1957 when Thurmond was setting his filibuster record, only one other senator came to aid him, offering to relieve him: Republican Barry Goldwater, an admirer of Thurmond's spunk. But even then, Thurmond refused the offer to permit him to physically relieve himself; instead, he chose to set a record filibuster of 24 hours and 18 minutes. This was a genuine filibuster without a filibuster bag attached to his leg for relief purposes.

The magnetic pull of the Republican party became even stronger on Thurmond in 1964 when the conservatives of the GOP took control of the convention and nominated Barry Goldwater to be their standard-bearer. Now Thurmond was becoming even more restless in his role of dissident Democrat.

But it was Johnson's nomination by the Democrats (and his record in office following Kennedy's death) and his selection of Senator Hubert Humphrey of Minnesota as his 1964 running mate that made Thurmond make his political switch.

Preparations for a possible switch in political party allegiance for Thurmond got under way.

Labor Day, 1964, Thurmond and I visited South Carolina to discuss with key Thurmond supporters the idea of changing parties. The move was frowned upon almost unanimously as too risky for the senator's political future. Most suggested that he stay completely out of the race, exercise golden silence (a la Harry Byrd Sr. of Virginia), or support Goldwater and remain a Democrat.

For a brief while, the idea of switching was cooled, but within a week Thurmond visited Goldwater in his Washington apartment. He requested that Senator and Mrs. Goldwater listen to his proposed statement of support and then decide if they wanted him to back Goldwater's candidacy only, switch parties in doing so, or give the proposed statement only with changes offered by the Goldwaters.

Senator and Mrs. Goldwater voted for all three. Goldwater felt that this could be the beginning of additional conservative political switchovers in the South. There was a belief that Senator Frank Lausche of Ohio might follow. In Alabama, George Wallace was being wooed by the Goldwater leaders. And Thurmond was certain Congressman Albert Watson of South Carolina would follow him with an in-party declaration of support to be followed by a switch at some appropriate time in the future. Watson subsequently resigned from the Democratic party and from Congress and won reelection as a Republican in early 1965.

After the Goldwater meeting, Thurmond attended funeral services for construction magnate and former U.S. Senator Charles E. Daniel in Greenville, South Carolina. Realizing that Thurmond would be confronted again by Democratic friends who did not want him to switch parties, Buzhardt and I determined to hold off with plans to mail the television speech and news release.

When Thurmond later called from Greenville to check on Senate business, he inquired whether the television speech had been mailed to the media with the embargoed dateline. I responded that we had held it up for fear he would be talked out of the party switch.

He retorted: "They met me in a group at the funeral, but I wouldn't talk to them. I told them I'd made my decision, and that was that."

Thurmond worked relentlessly for Goldwater all over the South. Our little group raised our own funds, sending the senator throughout the South and putting him on television and radio on virtually every broadcast station in Dixie. Thurmond's best job was persuading Governor Wallace not to be a presidential candidate.

The switchover speech on southwide television had a dramatic impact, especially when Thurmond surprised his vast television audience by switching parties to support Goldwater. They had expected when they heard of the forthcoming 15-minute show that Thurmond would announce his support for Goldwater as a Democrat. Few, except possibly those with whom we had spoken, suspected Thurmond would go all the way, and even they doubted he would do so.

One of those who had reveled at Thurmond's proposal to support Goldwater, but had balked at his party switching idea, was the late James F.

Byrnes, the former solicitor, congressman, senator, Supreme Court justice, "Assistant President" to FDR, U.S. secretary of state, and governor of South Carolina.

When Thurmond and I sat down to put our proposal to Byrnes, the state's No. 1 citizen remarked: "Well, I'll have to take a drink on that! Maude, Maude (his wife), bring me a drink! Why, Strom, that'd be audacious, that'd be a bold action, a daring action. But then, that's the only way I ever got licked in my political life—back in 1924, when Colie Blease whipped me for the U.S. Senate. He was bold, audacious, and by damn, he whipped me!"

Later Byrnes was to call Thurmond on prompting from a mutual friend to suggest that Thurmond support Goldwater as a Democrat.

After Thurmond rejected the advice of this sage political wizard in South Carolina, Byrnes even in his advanced years, joined arm in arm with Thurmond. Byrnes had led the South Carolina campaign for Eisenhower in 1952, declared himself an independent, and gave full support to the Goldwater campaign.

Thurmond had decided to go all the way with Goldwater out of sincere conviction and admiration for the senator and his cause. "How can I sit here and think only of my own political future when I face a choice of Goldwater and Miller versus Johnson and Humphrey?" Thurmond would ask.

On September 16, 1964, Thurmond told the people of South Carolina and the South:

> To my friends who have conscientiously advised me against this step, because of a sincere belief that I could best serve the country by following a course designed to keep myself in office, I can only say that I fully realize the political risk involved in this step; I could go down into oblivion. But in the final analysis, I can only follow the course which in my heart and conscience, I believe to be in the best interest of our State, our country, and the freedom of our people.
>
> I have chosen this course because I cannot consider any risks in a cause which I am convinced is right.

The evening following this speech all of us connected with the senator suddenly knew that not only had the right thing been done, but that we had gained the backing of the majority of the people who would hold the fate of

Thurmond's political future in their hands two years later when he would be running as a Republican for the first time. Hundreds of telegrams and telephone calls poured in, even the wife of our reluctant state GOP chairman admitted the speech was so moving and effective that she, like many others, had cried.

Thurmond performed magnificently in the Goldwater campaign and was well pleased when his candidate carried the southern states of South Carolina, Louisiana, Georgia, Mississippi, and Alabama, and also Goldwater's Arizona, by a narrow margin. Unlike many of the die-hard Goldwaterites, Thurmond had never expected a Goldwater victory. As conservative as he was, he was too realistic to expect miracles. This feeling was especially so after the senator's meeting with the Goldwaters in September. Surprisingly, even Goldwater expressed pessimism, acknowledging that he would go back to Camelback Mountain near Phoenix and play with his ham radio after the election. Buzhardt and I never forgot that comment, knowing he did not expect to win, but wondering if he wanted to win.

The Thurmond Speaks for Goldwater Committee concentrated on trying to win the southern states eventually carried by Goldwater. Thurmond made numerous public appearances in these five states and a few others. Television film clips and radio commercials were used featuring Thurmond speaking up for the Goldwater-Miller ticket.

All of this was done with funds raised by the Thurmond Speaks organization. No assistance came from the national Goldwater organization. The Thurmond Speaks committee was designed to supplement the Goldwater operation and operate independently.

I operated this special campaign, leaving my post on Thurmond's Senate payroll to do the job.

Ultimately, the campaign proved successful, and much of the success in the southern states was directly attributable to Thurmond's credibility and hard work.

Great rejoicing went on in the Thurmond ranks that election night, although Goldwater was taking a national drubbing. For one, Thurmond had enhanced his own prestige and political clout in doing what he believed was right. Once again he had swum upstream against the advice of his political friends. Most seemed to realize that night that although Goldwater had lost, Thurmond had won in 1964 and was on his way to becoming the first statewide candidate to be elected as a Republican in South Carolina in almost 100 years.

Again, Thurmond had done the unusual, the unexpected, and prevailed, which is how he got to the Senate in 1954. He acted with audacity to challenge the Democratic establishment in South Carolina, running as a write-in candidate and winning 2-1. He became the first major officeholder ever elected to office in this country without his name being on the ballot.

Goldwater had lost, but his friend Thurmond was a big winner on his own turf, the South.

In the next two years, the seed of the Republican Southern Strategy began to sprout and grow.

Thurmond returned to the Senate with more respect and comfort on the "right" side of the aisle. The Republicans welcomed him, doing their best to make up for the party seniority he had lost as a Democrat. They put him back on the Armed Services Committee with relatively the same position he would have had on the committee had he been a Republican all along. This was made possible by shuffling a few Republicans to other committees and by the loss of Goldwater and the late J. Glenn Beall Sr. of Maryland from the Senate. No one had to be dropped for the new convert—and none would have consented to such, even as popular as Thurmond was at the time among GOP senators. None seemed willing to surrender one iota of seniority or other senatorial perquisites in the Congress. This is why so few party switches take place.

Thurmond could not be given his same relative rank on the Commerce Committee, so he was shifted to the Banking and Currency Committee. Because of some vacancies there, he got a few notches up the seniority list.

To make it all go better, the Republicans put Thurmond on the Republican Policy Committee. The placement did not mean much, but it looked good.

These committee assignments were important to Thurmond, because he knew the loss of seniority would be an issue in his reelection campaign two years hence.

Although Thurmond initially had made his switch without knowing what effect his party-seniority status would have on committee assignments, everything worked out favorably. Thurmond could, therefore, campaign that he had not cost his state power or influence. In fact, he campaigned that his influence increased because he had little clout on the Democratic side, and the Republicans could not do anything to enhance the power of a dissident Democrat.

The good treatment the Republicans gave Thurmond showed their pleasure at the prospect of a developing southern power base, which might change the political picture in national and local elections.

When Thurmond changed parties in 1964, he became the first Deep-South Republican in the Senate in many years. Professor John Tower of Texas had preceded the senator as a Republican from an old Confederate state (Texas) when he won a special election in which he was the only Republican and thus was high man in a one-shot race with the Democratic vote being split several ways. He was able to go on from there and maintain the remainder of the term in 1966 and win reelection in 1972.

In 1964 the Senate had two conservative southern Republicans—Tower and Thurmond. In 1968 the count stood at six in the Senate, twenty-nine in the House. Additionally, Republicans held four governorships in the South and almost three hundred state legislative seats. Comparatively, in 1958 there were only two senators, eight congressmen, no governors, and less than one hundred state legislators.

It was coming to be true what the new breed of southern Republicans were yelling in the Goldwater campaign: "We're gonna' win from the court-house to the White House!"

After the Goldwater campaign, Thurmond made a second shift from a Goldwater Republican to plain Republican.

When the state Republican chairmanship came open in the fall of 1965, the Thurmond fans in the party convinced me to offer myself as a candidate against the party leadership's candidate, Arthur Ravenel Jr., who had switched a few years after serving as a Democrat in the state legislature from Charleston County. After a brief campaign Ravenel withdrew.

My election as chairman certified Thurmond as a bonafide Republican. I had told the senator when James B. Edwards, now South Carolina's governor, was talking Thurmond into letting me run for chairman that I would fight hard to develop a strong two-party system in South Carolina and throughout the South, and Thurmond had said he would help me recruit a quality team with which he would run for reelection in 1966 and that he would lead the team. He kept that promise.

As a result, the biggest statewide and local Republican ticket since Reconstruction was put together, called "the Quality Team You Can Trust."

Team members ran for most of the congressional seats, both U.S. Senate seats, governor, lieutenant governor, and state superintendent of education. All Thurmond insisted on was that the members of the team be honest and credible candidates. Each member was.

The team retained the Watson congressional seat easily, and Thurmond smashed his credible opponent, Senator Bradley Morrah, with 63 percent of the vote.

In addition, the state was stunned with Republicans moving from one to twenty-three state legislators and many more local offices.

The tree was bearing fruit. We South Carolina Republicans were now getting ready for the big coup—the White House—with this new southern strategy.

Meanwhile, other gains outside Dixie were being made for the GOP. The Republican party made a good comeback from 1964, picking up 47 seats in the House and 4 in the Senate. Leading the rejuvenation was another man on the comeback trail—Richard Milhous Nixon.

5
Victory
in
1968

A pproaching the presidential election of 1968, three Republican leaders were considered the most likely candidates to win the GOP nomination for president. They were former Vice President Richard M. Nixon, Governor Ronald Reagan of California, and Governor Nelson Rockefeller of New York.

The national Democratic party had overplayed its hand with the South by 1967. It had moved so far left that loyal southern politicians no longer found it possible to camouflage these conditions and hold the majority of southern voters in line.

Conservative Democrats in Dixie, the most loyal group the national party had ever had, were fed up, weary of being taken for granted. They were ready to play a major role in electing a Republican president in a mass desertion of "the party of our fathers."

The roots of political frustration in the South backtracks to the 1940s and 1950s, and even earlier.

Since the Civil War, the South had been treated as an illegitimate stepchild by much of the rest of the nation, particularly the Northeast. The only way the South could exert political power nationally was by means of solidarity. "Solid South" came to mean that voters elected only Democrats and those elected maximized their power in Washington by effective use of the seniority system in Congress.

This strategy worked for decades and probably would have continued to be effective long into the future had the national Democratic party not been taken over by ideologues from the left, or as sometimes called, the "wild-eyed liberals."

Southerners were gradually convinced by the "new" national Democratic party that the party was going to whip the South into line, even at the expense of sacrificing the South. Many, myself included, were amazed to watch many southern politicians allow themselves to be whipped into line. Two who bucked were Wallace and Thurmond. Contrary to the popular view fostered by eastern liberals, only Wallace's rebellion was based substantially on race. Thurmond's rebellion was fundamentally one emanating from other concerns affecting the national interest, like his fear of big government, excessive spending, and soft foreign policy.

Throughout the nation, a fast-growing number of voters was becoming so disenchanted with the uprooted Democratic party that it turned its support to the "fighters." Democrats who surrendered could not muster much support any longer, and the presidential election of 1968 was to prove that the South was available to the highest bidder. Dixie was no longer in the bag for the Democrats.

In the 1930s, 1940s, and 1950s, it was virtually impossible to defeat an incumbent southern senator or congressman, because his campaign would always be keyed to seniority, a code word for power in Congress.

Previous records support this. Olin D. Johnston, a New Deal-type senator from South Carolina in the 1940s and 1950s, campaigned on the twin themes of seniority and sobriety. He was so unbeatable that even then-Governor Thurmond suffered his only political loss to him in 1950.

But change has visited the political system. Now seniority is becoming less a tool of political power for southern Democrats. Liberals in the Democratic party have been gnawing away at the system that protected incumbent conservative Democrats. By the end of another decade only a few conservative Democrats will remain as head of major committees on Capitol Hill. And when this finally happens, many southern voters will have less reason to remain with "the party of our fathers."

The South's growing frustration with its loss of influence in the national Democratic party was demonstrated years ago in the 1948 presidential election. South Carolina's then-Governor Thurmond served as the focal point of this dissatisfaction.

Governor Thurmond agreed to lead the States' Rights Democratic party efforts of the 1948 presidential race. It was an attempt to wield southern power on a national scale again. The objective of the states' rights move was to capture the electoral votes of the South. The national Democrats, having been denied the South, would lack the majority necessary for victory. This would throw the election into the House where southern congressmen could assert their unified power to name a president.

The ticket of Governor Thurmond and Fielding Wright of Mississippi carried five states—North Carolina, South Carolina (three-fourths of the votes), Alabama, Mississippi, and Louisiana—and one errant electoral vote in Tennessee. Georgia was lost primarily because Herman Talmadge decided to stick with the national Democratic party.

Despite Thurmond's strong effort, the adventure failed in a close election won by President Harry Truman over Thomas Dewey.

Although the southern strategy of 1948 was unsuccessful, it offered a lesson. Twenty years later, Thurmond would make the lesson work.

Much of the South favored Thurmond in 1948. Dixie voters tasted independence for the first time. There was substantial southern support for Eisenhower in the elections of 1952 and 1956, for the 1956 Harry Byrd independent ticket, for Nixon in 1960; and then there were the wholesale defections to Goldwater in 1964.

From this point, southern conservatives have been well received in the Republican party. The 70 percent average vote among all southern states for Nixon in 1972 was historical. Here again was the Solid South—but solid for a Republican, for the first time in history.

Such a reversal undoubtedly changed the character of politics in America. By 1969 southern strategy had become a common expression. It was used as a term of derision by the Democrats and many in the national press and often with a look of complete innocence that the Democrats had used their own southern strategy for years to hold the South in line in national elections.

To some, especially Southerners, the emergence of a southern strategy with profound national significance was the salvation for America. Many believed that only in a return to conservative policies at the national level could the free enterprise system be preserved and individual freedoms protected in this country and around the world.

The national press could never understand that for most Southerners in the Republican Southern Strategy movement, the motivation was not racial. The collective efforts were not generated by a desire to turn back the clock pre-May 17, 1954, the date of the Supreme Court's desegregation decision. Had this been the case, the new Republicans would have gone with the Wallace tide. The fact is, the Democratic party is the one with the racial problem. It swings between love and hate for the Wallacites. Even Massachusett's Ted Kennedy can exhibit hatred when in Washington, but still journey to Huntsville, Alabama, for a love-in with Wallace in 1974.

The principal aim of southern conservatives has been the preservation of individual freedom, not only for Americans, but for people the world over. This group believes that the policies of liberalism on the domestic front and internationally result in the diminution of individual liberty.

Conservatives believe that liberal policies internationally usually result in weakening America's place in world leadership, thus increasing the possibility of domination by a potential enemy. Conservatives also believe that liberal domestic policies lead to a national welfare state in which workers lose their freedom through heavy taxation and that the recipients of the welfare state lose their personal liberty through bureaucratic regulation.

In the 1960s under the leadership of John Kennedy and Lyndon Johnson, it appeared to most conservatives that America had lost all its moorings. The streets were filled with radical dissenters, cities were literally burning down, crime seemed uncontrollable, and the vast social programs of the

Democrats were excessively expensive. And in the end, the only way Kennedy and Johnson could solve the problems of needy people was by putting them on the public payroll.

If social and welfare programs continue for the next 20 years at the same pace as the last 20, half of the American population, by the end of the century, will be working to support the other half according to former HEW Secretary Casper Weinberger in August 1975. At that point hardly anyone will have any personal freedom left.

When we southern conservatives took advantage of the 1964 Goldwater break, moving toward the predominant position held by one of the two major political parties, we did so grasping for the opportunity to help preserve a strong America and its place of meaningful leadership in the world. This was the message with which we kept delegates in line. We were playing for keeps from a sense of deep regional loyalty and American patriotism.

It was apparent to many of us that the Democrats would probably end up nominating Vice President Hubert Humphrey for their 1968 run for the White House; and if this were the case, Humphrey would have to run helter-skelter in search of ways to unite the badly factioned Democratic party.

On the other hand, all three of the serious Republican candidates for the nomination must have known that ultimately the battle would have to be won in the South.

So while Humphrey ran in every direction, Republican candidates traveled the "Chattanooga Choo Choo" in their race for the votes down South. Nixon, Reagan, and Rockefeller would be invited and would accept the opportunity to present their cases to southern Republican chairmen prior to the Southerners making a final decision on which candidate to support.

While Nixon was never unpopular among us southern conservatives, he was never our first love. Nevertheless, he, unlike other eastern Republicans, endeared himself to Republicans across the nation with the constant support for this party's candidates. In 1964, he impressed all the Goldwater devotees and Thurmond himself with his unrelenting support of the standard-bearer. Nixon helped make Goldwater look good in 1964, and we never forgot it; neither did Goldwater.

For Nixon, a simple twist of fate may have made a major difference in his political understanding of issues in Dixie. In 1966, as speaker for the South Carolina Republican fund raiser, Nixon addressed a good crowd and responded to a rousing reception for him in Columbia. He stirred us up and won points with our people by endorsing our conservative ticket down the line, being particularly complimentary of the Thurmond and GOP Congressman Albert Watson switches. When asked in a national interview if he were embarassed to have "ole States' Rights Strom" in his party, Nixon answered: "Strom is no racist. Strom is a man of courage and integrity." Thurmond never forgot those unapologetic, gracious comments by Nixon— nor did any member of the South Carolina GOP.

But following the speech that twist of fate happened. I drove Nixon to the airport for his flight, which was late, thereby giving me time to present the case for the South as rapidly and forcefully as I dared.

A *Washington Star* reporter on the trip with Nixon had graciously complimented me to Nixon, indicating that I was able to put a political operation together and score.

In the conversation Nixon made clear his intention to seek the top job again in 1968 and expressed deep concern about George Wallace. Could he win if Wallace made it a three-way race? This, he felt was his chief obstacle. Should Wallace take most of the South, he would be unable to win enough votes in the rest of the country to gain a clear majority and avoid having the election thrown into the Democratic-controlled House of Representatives; and there, the Democrats were sure to win.

I painted a picture for Nixon of what Thurmond had done for Goldwater in the 1964 race. I was careful to explain something Nixon either knew or accepted from me as fact—Thurmond was the only southern leader in the GOP who could rally Southerners to a Republican banner. (Many Nixonites then did not understand the political clout of Thurmond in Dixie). After all, I explained, Thurmond won 39 electoral votes on his own in 1948; and he did even more good for Goldwater in 1964.

I could tell Nixon was computerizing these ideas for recall in 1968. All my meetings with Nixon—from then through all my meetings with him in the first term in the White House—convinced me Richard Nixon could perceive a practical political point correctly and quickly. His antennae never missed a single beat of common sense political rhythm until he became engulfed in Watergate.

The twist of fate—a plane running late—launched the 1968 southern strategy. It taught me that Nixon knew where his Achilles' heel was; it also gave me the chance to show him how possibly his weakness could be protected.

Reagan also had been a hero in his support of Goldwater in 1964. A classic conservative in the philosophical sense, Reagan brims with charisma and good looks.

Conditions in South Carolina in 1967 required the services of the California governor. The state party was $40,000 in debt after the 1966 campaign, which was not too bad, except that my name was the only one on the note. I figured it was time to get Reagan to come South—and to get that note paid off.

Arrangements were made for the governor to appear in Columbia when I visited Sacramento in the summer of 1967.

A considerable amount of publicity was given in South Carolina to the Harry Dent visit to Ronald Reagan in California, making it appear that the Nixon-Reagan battle in the South Carolina GOP was underway.

J. Drake Edens Jr., the national committeeman, supported Nixon completely. Talk swept the state about how Thurmond and Dent were committed to Reagan and were busily stealing Edens's delegates for Reagan. But this was not so, although I liked Reagan more than Nixon, I was still uncommitted; so was Thurmond.

In retrospect though, I must allow for some confusion in me about whether I loved "Ronnie Baby" or the idea of getting my name off the $40,000 note. After the governor's appearance, the answer was clear: I loved "Ronnie Baby" because he got my name off the note. The note was paid in full.

Getting Reagan to speak to the statewide rally in Columbia in late September 1967 was a real coup. In his address, televised statewide, Reagan was magnificent, setting Republican hearts afire—and clearing up our debt. The governor's points were loaded with humor and facts that made the liberals look foolish, wasteful, and socialistic. He described the awful mess he found in California following the years of liberal Democratic leadership. His administration was working posthaste to save the state from impending bankruptcy, brought about principally by uncontrolled welfare spending.

In South Carolina, Reagan's speech further forced Democratic leaders to run for cover, doing their utmost to get away from Johnson and Humphrey.

During the months that followed, the Reagan forces continued to work toward a run for the nomination, staying in close contact with me. However, during this period the question, "Can Reagan win?" bothered me. So I started my own search to find out. The question became critical in finally settling on a candidate.

I found in South Carolina that, although Reagan was No. 1 in

Republican hearts, Nixon was the choice for president, with Reagan as his running mate.

The nationally published polls showed Nixon the first choice. Hale Greenleaf of Central Surveys in Shenandoah, Iowa, told me the same Reagan strengths and weaknesses were showing generally in other states. Unfortunately, in 1967, Reagan was being perceived as another Goldwater. He could arouse the GOP stalwarts, but he would be rejected in a national election because of his inexperience in national and international affairs.

Nixon was the one.

Governor Nelson Rockefeller was running strong nationally for the nomination, but not too well in Dixie. At the invitation of the southern conservatives, Governor and Mrs. Rockefeller came to a closed door luncheon in Columbia, where they met with the state convention delegates and alternates. Interestingly, Rockefeller revealed in his talk that he understood the problem affecting the southern conservatives in offering him support. He explained his problem in New York if he gave his unqualified support to a rock- ribbed conservative. He also explained that the problems and the constituencies were different in his region. The only way a Republican could win in New York was by winning the support of a lot of Democrats, many of whom are more liberal than the Democrats of the South.

We Southerners were gracious in our reception of the Rockefellers, and the Rockefellers were gracious in their acceptance of our southern hospitality, but this is all the occasion amounted to: a gracious affair.

Leaders in South Carolina did realize, however, that Nelson Rockefeller is without horns or a forked tail.

The Republican chairmen met in New Orleans in the spring of 1968. Senator John Tower and Peter O'Donnell of Texas and Fred LaRue of Mississippi were there trying to line up Republicans for Nixon. As in the past, I argued for the hang-loose strategy (that is, southern GOP leaders and delegates should "hang loose," but hang together) with support from Clarke Reed, the chairman of the group; and William F. Murfin, the Florida chairman.

My proposal was to invite the three big candidates to meet with us southern chairmen in the South to discuss their platforms. This would be a visible demonstration that the two-party system was to work in Dixie—and work for the benefit of the South. After all, a few national candidates, except Barry Goldwater, had come a courtin' in the South from either party for years.

We Southerners felt it was important to impress our southern constituency by showing that we were so desired by the big candidates that they would indeed come a callin', dressed up in their best bib and tucker.

Friends from the Nixon camp visiting the meeting could not resist this good rebel logic, so they gave up getting a ring on our finger just then.

The Greenville Group was made up of Clarke Reed, Bill Murfin, and myself. The group was so named because the meetings were held at Reed's home in Greenville, Mississippi, on the broad levee of the great Mississippi River.

In Greenville, a more careful job was done of mapping southern strategy. We determined to play hard to get. We vowed to keep the pact to "hang loose, but hang together" until we could reach the most workable decision on which man to go with—Reagan or Nixon? We were determined to accord Rockefeller every courtesy and every chance, but realistically, we all knew that he had only two chances in Dixie—slim and none. But anyway, although we were serious in our efforts, it was going to be fun to see how the "Big Three" looked when dressed in gray.

Reed invited the three South. And each accepted, but Nixon's people seemed chagrined to have to court something they thought was already available. Reagan and Rockefeller agreed to come to New Orleans; but Nixon insisted on Atlanta, since he was already planning to be there for reasons of his own. Thus the Greenville Group missed out on making Nixon bow by coming to New Orleans. It did, however, get a curtsey when Nixon consented to come to Atlanta.

Reagan's meeting was first. A full course dinner was prepared, with all the trimmings. It was grand, and very intimate. Reagan indicated that he would not be a candidate. But had he asked for support in the atmosphere of that occasion, charged with his presence, the Californian would have received it from us then and there. But a noncandidate can be a noncandidate too long.

The dinner was superb. But typical of the style of Reagan's staff, we received the final course—the full bill for the evening.

How can anybody top a dinner planned by Californians and paid for by Southerners? Rockefeller could and did. He entertained us for breakfast, serving steak and grits—all at his expense.

Back in Calhoun County, South Carolina, I had grown up on grits for breakfast and supper—but steak and grits was a plush touch only a

Rockefeller could bring into the experience of a southern boy and his southern friends.

Reed will testify under oath he caught Rockefeller trying to put sugar on his grits. Fortunately, Reed stopped him in time, preventing the emasculation of a southern delicacy.

Normally, I would have been for Reagan all the way, but several points about his candidacy bothered me. First, the polls were raising serious questions about his ability to win. Second, the candidate was playing too coy. He needed to say clearly that he was running. Third, an inner-office scandal involving one of Reagan's key staffers distressed me considerably. Fourth, Reagan's staffers were making too many political miscues, which were getting public attention.

Fifth, I was upset by a telephone call taken by Reagan's political strategist Cliff White, during a Washington visit I had with him. White had been titillating me with a Reagan candidacy, but without a solid commitment. We were specifically talking about a matter the Reagan staffers had hinted at previously, my handling the Reagan campaign in the South.

During the visit, a telephone call came through to White from a key Rockefeller campaign leader. Something was said which indicated to me that Reagan and Rockefeller were holding hands under the table with plans to stop Nixon. The reasoning was simple: If the two could prevent Nixon from achieving a first-ballot victory, the nomination could then be fought out between the two of them—Reagan and Rockefeller. The pair was working to force Nixon to win on the first ballot, if he were to win at all.

This event took place early in the GOP presidential sweepstakes when I may have been easy pickings for the Reagan people, but a telephone conversation, inadvertently overheard, disturbed me enough to make me retreat. My chief concern, I suppose, was that if the Reagan-Rockefeller strategy worked, my group might end up with Rockefeller as the standard-bearer; and while I personally liked Rockefeller, politically I did not feel he could win in Dixie.

Finally, Reagan was not my choice in 1968 because Nixon affirmed what people in the South wanted to hear.

Two weeks after the sessions in New Orleans, Nixon's meeting in Atlanta took place. The Nixon staff had evidently convinced their boss that the Southerners were his, but they were incorrect. At that time, many were closer to going with Reagan, the noncandidate.

Upon arrival, my group met the new campaign manager, "Big John" Mitchell, and H.R. (Bob) Haldeman, who few in the group knew.

I had been calling for a tough, but courteous approach in discussions with each candidate. The questions asked of Nixon were clear, direct, and on these subjects: balancing the Supreme Court, busing schoolchildren for integration, protecting textiles, law and order, communism, national defense, and pledges to build the party, especially in the South.

On the subject of the Supreme Court, Nixon answered with a sense of deep concern and force—conservative appointments only. This, he made clear, was his prime goal as president.

It was my assignment to ask most of the questions of Nixon, along with my invitee Joe Rogers. I tried to make sure the answers were forthright and unequivocal. Nixon did well.

I called Senator Thurmond and asked him to come to Atlanta. We southern GOP chairmen had found our candidate.

When the senator arrived the next morning, he was invited to sit in a meeting with some of the other southern leaders who had not been present the previous day. Most of the same questions were posed and the same answers given.

Nixon's position on the Supreme Court got the most enthusiastic response. Thurmond was particularly pleased to hear him declare that as president he would only appoint strict constructionists. On the vice-presidential question, Nixon said he did not believe in balancing the ticket, but that he would seek someone who shared his philosophy in the event he ascended to the presidency. This pleased everyone considerably.

Nixon made clear his support of the Supreme Court's ruling overturning the old separate, but equal, system of education for blacks and whites. He neither committed himself to retreat from that decision nor to suggest that he would support repealing the 1954 High Court decision, as has sometimes been speculated by some writers. Nixon did, however, express his opposition to busing as a means of achieving racial balance in schools.

After the session, Nixon asked Thurmond to accompany him in his car to the airport. Thurmond accepted. The press played up this ride to the airport as if some sinister deals were made between Nixon and Thurmond. This was not the case.

The majority of the southern chairmen and Thurmond were determined to go with Nixon as a result of the sessions the previous day and that morning. Senator Tower was already aboard the Nixon team.

Back in South Carolina, plans were formulated to have Thurmond as the favorite-son candidate declare for Nixon and carry all 22 convention votes from the state for maximum impact. A meeting of South Carolina's delegates and alternates was scheduled in Columbia when Thurmond and the only GOP congressman, Albert Watson, would make public their support for Nixon. The hope was for the entire delegation to go along.

Meanwhile, I communicated the decision to Tom Reed of Reagan's staff, hoping Reagan would follow suit and join in a Nixon bandwagon. I got the distinct impression that Reagan's team might join in the bandwagon, despite its personal loss.

A few days later the news broke of the assassination of Robert F. Kennedy, who was gaining fast in the Democratic struggle for the presidential nomination. Soon thereafter Tom Reed called me. He made no suggestion of joining a bandwagon for Nixon. He now felt that as a result of the Kennedy tragedy, Reagan's No. 1 issue, law and order, would catapult him into a much stronger position nationally.

Thurmond made his declaration for Nixon as planned.

> He (Nixon) offers America the best hope of recovering from domestic lawlessness; a bloody, no-win war in Southeast Asia; runaway spending and rising costs of living; strategic military inferiority; loss of influence in world affairs; and a power grasping Supreme Court.

> I do not intend to give the impression that on all issues I agree with Mr. Nixon, or he with me. I do say that Mr. Nixon is the best of the candidates of either party for America and the cause of freedom. He offers the best qualifications in terms of experience and preparation for the office of president. He is the most acceptable and electable candidate. He can fill the leadership vacuum in the White House and unify America in a time of crisis.

On Nixon's civil rights position, Thurmond said that Nixon's position was the most satisfactory of the candidates.

Then in a public statement I applauded the senator's endorsement, predicting that Thurmond's support of Nixon would win the 1968 election for Nixon and the GOP:

> Thurmond's sticking his neck out because he believes Nixon is the best man for the country. It's not going to be a plus for him per-

sonally because many people want him to support Wallace or do nothing. Thurmond's support of Nixon will effectively squash Wallace's chances.

Little did I know then how often I would have to declare "Thurmond is sticking his neck out" not for his own good, but for the good of America. This message enabled the senator to prevail for Nixon at the GOP convention.

My prediction proved accurate.

For Southerners, a struggle at the convention would be Thurmond versus Reagan. In the general election, it would be Thurmond versus Wallace; and in both contests Thurmond would emerge the winner—and Nixon, the big winner.

After the Reagan leaders finally decided to make the race—even though unannounced—they swiftly began an all-out effort to undo the Nixon coup and score in Dixie. Reagan's considerable charm and charisma were exerted upon southern delegates, many of whom were flown to see the governor personally in California. And Reagan personally made a tour of eight southern and border states and conservative Indiana. In this tour, the purpose was to meet with as many GOP delegates as possible, especially those who would be Reagan inclined. I considered Reagan's forces sharp in this effort to undo the strategy of Southerners hanging loose.

So now, the real struggle to keep Southerners linked together behind one man who was electable was facing its first test. But the test was to be repeated again and again, until ultimately, solidarity prevailed.

□ □ □

At the GOP convention in Miami, the strategy of Southerners was simple in design, but difficult to execute—hold the "Old Grey Line" for Nixon. We Southerners had to hold what we figured we had—the great majority of southern delegate votes. Yet we knew Reagan and his people would work all their candidate's charismatic powers to break our ranks.

Sure enough, Reagan although still unannounced was the first candidate to arrive. Fred Buzhardt, now a South Carolina attorney, and I decided to be in Miami the week before the convention to assess the situation before the delegates arrived—and with good reason. We saw Reagan's superb appearance before the Platform committee, when he strummed his law and order theme.

When the governor made this statement, he stirred the crowd and the committee:

> We must reject the idea that every time the law is broken, society is guilty rather than the lawbreaker . . .

> It is time to move against these destructive dissidents (in universities); it is time to say, "Obey the rules or get out!"

> It is time to tell friend and foe alike that we are in Vietnam because it is in our national interest to be there.

Later in the week Reagan went into neighboring states to stir delegate passions. Then the governor's managers let him talk freely with the delegations, especially southern ones, as they arrived the weekend before the convention voting. He spoke with delegates from Alabama, Georgia, and Mississippi— my group's weakest states—that Sunday. The Alabama chairman, Alfred Goldwaithe, clearly favored Reagan. My group had fairly good handles on Georgia and Mississippi with Howard "Bo" Callaway heading up the Nixon forces in Georgia and the South; and Clarke Reed, the Mississippi chairman in command in the rebel state delegation. However, we southern Nixon leaders were concerned about the minority factions for Reagan in Georgia and Mississippi, which were doing all they could to undo the work Callaway and Reed had done with their majorities. In Alabama, we had resigned ourselves to taking the hindmost part.

One place Reagan visited the week before the convention gave members of the Nixon camp considerable concern. This was the Reagan visit to Birmingham. Roscoe Picket of Georgia, a long-time party leader, flew eight delegates and five alternates from South Carolina to the Birmingham meeting.

The Evans-Novak column of July 28 addressed itself to the importance of this so-called raid on the Nixon camp. The columnists reported:

> What makes this a major breakthrough for Reagan is the strategic importance of South Carolina in Nixon's nomination strategy. Having coaxed Senator Strom Thurmond into dropping his favorite son status and endorsing Nixon instead, Nixon aides have been confident of all 22 South Carolina votes under the unit rule (which cannot be enforced if any member dissents).

This Reagan incursion in South Carolina is only the most important aspect of Reagan's Southern raids which are eroding Nixon's battle plan for a first ballot nomination.

Some 90 delegates and alternates from Alabama, Mississippi, South Carolina, Louisiana, and Georgia who met with Reagan at Birmingham's Tutwiler Hotel reflected a pattern of small Nixon losses and small Reagan gains throughout the South. The transformation in the Louisiana situation is most dramatic. Although one careful delegate count in June gave all 26 of Louisiana's votes to Nixon, Reagan now has nearly half the delegation and may move to a majority.

Apart from exposing new slippage on Nixon's sagging Southern front, the Birmingham meeting revealed just how carefully Reagan's clandestine campaign for President had been prepared in the South.

Reagan's raid into West Texas a few days earlier uncovered another cog in the undercover Cliff White machine. Frank Whetstone of Cut Bank, Montana, a long-time White lieutenant, was in charge of the Texas operation which has produced at least 20 Reagan delegates—twice as many as Nixon forces expected. Nor was Reagan's trip to Alabama the end of his pre-convention infiltration of Dixie. He plans a final raid in North Carolina this week.

All this has caused no little consternation in the Nixon camp. Two of Nixon's most important and most able Southern backers—State Chairman Harry Dent of South Carolina and National Committeeman Fred LaRue of Mississippi—were hurriedly summoned to New York for conferences at Nixon headquarters recently.

At the convention, Buzhardt and I began picking up the distressing, disruptive rumors about the vice-presidency. Word was passed that Nixon was indeed going to balance the ticket if he won the nomination. And there was no way we would know for sure until after Nixon was nominated. Balancing meant the use of Illinois's Senator Charles Percy, Governor Nelson Rockefeller, New York's Mayor John Lindsay, or Oregan's Senator Mark Hatfield. Circulated by Reaganites and Rockefellerites, these vice-presidential rumors unnerved my group throughout the convention. Repeatedly, the question would be raised: "Yeah, but how can you trust, Tricky Dick?"

As Thurmond was preparing to come to the convention, he was busy sending telegrams and making telephone calls to southern delegates. No chances were taken on the Reagan magic. Thurmond's telegrams read:

> Richard Nixon's position is sound on law and order, Vietnam, the Supreme Court, military superiority, fiscal sanity, and decentralization of power. He is best for unity and victory in 1968. Our country needs him, and he needs our support in Miami. See you at the convention.

Goldwater and Nixon also sent telegrams. Nixon invited everyone to a reception at the convention.

On the telephone, Thurmond used the key phrase for holding the line: "A vote for Reagan is a vote for Rockefeller." This was the same line later used against Wallace, only with a different theme: "A vote for Wallace is a vote for Humphrey." The logic behind all this was that if Nixon failed to make it on the first ballot, then Rockefeller would win the convention. Rockefeller and his strategists were convinced they could win if Nixon could be stopped on the first ballot. They had polls showing Reagan a loser in the general election, much like Goldwater in 1964. His weakness was apparent in the big cities, which in many cases provided the necessary Democratic margin to carry the state's big electoral vote by a small margin in the winner-take-all electoral college system.

Rockefeller's dependency on Reagan was best explained by George Hinman, the GOP national committeeman from New York, then one of the governor's closest and best advisers. After the convention, Hinman revealed that Rockefeller had come closer than many people realized. To the authors of *An American Melodrama* he said, "Actually Rockefeller came very close. There was a chance after Reagan's entry split the conservatives. That's the only condition on which a moderate can go through."

In *An American Melodrama* the authors pointed up the Rockefeller strategy with this assessment (pages 454-455):

> In short, Rockefeller's only chance of success depended, as it had for some weeks, on the sweet-talking talents of his ideological opposite, Ronald Reagan. If Reagan could chip away Nixon's Southern base and throw the convention open, then Rockefeller

would be in business. On Saturday, August 3, a story in the *New York Times,* based on information supplied by Leonard Hall, Rockefeller's floor manager, was headlined: "Rockefeller Aides Fear Reagan Is Gaining Rapidly." A more accurate label would have substituted "Hope" for "Fear."

The Reagan outfit was not entirely happy with all this gratuitous publicity—coming as it did from a source which most of the delegates they were appealing to would find unappetizing. For them, predictions by Rockefeller's staff that Reagan might pick up a prodigious 300 votes in the first ballot were entirely counterproductive. All along, the Reagan strategy had been firmly grounded on the "poor-mouthing" principle, designed to make small gains look wondrously impressive. F. Clifton White's predictions, therefore, rarely topped 180 on the first ballot (Reagan got 182), though privately he was hoping something nearer 250, more than enough to deny Nixon that crucial first-ballot majority.

As with Rockefeller, Reagan's cardinal weakness derived from his late entry into the race; he had only a meager base of committed delegates. Unlike Rockefeller, however, Reagan could expect that his proselytizing among the delegations could be converted into concrete votes. Outside the big industrial states, nobody thought Reagan had horns, though there were some in Miami Beach who seemed to think him capable of sprouting wings. His prejudices most nearly matched those of the average delegate. And the caucus setting was perfectly attuned to his talents. "There is nothing more impressive than Ronnie Reagan behind closed doors," according to South Carolina's Harry Dent.

On the other hand, Reagan and his advisers were convinced they could stampede the convention given Ronnie's charisma and conservative appeal—if only Nixon could be stopped on the first ballot.

To us southern Nixonites, our candidate was almost as conservative as Reagan and could be put over on the first ballot. Convention votes of the 13 southern and border states (Virginia, North Carolina, South Carolina, Georgia, Florida, Alabama, Mississippi, Louisiana, Texas, Arkansas, Tennessee, Kentucky, and Oklahoma) could virtually do the job alone. These states had 356 of the 1333 votes needed to nominate a presidential candidate.

Our "vote for Reagan and get Rockefeller" theme worked fairly well because of the strong resentment lingering among staunch conservatives over the governor's lukewarm, if any, support for the Goldwater-Miller ticket in 1964. Many southern delegates had a stronger resentment against Rockefeller than love for Reagan.

What gave the theme even more credence was all the talk of a Rockefeller-Reagan "dream ticket." *Time* magazine had virtually nominated such a ticket, and the Nixon forces were spreading this possibility all over the place. In interview after interview, Nixonites deplored the thought that this might happen. After all, the logic of a ticket of this sort was fairly solid. It would tie together two top GOP superstars, the governors of the two biggest states, and the left and right of the GOP.

At this point, some information about Thurmond not generally appreciated is in order. One of the most remarkable specimen of physical energy around, the 65-year-old senator put in intensive duty night and day at the 1968 convention, and not once did he falter from fatigue.

Thurmond's political opponents through the years have learned to their own dismay and defeat that "ole Strom" can outwork and outfight them all.

Those who know the Senator have learned not to be surprised when there comes the announcement in 1975 that the senator, at age 72, and his young wife, Nancy, are expecting their fourth child in a marriage only six years old.

He put out fires Reagan generated among conservatives and especially Southerners. Whenever Reagan worked his charm on a southern state delegation, Thurmond doused the fire. At the convention, Thurmond became known as the chief of the Nixon fire brigade. He was used repeatedly all over Miami in the next few days and nights, right up to the presidential nomination vote. Usually, I took the senator to a delegation meeting and presented him, saying all the things he could not afford to say. In other words, I built up the senator and his conservative credentials and credibility and why he was risking his all for Nixon.

Then Thurmond would appear and talk about substantive issues like national security, the Abe Fortas battle (Thurmond and Senator Robert Griffin of Michigan led the fight which stopped liberal Fortas from being confirmed for the U.S. Supreme Court).

The Thurmond-Dent appearances were called "the Dog and Pony Show." I made the sales pitch, and Thurmond's presence reflected his prestige and credibility. Without that Thurmond appeal, Nixon would never have made it on the first ballot—and if not then, never. The Nixon leaders were using Goldwater and Tower to influence Southerners, but Thurmond carried the most weight among southern delegates, and in many cases with conservative delegates elsewhere. Thurmond's political motivations were the least subject to question, considering all the conscience actions he had taken, like risking all to switch parties for Goldwater's hopeless campaign in 1964.

Thus when the Nixon leaders needed help, they usually yelled for the Thurmond fire brigade, which most of the times did the job, even outside the South. Thurmond's fire brigade was Nixon's magic potion.

Since everything depended on the first-ballot victory, the 300-plus Nixon staff and workers had to put on an air of great confidence. The whole psychology of the convention was wrapped around this point. It was built up by hostile news people and also Nixon's rivals, Reagan and Rockefeller. It was a point of weakness, but also one of strength. It gave us southern Nix-onites our greateast selling point to hold a Solid South on the first ballot. We Nixonites in the South Carolina delegation had been forced to concede to the Reaganites that we would probably go for Reagan on the second ballot if they would help us hold the line and try for our moment of greatness on the first ballot.

The psychology laid down in the press on Nixon's imperative first-ballot victory played a role for and against Nixon's candidacy. It was the come-on for the Reagan and Rockefeller forces: If we can stop Nixon, then we will win for our man. Each Rockefellerite and Reaganite was led to believe this. At the same time, it underscored to Nixonites the vital role we had to play in putting across our "loser" on the first ballot, if we stood any chance of winning. Thus the lines were drawn—win or lose on the first ballot. And this applied to all three leading candidates, because even Nixon believed he would win or lose on the first roll call and Rockefeller supporters were equally convinced that once Nixon failed on the first ballot, their man would make it on some successive ballot.

The Nixon camp had to maintain an air of invincibility. However, behind-the scene members of the camp were deeply concerned whether they could hold off the Reagan raid on their soft underbelly, the South. Yes, they were concerned about their holdings outside the South, but their southern strategy was the ultimate key to winning or losing. And Reagan was the real threat.

In *An American Melodrama,* the problem for Nixon and the strategy for Reagan got this summation (page 457):

The chances of a breakaway in the South had suddenly, and nightmarishly, become a very real possibility. Reagan, now an open candidate, was going the rounds of the delegations, and his pitch was brilliantly seductive: they should let it go for a couple of ballots "just to get an open convention, so that all views get a chance to be expressed." This was backed by the disingenuous assurance that "nobody had anything to lose," because, sure, if nothing emerged by, say, the third ballot, then we can all go back and rally around Dick.

The vice-presidential question particularly disturbed Callaway. Although a staunch Nixonite, even ahead of many of us, Callaway wanted some reassurances from high up in the Nixon camp. He and a few others of us talked with Nixon campaign manager John Mitchell about the running-mate rumors we knew would be even more disturbing when the main portion of southern delegates arrived in Miami. The Sunday before the convention, Mitchell sought to reassure us that the ticket would not be a balancing act— the same thing Nixon had said in Atlanta earlier. This was a little reassuring, but only because it was current. Still, Nixonites did not know what the prevote pressures might be, and we were not told who the choice would be. Mitchell was evidently keeping the Nixon options open because he, and Nixon, did not know what might be required to assure the absolutely necessary first-ballot win.

When the South Carolina delegates arrived Sunday morning, members of the Nixon forces began counting to determine if everyone was present and if there were any more Nixon reluctance. Some Reagan strays were still present. One group, led by Howard Poston of Kingstree, stated its devotion for Reagan. After a while of persuasion, Poston's group joined the Nixon team.

Still to be dealt with were two principal Reagan holdouts, Jim Edwards and Bill Hunter. Edwards was rigged up with a Reagan walkie-talkie. He was to be Reagan's contact in the South Carolina delegation. Finally, an agreement was reached with Edwards and Hunter. If the unified move for Nixon failed, everyone would support Reagan on the second ballot, regardless of Nixon's position at that time.

To keep some controversy swirling in the delegation for the Nixon leaders to see, an agreement was made to have the formal meeting of the delegation open to the press with Edwards and Hunter advocating for Reagan. The two had insisted on making one more appeal before succumbing.

Present for the meeting was pipe-smoking John Mitchell, Nixon's No. 1 campaign heavyweight. Representing Reagan was Robert Walker, who had been Nixon's number two man early in the nomination maneuvering. However, he had since turned bitterly against Nixon.

Mitchell's single purpose was to quiet the rumors about a liberal running mate. He said, "I talked with Dick Nixon this morning and it's not his intention to cram down your throat any candidate not fully acceptable. His aim is that the party leave here unified. To this end, the vice-president will be considered."

Continuing, Mitchell said, "You can expect he'll be a man chosen after consultation with all segments of the party, including Senator Strom Thurmond."

The delegates applauded. We South Carolina Nixonites knew we were helping to put our senator in the catbird's seat. The strategy was working smoothly.

Bob Walker spoke after Mitchell. He appealed to the delegation to revert to an uncommitted position until they could hear from Reagan.

After further discussion, speaking, and so on, the delegates reaffirmed their allegiance to Nixon on the first ballot. It was decided to nominate Thurmond as favorite son and then have him withdraw and give the 22 votes to Nixon.

The delegates were informed about the afternoon Reagan meeting and also a morning meeting with Nixon in conjunction with other southern delegations.

Then Reed, Murfin, and I had lunch with Reagan and Goldwaithe of Alabama, our only Reagan-committed southern chairman. We decided to try to talk Reagan out of his likely candidacy. We liked him more than Nixon and did not want to see him hurt.

At the luncheon, Reagan asked whether he should announce as a candidate.

I led off speaking in the negative, assuring the governor how much we admired him and wanted him on the ticket. But I explained that we had found a weakness in his ability to win in November and win we must to save America. I stressed that Thurmond was the key to most southern delegates and that he had committed himself absolutely to Nixon. I underscored this point: "Thurmond has given his word, and he's not noted for backing up on his word." I assured him a Reagan announcement would stir things up, but the result would be the same.

Evidently, Reagan did not think too much of our advice, for later that day he announced his candidacy on television.

The Reagan announcement shook the southern strategy group, which knew the still shaky delegates would be affected by the announcement. Thurmond was put to work even harder. Reed panicked over the Reagan shock waves in his delegation, at times questioning how he could ever return to Mississippi after having led the battle for Nixon over Reagan.

Later while attending a big social affair, Thurmond, Buzhardt, and I ran into Phyllis Schafly, the conservative writer and speaker, and a few of her conservative friends. Schafly favored Reagan and was concerned about our support for Nixon. William Rusher, the writer and publisher of *National Review* magazine, favored Reagan too. Both were basically making the same point: Sorry you're for Nixon and not Reagan, but you'd better get your "pound of flesh" from Nixon if you're going to stay with him because he'll mislead you. By "pound of flesh" they meant making Nixon give us specific promises in writing on specific issues in return for our support.

Rusher tried repeatedly to turn us around, but Schafly realized this was hardly possible. We told both we were planning to see Nixon the following day. This is when Schafly bore down hard on getting Nixon to commit himself on certain issues, particularly national security.

Jean Dixon, the prophetess, also worked on us that day. Twice Dixon had previously told Senator Thurmond that he was destined to play the key role in nominating and electing the next president.

When I was still the senator's administrative assistant in early 1965, Dixon visited the office. She told me then of her powers of prophecy. To the senator, the prophetess said she had strong vibrations about him. She said he would play the key role in nominating and electing the next president, who would be a Republican because sentiment would change between 1965 and 1968. At that time Lyndon Johnson was strong as president, having just been elected over Goldwater with the biggest victory in history. Johnson's legislative program was moving through Congress with great dispatch. The new president was turning the New Frontier into the Great Society with far more momentum and effectiveness than John Kennedy ever imagined.

I thought to myself: How in the world can it be possible for us Republicans to win in 1968 with things as they now are?

A year after I had left the senator's staff, Dixon saw him again, making the same prediction—this time more confidently. This was in 1966. The senator told me about the second prediction immediately.

In Miami, and just before we arrived there, Dixon had been calling Buzhardt and me. She was trying to influence us to go with Reagan. I think she was trying to say that Reagan was the one, not Nixon, who was to carry out her prophecy regarding Thurmond.

Before that, I believed Dixon indeed had extraordinary sensory powers. But after we had committed to Nixon, vibrations were not going to dissaude us. In fact, the prophetess lost some credibility with me, since I felt she was being used by some of the Reagan people to mislead us.

While Dixon proved right in her prophecy regarding Thurmond, she had forecast the wrong horse. Even she admits to fallibility on some vibrations because she cannot always focus in 100 percent.

In 1971 Dixon proved to be a prophetess again, when she visited with me concerning potentially diastrous consequences for the president, which could be caused by White House staff members. She referred to a number she had perceived through her ESP powers. This number represented the particularly dangerous staffer. I assumed it to be Henry Kissinger, but the identity was never made clear. I tried to help Dixon gain access to President Nixon as a White House counsel, but my efforts were unsuccessful.

Meanwhile, Buzhardt and I thought carefully on what Schafly had warned about "the pound of flesh." We were concerned about the consequences to Thurmond if Nixon won and proved to be anti-South and liberal like LBJ. The term "Tricky Dick" kept cropping up all over Miami, especially when people talked to us. Buzhardt and I had been involved with the senator in a number of daredevil ventures—like switching parties, launching the U.S. Senate's muzzling of the military investigation in 1961, challenging Kennedy and Robert McNamara on missiles in Cuba, and many more. In each foray, we had helped convince the senator to charge out in the style of Sir Lancelot. If the plans did not go well, it would be the senator hurt—not such nonelectives as Buzhardt and Dent. Because this consideration weighed heavily on our minds, Buzhardt and I always tried to cover every base for the senator. It was not just a case of protecting ourselves from the senator's wrath, if the action were a political minus. When Thurmond made a decision it was all his; no one who contributed to the decision need fear that the senator would use him as a scapegoat.

So Buzhardt's and my concern was for our daredevil leader. We respected his raw courage, his willingness to carry out bold ideas.

While preparing for the first night's session of the convention, Buzhardt and I discussed "the pound of flesh" strategy for Tuesday's meeting—or should we do it differently? Perhaps the better way would be different. Go in there and tell Nixon: "We're for you—win, lose, or draw—because we have faith in you." The latter course, the two of us thought, would be more appropriate than trying to strike a bargain with Nixon.

En route to the convention session Monday evening, Buzhardt and I ran into James Gardner of North Carolina. Gardner, a successful young quick food franchiser who had won a seat in Congress, was now trying to win the state's governorship.

In 1968 Gardner had been invited to speak at the State GOP Convention. But knowing he was then a Nixon man, he was asked not to make a Nixon speech, since, at that time, South Carolina was uncommitted and we did not want to appear to be taking sides. However, at the convention Gardner made a very pro-Nixon speech.

Now on this first evening of the national convention, Gardner was telling Buzhardt and me that he was going to take most of North Carolina's delegates to Reagan.

Finding the Gardner decision incredulous, I talked to other North Carolina delegates, who said the rumor was that Reagan had agreed to campaign for Gardner after the convention.

On the convention floor, I sent an urgent telephone message to John Mitchell: "We need to see Nixon tonight, not tomorrow as I had previously requested as things are taking a turn for the worse." Ever since Reagan announced after lunch, the Reagan passions were stirring in Miami. Gardner had created the most traumatic shock wave we Nixonites had felt. Delegates from all over the convention floor were telling of more and more possible defections from Nixon to Reagan.

Nixon was not aware of all this. He had just arrived at the airport late in the afternoon. Large crowds with great fanfare had met him, including Thurmond as one of the principal greeters. The reception was so good Nixon must have felt fully confident about the decision to be made at Miami.

Buzhardt and I knew Nixon's top people would believe we were only panicking as extremists. Yet we felt we had to get to Nixon—not just Mitchell—that night, because it was vital he say the right things to the southern delegates the next morning at the scheduled meeting. Also, this would be the chance to let Nixon know Thurmond was putting it all on the line out of faith—pure faith in "Tricky Dick." Buzhardt and I were not going to seek the pound of flesh.

Later in the session, Mitchell's response came: "Yeah, come on up. We'll send for you at 10 P.M."

Nixon was headquartered at the plush Hilton Plaza. En route, Buzhardt and I talked over our strategy. It was agreed I would do most of the talking because the senator could not stress how much he was risking. It would be better coming from me. We decided again not to use the pound-of-flesh strategy.

John Mitchell met us and escorted us to Nixon. Already present were Haldeman, Nixon's chief of staff; and John D. Ehrlichman, Nixon's tour chief.

After thanking Thurmond for his efforts, Nixon asked for a report on how things were going with the hunt for southern delegates.

I responded by reporting that all was not well as a consequence of the *New York Times* article on Monday quoting someone close to Nixon as saying the vice-presidential choice was down to Senator Hatfield of Oregon, Senator Percy of Illinois, and Mayor Lindsay of New York. (We learned after the convention that long-time Nixon press aide and friend, Herb Klein, had circulated the story. Whether with or without Nixon's consent, I have never learned. From what I know now, it probably was part of an overall strategy, although Klein would have been personally inclined in that direction.)

I told Nixon that Reagan's announcement had stirred all conservative delegates and alternates and that some defections were already taking place. I mentioned the Gardner switch, which startled Nixon. Mitchell reacted with strong language, indicating a double cross. Nixon stopped the conversation and barked some orders on the Gardner problem.

The Gardner report got Nixon's attention and concern, thereby giving our trio more credibility than we would have had otherwise.

Nixon's reaction also permitted me to launch into my spiel about Thurmond tearing his shirt for Nixon. I explained that the senator had faith in the candidate, despite all the "Tricky Dick" talk. I said, "We're with you, and we're going to stick with you." Nixon then asked what he could do to help. He seemed to be asking for my next line.

I said: "Mr. Vice President, the Senator's been trying to hold the line by just telling the delegates that he's standing firm for Nixon despite all the pressures. What we need is to be able to answer some of the questions we're being asked about you."

Thurmond chimed in here to emphasize that we in the South were not looking for any special treatment—we just wanted to be brought back into the Union and treated as an equal section of the country. To this, Nixon readily agreed.

Then Nixon volunteered a rundown on all the key issues. He covered virtually everything, and we were overjoyed with his positions. No questions were necessary.

With regard to the vice-presidency, Nixon repeated his previous private statements about not wanting to balance the ticket or "to cram anyone down anyone's or any section's throat." He wanted someone who could run well in all sections. Again, he was not specific, but that all sounded mighty good.

Nixon reiterated his determination to balance the U.S. Supreme Court with some conservatives, to campaign in every section, to maintain a strong national defense, to restore law and order, and to build a stronger Republican party, especially in the South.

On the subject of civil rights, he let us know he favored the Supreme Court school desegregation decision and the general move to desegregate public life in all sections. However, he did not favor forced busing of students. He said that just as he favored civil rights he was also opposed to "civil wrongs," such as lawlessness in the streets. He deplored the actions and words of the current attorney general, Ramsey Clark, who he said was "no Attorney General at all." He said, "We'll have a real Attorney General who'll enforce the law!"

When he finished his speech he asked again what he could do to help. I responded: "Tell all that directly to the delegates you'll be speaking with tomorrow morning. It'll have much more impact coming from you rather than a conduit, even though Strom Thurmond is the best conduit possible to the southern states' most conservative delegates."

The suggestion put Nixon on the spot initially. This was a test of whether Nixon was going to tell his conduits one thing and then give a nice pep talk to the southern delegates the next morning, avoiding specifics.

I told him I felt candid statements made directly to the delegates would "wrap it all up."

Thurmond and Buzhardt agreed emphatically.

Surprisingly, Nixon, without hesitation, said, "OK, I'll do it." He then told Mitchell that this would be his approach the next morning. The meeting ended with everyone happy, confident.

The next morning all the delegates assembled as scheduled at the Hilton Plaza to meet and confer with Nixon. The southern and border states were in two separate groups, with some nonsouthern delegations in each. The District of Columbia was in the same group as South Carolina.

Thurmond, Buzhardt, and I arrived early, happy and excited. We knew our candidate would help us hold the "Old Grey Line" in accord with the carefully laid strategy.

The three of us slipped into the other southern meeting, which preceded ours. This was the meeting recorded by the *Miami Herald* and published the next day as Nixon's commitment meeting with the southern delegates. While Nixon's statement and his answers to questions were good in this meeting, the presentation in the second one was better.

In this meeting I stood on the front row and prompted Nixon or asked questions that brought out the key points I wanted made. And sure enough, every time Nixon spoke, his words were the right ones. He got a rousing reception, since I had prompted our delegates and others to cheer and applaud, because the answers were supposed to be good.

The next crisis was the Reagan meeting with Thurmond and then the South Carolina delegation immediately thereafter.

After an hour, Reagan emerged with a long face from the meeting with Thurmond and himself. He had failed to move the immovable, determined senator.

Downstairs at the delegation meeting, Reagan was not at his best. The Thurmond session had evidently drained and distressed him.

Reagan began by telling the South Carolina delegates there were "no circumstances under which I would exchange my position as governor of California for the Vice President on any ticket." When pressed, he said he could become the third person in history to refuse to be drafted.

The governor answered right on all the questions of the delegates, but the Nixon answers earlier that morning and the Thurmond leadership were too strong for Reagan to overcome. Bill Hunter, one of our last Reagan holdouts, told a reporter after the meeting that the delegation was now convinced that "Nixon is the best man to lead the United States out of this morass." He predicted a first-ballot victory.

On Tuesday evening at the convention more anxious moments occurred over the Reagan threat to Nixon's southern strategy. More rumors and questions developed about whether Nixon's statements would hold up in the White House. The most excitement came in the Florida delegation, where Reagan kept calling delegates off the floor and into his trailer behind the convention hall. He was particularly effective with the women delegates. By Florida law, half the delegates had to be women. The women delegates would come back from the Reagan trailer virtually swooning. This meant more work for the Thurmond fire brigade.

Florida chairman Bill Murfin was very concerned about being able to hold his Florida delegation in line for Nixon. He told of the attraction of Reagan for his women delegates and that former Senator William Knowland of California (now deceased) and Max Rafferty, the outspoken super-intendent of education in California, were coming to finish the Reagan job early Wednesday morning at the Doral Country Club, where the Florida delegates were housed. Rafferty was at that time very popular among con-servatives.

Murfin wanted Thurmond. He was confident the Florida delegation, operating under an agreed-on unit rule, would be swung to Reagan, except for Governor Claude Kirk, who was pledged to Rockefeller's futile candidacy in order to try to get the vice presidential nod for himself.

Thurmond and I arrived at the country club slightly ahead of Knowland and Rafferty. Murfin put us on first, and off we went again on "the Dog and Pony Show."

I hinted strongly in my remarks that I felt Nixon had given Thurmond a veto essential to hold the delegates in line for Nixon. I believed Nixon would not name anyone to whom Thurmond objected. Nixon had in effect said as much, but he had never said absolutely that Thurmond was holding such a veto.

We scuttled the strategic Reagan move, and when the delegates voted after hearing both sides, the vote was still Nixon 19, Reagan 14, and Rockefeller 1. Murfin was most pleased and relieved because this meant a final vote of 33 for Nixon and Kirk's lone vote for Rockefeller.

But this sigh of relief was to be brief for Murfin. Reagan entertained half the Florida delegation at lunch in his hotel and then kept working them over in his trailer during the evening session at the convention. We were pressed into service a few more times during the evening to work on Florida delegates, as Murfin continued to sweat out the Reagan assault on his delega-tion.

Reagan concentrated most on Florida, Mississippi, and Alabama on Wednesday and that evening at the convention. If he could turn around Florida's unit vote, steal some from Mississippi, and hold his ground in Alabama, he could stop Nixon on the first ballot.

Jim Martin, the man who almost unseated Senator Lister Hill in 1962, was the Nixon leader in the Alabama delegation. However, even Martin, a staunch conservative, had his doubts about Nixon from hour to hour.

A question arose as to the supposed importance of getting Alabama to yield to South Carolina so South Carolina could nominate Thurmond as the

first name who would give our 22 votes to Nixon. It would be as good as getting Nixon nominated first. However, Martin concluded correctly that by forcing a vote, which could be won, we Nixonites would risk alienating some pro-
Nixon delegates in the Alabama delegation. Instead, he suggested proposing
that Alabama yield to California, letting Reagan be nominated first. Under this
strategy Martin concluded he could gain more Nixon votes or better hold
what he had. The reasoning was that while most of the Alabama delegates
understood the Thurmond pragmatism exhibited at the convention, the people back home in Alabama just might not understand, since most of their
hearts belonged to Reagan. Clarke Reed had the same problem in Mississippi. Still Martin's assignment was more difficult, because his delegation was being led by the only Reaganite state party chairman in the South, Alfred
Goldwaithe.

In the end Martin's strategy proved good, because he carried Alabama
for Nixon by a two-vote margin, under difficult circumstances.

While I felt fairly secure Wednesday afternoon about Nixon's first-ballot
nomination and the South's key role in that victory, I suddenly got panicky
again when arriving at the convention that evening. Rockefeller and Reagan
people were distributing copies of the next morning's *Miami Herald* that carried a disturbing headline. It was a page-one streamer by Don Oberdorfer saying Nixon had decided to go with Senator Mark Hatfield of Oregon as his running mate. And Hatfield was sitting right in front of us. The story read most
convincingly, just as had an Evans-Novak column the previous morning. It
said Nixon was moving to go with Mayor John Lindsay. The column quoted
from a "secret letter." The two columns taken together had a strong emotional impact on conservatives. It was a false alarm, but I knew the basic
distrust of Nixon would set off another big job for the Thurmond fire brigade.
And it did. Congressman Rogers Morton, Nixon's floor leader, was busy that
evening running to and from the South Carolina delegation with Thurmond
on his arm to visit other southern delegations.

The major panic, however, came from Clarke Reed and Jim Martin,
who thought they needed to pass on the first ballot and see how the other
delegations voted. Things were tough in those two delegations as a result of
the two authentic reading and devastating news accounts.

Still, Reed and Martin's strategy was rejected as being potentially
catastrophic and precisely what Rockefeller and his forces wanted. Branding
the articles as totally false, I pointed out my conviction that Evans and Novak
favored Rockefeller and that this column was all a plant to panic us into just

such a strategy. Thurmond pledged to talk to each of the Mississippi and Alabama delegates to help Reed and Martin hold the line.

Don Oberdorfer, author of the *Miami Herald* story, showed up on the convention floor, playing right into my hands.

The idea for using Oberdorfer to my advantage came from something I saw Clarke Reed do. Reed had offered a $100 wager to anyone in his delegation that Hatfield would not be the veep candidate. He got no takers.

I cornered Oberdorfer in front of the Louisiana and Georgia delegations since Charlton Lyons and Bo Callaway were having a tough time with the two groups, respectively, because of the *Miami Herald* and Evans-Novak articles.

Forcibly, I pulled Oberdorfer over to the two delegations and took a risk that was to pay good dividends. I bet Oberdorfer $300 that his story was wrong and dared him to take me up. He refused. The natural suspicion of southern delegates over eastern establishment newsmen, coupled with Oberdorfer's apparent lack of confidence in his own story, seemed to turn the trick.

With this, Buzhardt, Callaway, and I went running among the southern delegations telling how Oberdorfer failed to back up his own story. This gave us renewed confidence as we sat down to listen to the roll call of the states.

The vote count in the 13 southern caucus states turned out almost exactly as we had projected.

State	Nixon	Nelson Rockefeller	Reagan	Rockefeller	Total Delegate Votes
Ala.	14		12		26
Ark.				18	18
Fla.	32	1	1		34
Ga.	21	2	7		30
Ky.	22	2			24
La.	19		7		26
Miss.	20				20
N.C.	9	1	16		26
Okla.	14	1	7		22
S.C.	22				22
Tenn.	28				28
Texas	41		15		56
Va.	22	2			24

As the Wisconsin delegation cast its 30 votes for Nixon, the former vice-president had performed his miraculous comeback and scored his first-ballot victory. When all the votes were counted, he had eked by with a margin of 25 votes. We knew that all those long hours and anxious moments of trying to cover every base and put out every fire had made the vital difference.

Soon after we southern Nixon leaders were congratulating ourselves in delirious satisfaction on the convention floor. A Nixon messenger gave me two envelopes, one addressed to Thurmond and one to me. I opened mine and was most surprised to read an invitation to meet with Nixon in his hotel suite right after the balloting. This meant participation in the selection of the vice-presidential candidate.

The senator and I left immediately for the Hilton Plaza. Nixon was delayed in coming into the meeting. At the time, Thurmond and I did not know Nixon was 30 feet down the hall talking over his vice-presidential potentials with his top staff members. Evidently, no consensus was reached; so Nixon came to meet with Thurmond and me and the others assembled: Lt. Gov. Robert Finch of California; Senator Hiram L. Fong of Hawaii; ex-Senator William Knowland of California; Leonard W. Hall of New York, former national Republican chairman; Senator Barry Goldwater of Arizona; John Mitchell; ex-New York Governor Thomas E. Dewey; William F. Murfin, Florida chairman; Congressman John J. Rhodes of Arizona; ex-Attorney General Herbert Brownell; Congressman Leslie Arends of Illinois; Senator Karl Mundt of South Dakota; Billy Graham; Governor James Rhodes of Ohio; Senator Jack Miller of Iowa; and Congressman Don Rumsfeld of Illinois.

After thanking each of the 18 people in the room, Nixon started his talk by giving his general views on the kind of vice-presidential candidate he had in mind. He mentioned several names and asked each person in the room to give his comments on the names and to add any others.

The sentiments for Reagan were strongest, but doubt was expressed that he would accept. Of course, Thurmond and I plugged for Reagan. And we also suggested Senator Robert Griffin of Michigan, Congressman George Bush of Texas, and Senator Howard Baker of Tennessee; Thurmond repeated what he had told delegates about no obnoxious candidate being selected, that the candidate would be one who could run well in every section.

Reagan got bad marks from Governor James Rhodes of Ohio, the man Reagan had told me was encouraging him to run for president and would probably join him as his running mate. Rhodes pulled his top aide, Ohio Chairman John Andrews, into the room with him, seemingly as a backup for his anti-Reagan statements. He claimed to have polls showing Reagan would be a bad drag in the industrual cities.

Billy Graham was the last to speak, strongly supporting Senator Mark Hatfield.

After everyone had spoken, I got the impression four frontrunners were emerging, since their names had been mentioned by Nixon in the beginning and had not been shot down in the meeting or tabbed too controversial. They were Governor Spiro T. Agnew of Maryland, Governor John Volpe of Massachusetts, Congressman George Bush of Texas, and Senator Howard Baker of Tennessee.

On the way out the door, Thurmond pressed into Nixon's hand a small piece of paper on which he had three columns of names. On it were the acceptables—Reagan, Tower, Bush, Baker, Griffin, and Morton; the no objections—Agnew and Volpe; and the unacceptables—Hatfield, Lindsay, and Rockefeller.

This was Thurmond's way of casting his veto without any doubt.

Thurmond and I did not know much about Agnew. Earlier Agnew had been for Rockefeller, but abandoned his favorite-son status to Nixon at the convention. He had been the open housing candidate for governor of Maryland, yet he had stood up against civil wrongs and riots as governor. And he was from a border state, Maryland, although more yankee today than southern. Thurmond had already listed Bush and Baker as "acceptables" on his list before the meeting. After hearing Nixon mention Agnew and Volpe, the senator created the "no objections" column and inked their names there.

At mid-morning, Thurmond got two calls from Senator Tower. After telling Thurmond of a very small and final meeting then in progress, he wanted to know Thurmond's feelings about Agnew and Volpe. Thurmond favored Agnew, although both men were now acceptable to him.

At 1 P.M., Nixon finally announced his choice of Agnew, and Thurmond and I felt we were now in fairly good condition to face our next problem— George C. Wallace in the general election.

The Agnew selection looked even better for the southern strategy after a group of liberals blasted the selection and staged a brief effort to defeat Agnew with Mayor John Lindsay of New York City. Lindsay withdrew after being nominated and seconded Agnew's nomination; however, it all made the Agnew selection more salable in Dixie and also enhanced the idea that Thurmond's veto power had been real and had worked against the liberals.

The final moment of glory came when Thurmond, Murfin, and a few others were selected to escort Nixon to the rostrum to make his acceptance speech. Frankly, it was never expected that the Nixon high command would permit Thurmond's role to be acknowledged so obviously.

Most of the key news media reporters had reported the Thurmond role as "kingmaker," or as I preferred "kingsaver"; but some raised the question of whether this role would spell the doom of Nixon in the general election. Some of Nixon's staffers shared this view.

The *Los Angeles Times's* headline on a Thurmond feature story read: "Nixon Tieup with Thurmond: Master Stroke or Blunder?" Tom Wicker in the *New York Times* asked, "Has Nixon Sold GOP's Soul to South Carolina's Strom Thurmond?"

This was the type of impression I wanted created in South Carolina and the South—and in South Carolina, especially it was. The Nixon staffers were much concerned about such stories and hoped to hear no more speculation on the subject of "Kingsaver Strom."

Doug Kiker of NBC-TV News made the Nixon forces shudder when he interviewed me on NBC-TV and I claimed full credit for Thurmond, pointing out that the senator had determined the outcome at his first GOP convention. Kiker made me credible with his commentary which followed. Indeed, it was paradoxical that the maverick Thurmond with his strong conservative and southern views should finally be the kingpin of the GOP after being a Democrat for most of his life and the Dixiecrat leader 20 years earlier. To those of us who worked with and knew Thurmond, it was neither funny nor paradoxical. It was fabulous, working out just as it had been planned, with "ole Strom" in the catbird's seat.

□ □ □

Now that Thurmond had held his good and admired friend Ronald Reagan at bay he suddenly found himself confronted with an even bigger assignment—cutting George Wallace down to manageable proportions.

Thurmond's most devout followers in South Carolina were Reaganites and/or Wallacites. He had cooled off his Reagan admirers. Now he would have to risk the friendships of his Wallace fans.

While Thurmond was resting up back home and enjoying his new role as top elephant, I was following the Nixon campaign staff to Mission Bay in San

Diego for their strategy planning in a relaxed atmosphere. Nixon had invited me as I was moving through his receiving line at the convention. He had said: "Harry, come on out to Mission Bay after the convention and let's see what we can do about the textile problem."

So I got together a few textile executives, and we flew to San Diego for the textile session. The chief textile spokesman was Fred Dent of Spartanburg, South Carolina, later Nixon's 1973 secretary of commerce and Ford's trade ambassador. When we met with Nixon we presented a reasonable stance, and Nixon, evidently expecting something less reasonable, quickly assented. The idea was that Nixon would pledge to work to achieve voluntary limitations on textile imports in cotton, wool, and man-made fiber textile products. We explained how President Kennedy had obtained an agreement with the Japanese to limit cotton textiles, but how the Japanese had skirted the agreement by flooding us with man-made textile fibers and blends of cotton and manmades above the cotton quotas established. They had also sent in more woolens. Thus what we asked for was an all-fiber limitation with all countries exporting textiles to the United States so no country could get around the agreement by transshipping through another country—again, a Japanese way of bypassing the agreement—or by switching from one category of fibers to another.

We were surprised that Nixon made the agreement himself without a delayed staff study. After an hour's discussion, he called a former congressman, Robert Ellsworth of Kansas, then a key Nixon strategist. Nixon told him to get a few economists and staffers to sit down with us and work out the details for a telegram to be sent to Senators Thurmond and Edward Brooke of textile-conscious Massachusetts and other textile-area GOP leaders.

Later in the day we completed our work, and the telegram was released as Nixon's pledge to try to solve the textile problem with a voluntary approach.

While I was at Mission Bay, I told Nixon and Mitchell I would put together the same kind of special southern operation for the general election as we had used for the Goldwater campaign in 1964. I explained it would be a separate operation, raising our own funds but checking our major actions with Mitchell.

Had my proposal been voted on by the Nixon campaign staff it would have been rejected overwhelmingly. They were leery of being associated with Thurmond and Dent, especially turning us loose to run our own southern operation.

The textile executives returned East without me. Before leaving, they signed up to help with the special southern operation.

For the next several days, I met with the Nixon strategists. They were studying an in-depth Nixon poll. My interest centered on the part having to do with Wallace and Nixon. It revealed what our polls had been showing at home—Wallace was first in Dixie, and something had to be done about it—fast.

The poll indicated no one could particularly help Nixon with an endorsement except maybe former President Eisenhower. I disagreed. My position was that Thurmond could help more than anyone, regardless of what the poll showed. I explained his infuence on southern voters and what he had done for Goldwater in 1964. However, the staff was not much interested. Thurmond had served their purpose very well at the convention, and most wanted to leave it there.

The in-depth look at Wallace showed his admirers were divided into three groups—the hard core, the favorers, and the leaners. They divided almost evenly one-third each.

The pollster said we could do nothing about the hard core. The leaners were the least committed and thus could be wooed away the easiest. The favorers were a little more committed, but they too were vulnerable to the right kind of campaign. However—and here was the main caveat—a strong anti-Wallace pitch could push the favorers and leaners right into Wallace's arms with the hard core. Thus the approach had to be soft.

On the return trip to South Carolina I gave much thought to the Wallace poll data. I concluded we would have to be very careful. Wallace would have to be pictured as a good guy who unfortunately was only helping Hubert Humphrey, the Democratic candidate, by taking votes away from Nixon, who was not our ideal candidate but much more acceptable than "Triple H," the bad guy. It sounded exactly like the theme we used at the convention with Reagan, Nixon, and Rockefeller. That had worked; why not the same strategy in the general election?

Back home I set up the necessary machinery for the southern operation, establishing a small political committee called "Thurmond Speaks for Nixon-Agnew."

The headquarters was my law office in the Palmetto State Life Building in Columbia. We convinced General Mark Clark of World War II fame to be our committee chairman. We enlisted Bobby Richardson, the ex-New York Yankee star second baseman as chairman of our statewide citizens group. We used Clark, Richardson, and Thurmond on TV, radio, and in newspaper advertisements throughout the South.

Our committee concentrated on south side Virginia, North Carolina, Tennessee, South Carolina, Georgia, and Florida. We decided not to waste our efforts in Alabama, Mississippi, and Louisiana because of the strong Wallace tide in those states. We shared our campaign materials with Clarke Reed in Mississippi and others in the Wallace hard-core states, at their expense.

Our polls showed we had a chance to peel back some of the Wallace vote in the target states, all of which were Wallace territory as the campaign got underway. In the end all of the target states were carried by the Nixon Agnew ticket except Georgia, and even that was close for traditionally Democratic Georgia.

Shortly before the Republican National Convention, I commissioned Central Surveys of Shenandoah, Iowa, to run a poll in South Carolina. My aim was to determine the relative strengths of Nixon, Reagan, and Rockefeller versus Humphrey and also third- party candidate Wallace.

Here is what the pollster concluded:

Richard Nixon runs the strongest of three possible Republican candidates, both in the three-way trial heats (against Hubert Humphrey and George Wallace) and in the two-way trial heats against Humphrey.

George Wallace shows more strength than either Humphrey or any Republican, consistently in the three-way trial heats.

Comparing these results with similar tests in February (with Lyndon Johnson as the Democratic candidate in February, Hubert Humphrey in the current survey) Wallace has improved his position by anywhere from 11 to 14 percentage points.

In the present survey not only does Wallace lead in all three races, but Humphrey is in second place, ahead of both Reagan and Rockefeller. Nixon and Humphrey are tied in second place behind Wallace in that combination.

Most of the Wallace support would go to the Republican in a two-party race, in any of these combinations—by about a 3 to 1 ratio when his votes are allocated in a Nixon-Humphrey race, and by smaller margins when they are allocated between Rockefeller-Humphrey or Reagan-Humphrey.

Combining results, this means that in a two-way race (without Wallace) Humphrey falls far behind Nixon, as did Lyndon Johnson in the February survey. A two-way race between Reagan and Humphrey would be very close, while Humphrey has a lead of 9 percentage points against Rockefeller.

I was particularly interested by the impact of a Thurmond endorsement. On this point, the pollster wrote:

About one fourth (24%) say Strom Thurmond's endorsement of Nixon affects their outlook favorably toward Nixon . . . about half of those favorably influenced by Thurmond's endorsement are Wallace supporters or undecideds. Thus, if all the Thurmond "fans" were to switch from Wallace to Nixon, it would put Nixon in first place over Wallace and Humphrey.

Thus a few points were clear: (1) Wallace had strengthened himself to the point where he was the clear favorite in this state midway between the upper and lower South (meaning he was No. 1 in the South); (2) Thurmond could make the vital difference; (3) Wallace would elect Humphrey in a three-way race; and (4) Nixon was the only Republican winner in a two-way race with Humphrey.

During the course of the campaign other polls taken nationally and regionally by the Nixon organization showed we were constantly whittling away Wallace's lead.

Finally, in another poll by Central Surveys taken October 9-12, 1968, we saw the first ray of hope. We had pulled ahead 32 percent for Nixon, 29 percent for Wallace, 20 percent for Humphrey, and 19 percent no preference.

The pollster concluded:

While Richard Nixon now enjoys a narrow lead for president in South Carolina, survey results (based on a comparison with a July survey) indicated a good possibility that the margin will widen. Nixon has gained votes since July while George Wallace and Hubert

Humphrey have lost support. Nixon has gained half of the total loss of the two and the other half had shifted to undecided.

Campaigning of Senator Thurmond in behalf of Nixon is favorably considered by three times as many voters as are unfavorably affected. Half of those unfavorably affected are now supporting Humphrey. Neither does Thurmond's effort seem to damage his image because twice as many say they are favorably affected toward him because of this activity than say they are unfavorably affected. Most say they are not affected at all.

The pollster recorded a six-point increase for Nixon since the July poll and six-point drops for Wallace and for Humphrey.

He also found that Wallace voters and the undecideds would vote overwhelmingly for Nixon were Wallace not on the ballot.

With regard to Thurmond's impact, he reported:

Another factor is that 53% of these "soft" Wallace voters think Nixon will be the next president, and only 37% believe Wallace will be the winner. The activity of Senator Thurmond on behalf of Nixon is favorably accepted by 26% of these respondents, and none say they are unfavorably affected.

Our Thurmond Speaks for Nixon-Agnew committee was determined to make our contribution to the Nixon victory without being in any way labeled an albatross. So I took every key speech and advertisement to Mitchell for his personal approval. While in New York on one trip I found a tape recording of some radio commercials of Stewart Hamlin, a country music star. He had made some recordings for the Nixon advertising people. The proposed commercials effectively pointed up to our textile and other working people the futility—and in fact the detrimental effects—of a Wallace campaign on "acceptable Richard Nixon" as against the "unacceptable Hubert Humphrey." One commercial had Hamlin strumming a guitar and talking in country music style about chasing a rabbit—George Wallace—while the battle was being decided in favor of the real enemy of the South—Humphrey. Wallace was pictured as the rabbit who was being used as a decoy the same as Teddy Roosevelt in his 1912 Bull Moose campaign where Teddy received enough votes to elect the Democrat Woodrow Wilson over Republican William Howard Taft. It was great for getting through to the working man and woman, especially in the South. Roger Milliken, the sophisticated textile industrialist, understood the potency of this appeal better than the Nixon aides. When they indicated a hesitancy to use Hamlin we arranged to run the commercials at our expense.

These radio commercials, plus Thurmond's 30- and 60-second TV spots, got across the message that Wallace in effect was a Democrat decoy for "Triple H."

A few years later Tom Turnipseed, our only South Carolina Republican to defect and offer his services to George Wallace's campaign on a full-time basis, told me of the devastating effect our commercials and our campaign had on the Wallace campaign. Turnipseed, who became in effect Wallace's campaign manager, told me he realized early in the campaign that the Wallace aim to be the deciding factor in the 1968 election was being effectively undermined when he watched several Thurmond Speaks for Nixon-Agnew commercials on TV. When he saw Thurmond making the point that Wallace could only elect the feared Humphrey, Turnipseed realized this was the one Nixon answer to Wallace they could not overcome. He felt that only Thurmond, the 1948 Dixiecrat, could punch across this point. The TV message was logical and penetrating enough that even a Wallace devotee such as Turnipseed—and none was stronger—saw that the Wallace effort could succeed except for one most vital ingredient, Thurmond. All Thurmond had to do was point up not only the futility of the Wallace campaign—"George can't win"—but also make the point that Wallace could only succeed in throwing the 1968 presidential election into the Democratic House where the "evil" Humphrey would surely win over the "OK" Nixon. To get across this vital message, we had to saturate the media, especially TV, with Thurmond spots in vote areas where it was reasonably certain we could reverse the Wallace tide. Had we spread our anti-Wallace money too thin, we would have lost the war. We sent materials and commercials into states like Mississippi and Alabama only when Reed and other leaders had the money to defray our costs. They understood our practical position. The Nixon staff did not believe we could be so practical, although they had witnessed quite a performance in pragmatism at Miami Beach. Thurmond had such a reputation as a conservative ideologue that few realized he could be so practical. What they did not know was that Thurmond, the staunchest of conservatives, is as pragmatic about winning as anyone, especially when he is convinced that "the American way of life" is at stake. Ideology was important to Thurmond, but unlike some conservatives, he is too smart to trip up on philosophy.

In 1968 Thurmond was so convinced that "the American way" was in danger that he short-circuited his love life to "do his thing for Nixon."

As I traveled the state of South Carolina in the Nixon campaign, I heard a recurring rumor that widower Thurmond, age 67, was seeing, as we Southerners say, Miss South Carolina of 1966, Nancy Moore of Aiken, South Carolina. Republican women who were great admirers of Thurmond were distressed and distraught at the mere idea that their senior senator widower was seeing Miss South Carolina.

I was not sure this was the case, but I had to deny it everywhere I went. The women seemed jealous, and the men were downright envious. I became concerned Thurmond's influence would be curtailed. So Buzhardt and I had a sons-to-father talk with Thurmond. We were deeply concerned about his ideas or actions regarding courtship or marriage. All that would have to wait until after he had finished saving the country in the general election of 1968.

We warned him that Nancy Moore could ruin all he had accomplished. We knew that there was truly one thing that came ahead of everything else with Thurmond, noted for his prowess as a ladies' man, and that was his basic sense of patriotism.

So we kept him out of sight from lovely Nancy for the duration of the campaign—and we hoped forever. Being as pragmatic as he was, Thurmond agreed not to pursue Miss South Carolina until after the election.

In the early days of the campaign I tried to get the Nixon staff to go along with a statement from Nixon indicating some favor for "freedom of choice" in public school desegregation and against forced busing of school children. We were told there was no way to get such statements and that we should not even breathe anything in this regard.

Then on the morning of September 13, 1968, I heard on the TV news that Nixon, in a TV interview in Charlotte, North Carolina, had just said what I wanted to hear. I got a *Charlotte Observer,* and there was the statement in print:

> Richard M. Nixon said Thursday that, "I look with great concern whenever I see federal agencies or courts trying to become local school boards.

> In an interview with WBTV of Charlotte and WFMY-TV of Greensboro, the former vice president criticized the federal Department of Health, Education and Welfare (HEW) for guidelines and for using federal funds as a way of forcing its wishes.

"There has been too much of a tendency," the Republican presidential candidate said, "for our courts and our federal agencies to use the whole program of school integration for purposes which have very little to do with education and which do not serve a very useful purpose."

Nixon, who left Charlotte Thursday for New Orleans after campaigning here Wednesday afternoon, said he supports the 1954 U.S. Supreme Court ruling prohibiting school segregation and favors "freedom of choice" plans that are not just "used to perpetuate segregation."

But he also spoke against busing children to achieve racial balance and said that most school districts could solve their problems on the local level. He said that when HEW withholds money from a school district only because it is violating HEW guidelines, "that activity should be completely examined, and, in some cases, rescinded."

"I wouldn't want to see a federal agency punish a local community," he said.

Nixon added that he has no timetable for nationwide school integration other than to move forward on a basis that puts primary emphasis on the quality of education. He said that busing slum children to schools in wealthier areas is useless because "they are two or three grades behind, and all you do is destroy their ability to compete."

I called Nixon's New York headquarters asking permission to use something already in print and on videotape. The answer was a resounding negative. They wanted me to forget the statement.

I then went to Charlotte, bought a copy of the videotape, and from there I flew to New York to see Mitchell. There I pleaded for permission to run the whole interview, or, in the alternative, excerpts. Finally I was permitted to use a few abbreviated excerpts which carried less impact than the full statement. I stuck with the agreement. However, I did reprint the *Charlotte Observer* article in handbills and advertisements. It seemed strange Nixon aides agreed to the article but cut back considerably on Nixon's full videotape statement. They just did not want him saying anything about favoring freedom of choice in public school desegregation and about being against forced busing directly on TV.

Wrestling with us step by step were moderate Peter Flanigan and liberal Leonard Garment, both later to be colleagues of mine on the White House staff.

By far, however, our most effective message stated repeatedly by Thurmond and all our literature was this message: "Wallace can't win; he can only elect Humphrey."

A direct mail postcard wrapped up the best of our argument. In South Carolina, we sent the card to the voter registration list. Other states were given the card to do likewise and adapt to their states. Some did, but none used it as extensively as we. The card read:

> On November 5 it's either Nixon . . . or Humphrey. The next President of the United States will be decided by your vote on November 5. Your real choice will be either Republican Richard Nixon or Democrat Hubert Humphrey. The third party candidate cannot be elected. After the Chicago Convention riots, public opinion polls show Nixon to be the strong choice of the people. However, Humphrey can still win, if he can split the vote of his opposition . . . or, if he can get the election thrown into the U.S. House for the politicians to make the choice. Let's don't let Humphrey divide and conquer us! Make sure that the people decide on Nov. 5, not the politicians in Washington. Make YOUR vote count for Richard Nixon to insure change and a return to order in America. This time, you can make your voice heard in Washington.

While Nixon visited South Carolina, he did not mention freedom of choice or textiles. So the Humphrey chairman issued a statement questioning Nixon's sincerity. The Democrats must have realized what we knew—that the Nixon staff was determined never to hear freedom of choice again.

However, four days later on October 7 in a meeting with United Press International (UPI) editors in Washington, Nixon reiterated his freedom-of-choice position. He told the editors he thought HEW had been "overzealous" in its efforts to implement guidelines, specifically as they related to "freedom of choice." He charged the department with going beyond the law in some cases by withholding federal funds to impose its own standards. He said he would favor deferring money but only where "free choice" is used as a "subterfuge for segregation." He reiterated his strong support of "true freedom of choice."

The following day, October 9, Vice President Humphrey told the same group there would be no letup in pushing desegregation. He claimed full credit for all civil rights legislation and endorsed the Supreme Court's recent decision outlawing the Court's earlier "freedom of choice" ruling.

Naturally, I made use of the statements before the UPI editors. I ran an ad displaying the Charlotte TV statement by Nixon and the UPI statement by Humphrey. The ad concluded by saying:

> Richard Nixon will be our next president, unless we allow Hubert Humphrey to divide and conquer us or throw the election into the House where Hubert Humphrey will be elected. Make *your* vote count! Nixon's the One!

Spiro Agnew was a big favorite for southern audiences. However, it was difficult to get visits from both Nixon and Agnew in smaller electoral vote states.

When I got the mid-October Central Surveys poll showing Nixon had finally moved slightly ahead in South Carolina, I used this to get Agnew. However, I had another verbal wrestling match with Peter Flanigan, the deputy campaign manager. He did not believe Nixon was ahead. In fact, he made me mail him a copy of the poll to confirm what I was telling him.

We finally prevailed, and Agnew was sent to Charleston on September 9. The reception was big and warm. Agnew's main theme was a warning against helping Humphrey by voting for Wallace. He said: "Wallace is dangerous because he is not electable. He will divide the vote.

"If you want Humphrey for four more years," Agnew warned, "vote for Wallace; if you don't want him, vote for Mr. Nixon."

Meanwhile, the South was still appearing to be Wallace country. On October 2, columnist David Lawrence reported on a Gallup Poll showing Nixon to be leading in all sections of the country except the South. Gallup had Wallace ahead with 38 percent to 31 percent for Nixon and 24 percent for Humphrey.

As late as October 21, UPI writer James K. Cazalas wrote from Atlanta that "subtle shifts are taking place in the South during the final days of the campaign, but George C. Wallace is still the man to beat."

He reported: "Richard Nixon and Hubert Humphrey have made some gains in Dixie but Wallace still has a healthy lead in most states."

He cited a recent North Carolina poll showing Wallace with 38 percent, Humphrey with 19 percent, and Nixon with 27 percent.

An Associated Press news story in South Carolina on October 20 called the race a three-way toss-up.

What was happening was this: Nixon was rapidly fading in the rest of the country while he was rising equally as fast in the South. Toward the end, the Nixon campaign team came to have a healthier respect for our virtually unwelcomed efforts up to that point. Flanigan asked me on my last visit to the New York headquarters: "Do you fellows really believe you can pull it through down there?" He could not believe me because the staff strategy was to win the election for Nixon in the rest of the country and "catch as catch can" in the potentially embarrassing South. This was neither Mitchell's view nor Nixon's.

In the last few days my telephone rang constantly with calls from New York wanting to know what Nixon headquarters there could do to help us pull it through.

And pull it through we did!

On November 7, 1968, Hugh E. Gibson, reporter for the Charleston (South Carolina) *News and Courier* told the story this way:

Sen. Strom Thurmond shifted from a "king-saver" to a "kingmaker" Wednesday as Republican Richard Nixon emerged the victor in the cliff-hanging presidential race. Although Illinois' 26 electoral votes clinched Nixon's narrow victory over Hubert Humphrey, they would have been meaningless had not Thurmond already helped to snatch 67 votes from third party candidate George C. Wallace.

There was no question that Thurmond almost single-handedly carried Nixon to victory in South Carolina, handing him eight electoral votes.

And few would dispute that he had carried the brunt of the battles that also gave Nixon victories in Virginia, North Carolina, Tennessee, Florida, and Kentucky. Either by personal appearances or providing campaign material from "Thurmond Speaks" headquarters, the Senator had used his prestige and influence to blunt the Wallace appeal.

Thurmond and state GOP chairman Harry S. Dent, well aware Humphrey had surged ahead in the Northeast, pinpointed southern and border states on election eve as essential to counterbalance the vice-president's gains.

On election day Thurmond was concerned we were going to lose the South and even South Carolina. In all his campaigning he had run into so many more Wallace bumper stickers than any others. This was especially so on pickup trucks with shotguns or rifles displayed in the back window. The psychology of all those bumper stickers got to all of us in the Thurmond Speaks for Nixon-Agnew operation. However, I had confidence in our poll of mid-October, and I could feel the tide changing from Wallace to Nixon.

Actually in the states we won, the end results showed a virtual reversal of the Nixon and Wallace percentages from the beginning to the end of the campaign. Wallace generally had 38 percent in the beginning and Nixon was fighting with Humphrey for a poor second. In the end it was Nixon with 38 percent and Wallace and Humphrey were fighting for a poor second.

Thurmond got a call from Nixon's headquarters for him and me to fly to New York to watch the returns come in for what was hoped to be a victory celebration. But I stayed in Columbia because of all the work to be done even on election night.

When Thurmond arrived at the Nixon celebration in New York City, he was ushered in to see Nixon, Mitchell, and some others. They profusely thanked the senator for his dedicated and—as they could then see—successful efforts. Nixon told him: "Strom, you did a fabulous job!"

Now that the 1968 general election was concluded, I was ready for rest and relaxation, and certainly no more political crises to face for a while. When Thurmond returned from receiving the Nixon and Mitchell plaudits in New York, a new political crisis was thrown in my lap by the senator himself.

Thurmond called to report on his New York trip. As he was concluding, he dropped his bombshell.

"Harry, now that the election is over, guess what I'm going to do?" he asked.

I said, "Rest, senator, get plenty of rest. You deserve it, and more."

"I plan to do that, Harry," he responded, "when Nancy and I get married."

I said, "Oh, senator, you can't do that!"

"But," he exclaimed, "you and Fred said if we waited until after the election it would be OK."

"Oh, no, senator," I groused, "we said that just to get you past the election so you could play the role destiny decreed for you in the 1968 election. You can never marry that girl. It would ruin you politically, destroy everything you've worked for in your political life. If you do this just don't plan to run again in 1972. In fact, you might as well resign now like King Edward and get public sympathy to offset all the public wrath that'll follow."

I hung up the telephone and then found Buzhardt to tell him how our "hero" was going to turn himself into a "goat" right away. We quickly arranged to meet with the senator in his hotel room. We gave him the lecture of his life. When we had finished, he meekly told us: "OK, boys, I'll tell you what you do, go talk to Nancy. Tell her everything you've told me and if you can talk her out of it, it'll be all right with me."

So off we went to find Nancy. We painted every horrible consequence possible, including how their children would be abnormal. We had four sessions with her over a two-week period. Finally, in the meeting, we became convinced of her deep love for the senator when she broke down and cried as I urged her, "If you really love the man, for goodness sake, leave him alone!"

So we then reconciled ourselves to a dreaded wedding. We would just have to minimize the adverse impact as much as possible.

Then the senator threw us another problem. "What about a big church wedding," he asked?

Again, we responded, "Oh, no, senator. You'd have *Time, Life, Newsweek,* and the networks down here ridiculing you like they did in 1947 when you married Jean (his late wife) while governor. Remember how the *Life* picture of you standing on your head next to your bride caused the only election loss of your career?"

Again, Buzhardt and I lost. The big church wedding was held in Aiken with all the big news media as we had expected. Buzhardt and I will always believe Nancy timed it for maximum political impact to show us how wrong we were in 1968 as the senator rolled to a 1972 reelection victory margin of 2-1.

Buzhardt's late father, the first law partner of Thurmond, once told me that Thurmond always had a little bit of luck to go with all his abilities. He said, "Strom's like a cat. You could throw him off the Empire State Building any number of times, and everytime he'd land on his feet."

In 1968 Thurmond had rolled the dice three times—against Reagan, against Wallace, and for Nancy—and each time he had landed, as the elder Buzhardt had said, "like a cat . . . on his feet."

6

Nixon Delivers on Desegregation

W ithin 30 days after the 1968 election victory I was installed in the Pierre Hotel in New York City as a deputy counsel to the president-elect in the transition government. Southern Republican leaders, led by Thurmond, proffered my services to Nixon, Mitchell, and Bryce Harlow. Southerners were concerned that Nixon, Mitchell, and company might forget all those campaign promises without a southern face nearby to remind them. Since I had done most of the talking with the Nixon campaign team about the promises, I was the choice over the objections of my family.

Furthermore, Nixon had earlier indicated he might want me on his White House staff. Thus I was the logical candidate. Even so, the fact that I was so closely identified with Thurmond could—and did—create an impression that Thurmond was going to wield a strong influence on Nixon. This would be proof that there were deals made with the southern GOP and that there was indeed a Nixon Southern Strategy.

As a consequence the Nixon staff shrewdly waited until they had a few more appointees to announce before presenting me to the news media. They downplayed my presentation to the media, emphasizing John Sears and the other two appointees. However, the *New York Times* caught the ploy. Reporter John Apple referred to my appointment as a "small quid for a big quo."

When we moved into the White House on January 21, 1969, we found the Johnson administration had left behind some desegregation booby traps to test the Nixon campaign rhetoric on school desegregation guidelines. Thus we were immediately at odds with what we came to call "WHEW!"—the bureaucrats at the Department of Health, Education, and Welfare.

Nixon named his good liberal friend, Lt. Gov. Robert Finch of California as the HEW secretary. Finch was expected to control HEW and insure that Nixon's views were made to fit the law as much as possible and vice versa.

After skirmishing with HEW and Justice Department officials over several deadlines for cutting off federal aid to southern school districts, the president determined it was necessary to promulgate new school desegregation policies in a lengthy policy statement.

Finch's general counsel and Mitchell's confidant did the prime work on the statement giving the Administration's position. Robert Mardian, Bryce Harlow, and I assisted with input from Finch and his associates, as well as suggestions from Jerry Leonard's civil rights shop at the Justice Department.

Already in a memo I had outlined my views on devising the long-awaited school desegregation policy statements to the president. However, with all the controversy over the proposed statement, nothing had been accomplished.

I had suggested that the president be aware that "southern leaders are expecting some changes toward more reasonable implementation of the law and that he consider these basic points: (1) what the law requires; (2) what was said in the campaign and since; (3) what can be done as a practical matter to achieve total desegregation, when, and its effects on quality education; (4) what effects this policy may have on southern cooperation on Capitol Hill; (5) what political effects this could have in 1972; and (6) what is right and in the interest of all the people."

I cautioned the president in the memo to consider several observations, which I felt reflected my understanding of the southern mind, the problem, and the law, saying:

1. Quality education on an equal basis for all is the primary aim of federal aid to education programs. 'Education must come first.' (The Southern leaders want true freedom of choice but recommended in their last meeting that this quoted phrase might form the basis of new guidelines.)

2. Control over education must be maintained at the local level as much as possible.

3. The law must be enforced in all areas, not just the South. It is apparent that previous enforcement has been aimed solely at the South. Even Ruby Martin (civil rights chief at HEW) says the south is doing better than the rest of the nation.

4. The guidelines must be administered with the end of winning compliance and cooperation. Instead, they have been administered with an apparent attitude of retaliation in many cases.

5. Southerners can best persuade other Southerners. Too many 'outsiders,' apparent pro-hippie types, and Negroes have been sent South to do the job.

6. Not much can be changed at HEW unless there is a good personnel turnover (transfer, if necessary). The basic ideology among personnel is much left of center—zealots.

7. HEW educators (Title IV people) should have more say than HEW civil rights complaince (Title VI) people. The latter are more concerned with total integration 'now' than education.

8. Deliberate segregation and the dual school system concept must be eliminated. When this is accomplished in each case is a subjective question.

9. As a practical matter, it is impossible to achieve the guideline goal of total integration this fall. The major problems come where Negroes constitute more than 30% in previously all-white schools and where whites are ordered to go to previously all-black schools.

10. Private schools are now growing in the South. Many of the best teachers are going there. The people affected most are poor whites and Negroes, who cannot run from the problems created in desegregating.

11. People in HEW are pushing busing. This was recommended recently in a Newport News, Virginia, case. The Raleigh case ruling can only result in busing.

12. The British ran ahead of us, even to busing, and now are heading back to local control. The people think the President will slow up on this subject. All previous surveys show the majority want gradualism more than the LBJ-type policies.

13. Action should come this month before Mr. Finch goes south on April 25 to meet with educators and before the April 30 court-ordered deadline on 22 cases. These cases have been turned over to HEW to negotiate, putting us on the spot.

Also I had sent the president a memo with an attached Gallup poll on George Wallace, which indicated that "although he finished a weak third in last November's presidential election, George Wallace can still boast the support of sizeable minority of voters in the 13-state region of the South."

A final Gallup survey, published the Sunday prior to the election showed this: Wallace, 15 percent of the vote; Nixon 43 percent; and Humphrey, 42 percent. These figures indicated almost exactly the division of the vote in the election: Wallace, 13.6 percent; Nixon, 43.5 percent; and Humphrey, 42.9 percent.

The key to the policy statement was the relaxation of deadline dates for ending the dual-school systems in school districts. This was what the news media played, much to the horror of Leon Panetta, chief of HEW's Office of Civil Rights.

The southern headlines and reaction were great. In a memo I told the president of the favorable southern reaction he was getting. And his reaction in turn was favorable.

The statement was issued on July 3. And it brought sharp adverse reaction from civil rights groups despite all the consessions won by Leonard Garment, a recent liberal addition to the White House staff; Panetta; and Jerry Leonard.

Although the statement was issued, Panetta and HEW's Office of Civil Rights refused to let the statement speak for itself. In a background news conference and a later news conference at HEW, Panetta and Under Secretary Jack Veneman stressed that the guidelines were not changed by the statement and that Panetta's office would continue as before. Jerry Leonard of the Justice Department conceded there would be a shift in emphasis from fund cutoffs to court suits and that there would be some leniency on deadline dates.

Panetta declared the deadline date of 1970 would not be changed—no extensions. However, Panetta and his people viewed the statement privately as a sellout. They determined that what was important was how they administered the new policy, and that is what Senator Thurmond feared. His reaction was one of caution: "I reserve further judgment until I see how the policy is administered."

Southerners were concerned over the administration of policy; they could not understand how Nixon could say one thing in the campaign, back it up as president in news conferences, and then have HEW—and in some cases the Justice Department—executing actions to the left of LBJ.

Of course, court decisions kept crowding Nixonian positions. But Panetta was causing Nixon the most discomfort, since his actions demonstrated as much fervor as, or more than, the Johnson enforcers. True, Panetta had inherited the LBJ bureaucrats. However, Finch, Nixon's old buddy, had caused much of the problem by appointing top people as zealous, or more so, as the bureaucrats who carried out the LBJ policy directives.

When Finch became HEW secretary, he set up a liberal cabal under him. Jack Veneman became under secretary; Pat Hitt, an assistant secretary; James Farmer, a radical black leader, assistant secretary; and James Allen, the busing educator from New York, became an assistant secretary and commissioner of education.

Finch had intended to keep Ruby Martin, the holdover civil rights chief at HEW. To Southerners, Martin exemplified their worst fears. Thus the first action expected to come at HEW was the release of all the schedule "C" political employees of the previous administration, the ones Nixon had accused in the campaign of having gone too far.

But Finch's advisers had no such plans. He had been told by Veneman and his transition advisers that his liberal credentials would be destroyed unless he kept the Ruby Martin types and filled the presidential appointments at HEW with equally liberal types.

The president had his views and obligations, and they called for changes at HEW—changes toward moderation and reason. So it came to be Nixon's interest versus Finch's interest. The pressures on Nixon were from both directions—left and right—but he chose right in the campaign and got elected that way. When Nixon added the Wallace and Nixon vote, he got a good mandate. When he read the public opinion polls sent him, he found what he had said in a September 1969 news conference, "The people want a middle course."

Yet the courts kept pushing left, and the civil rights leaders and many newsmen put the segregationist tag on those in the middle or on the right.

Finch wanted to be on the liberal side for ideological and political reasons. In private conversations, he indicated no zealotry. In fact, he indicated softness. He certainly never fought with any relish or conviction in meetings I attended, especially with the president. He was easy to overcome, if indeed that was necessary.

Nixon's critics ascribed political motives to his middle course on school desegregation. To some degree this was true. After all, he did not have to run in California again—as Finch planned for himself—but the president did have to run nationally again in 1972. And he was clearly in step nationally according to the public opinion polls and the latest and most accurate national poll, the presidential election of 1968.

Attached to the April 9 memo I sent the president was also a February 9 Gallup poll showing the following national feelings toward integration:

Question. "Thinking of the new administration . . . it's too early to have a definite opinion, but just your best guess—do you think integration will now be pushed faster, or not so fast?"

Faster	Not So Fast	About Right	Don't Know
%	%	%	%
16	48	28	8

Regardless of all the presidential votes and public opinion polls, Panetta and company were armed with a cause and what their commander in chief wanted did not matter.

In his book, *Bring Us Together: The Nixon Team and the Civil Rights Retreat,* Panetta exposes the ways in which he willfully disregarded orders, finagled Finch to get his way, leaked to the press, and worked against Administration policy on Capitol Hill and elsewhere. Panetta switched to the Democratic party in 1975, and in 1976 won a seat in Congress in California's Sixteenth Congressional District.

Finally, on February 17, 1970, Panetta was fired, after several wishes by the president had not been carried out by Finch. These generally concerned efforts to give southern school districts with special problems more time to desegregate fully.

Had Finch felt strongly about Panetta he could have tried to block the firing with his own resignation. Instead, in an earlier meeting in his office, he accepted the resignation. Finch's problem, however, was Veneman, who had vowed to resign if the White House insisted on eliminating Panetta. Thus Finch was caught between Nixon and Veneman. He was a victim of his decision to appoint Veneman.

After Panetta departed, it was only a short time after that Finch resigned. The Panetta firing resulted in personnel turmoil at HEW. The Office of Civil Rights people sent the president a strongly worded letter. The 1800 HEW employees petitioned Finch to come to a meeting with them and explain the administration's civil rights policies.

Finch postponed the meeting a few times because of illness. Then on the day of the meeting he went to the hospital with a numb arm. Thus in March 1970 Finch was relieved of his duties as secretary of HEW. He was designated as a counselor to the president with Cabinet rank. His impact was never the same.

Elliot Richardson, Finch's successor, was another liberal Republican Nixon put in sensitive spots to do the job the way Nixon desired. Once when Secretary of State William P. Rogers would not order an honorary political appointment because he did not want to stir up state's bureaucracy, the president told me to call Richardson, the under secretary at the time. Nixon said, "Get Elliot, he'll do what I want." And he did. Thus Nixon subsequently used Richardson as top man at HEW, and the Defense and Justice departments. However, while attorney general, Richardson did not live up to Nixon's expectations. He appointed Archibald Cox as special prosecutor and then made a hero of himself when he defied Nixon's order to fire Cox.

Thus the president's tactic of using liberal friends to execute his conservative will without showing Nixon's hand did not prove too successful. Finch was the prime example, with Richardson a close second.

Finch's question of what to do with Ruby Martin became a pressing problem. The southern GOP said, in effect, "Hell, no!" Finch not only proposed to keep her, but to promote her to a higher grade and title as chief desegregationist.

In his book, Panetta gives this account of the fear Ruby Martin generated even in HEW types. "I checked my conscience every time I saw her," said one of her top desegregation staffers. "She scared all the old stodgy Office of Education types and hangers-on. She demanded performance. If other directors approached their task stressing education or law, Ruby reminded everybody we were retrieving stolen civil rights."

I called the Ruby Martin matter to the attention of the president and John Ehrlichman. Instead of the promotion, Martin submitted her resignation, effective March 7. Still, she was there long enough to participate in the initial HEW crises. The first were the five southern school districts scheduled to have their funds terminated nine days after the inauguration. One district was in North Carolina, two were in South Carolina, and two were in Mississippi. The time bomb was ticking.

Bryce Harlow, Bill Timmons, and I pushed for no cutoff and at least a reprieve. We prevailed over Finch's resistance, but not completely. Martin, Panetta, Veneman, and others at HEW were working feverishly to save as much as they could.

It was finally concluded to grant a 60-day reprieve and have the school superintendents hold the money while they negotiated with HEW desegregation teams.

Panetta and his people felt they had saved the day for HEW. However, Thurmond and most of the press viewed the concession as a victory for the South. This event did, however, point up the problems to come in the Nixon Administration as the behind-the-scene struggle was now underway between the hard and soft approaches within the Administration.

Within the 60-day period, the five districts negotiated plans deemed acceptable by HEW. But then seven more districts ran up against deadline dates.

In his book, Panetta aptly expresses his expectations in dealing with the seven southern districts: "I'll have to prove these are the most segregationist, bigoted sons of bitches in the world."

Panetta and Veneman convinced Finch to focus on three of the districts for the purpose of showing the HEW civil rights muscle. The announcement of fund cutoffs with no grace period was made on February 13. Sparks flew in the South, especially on top of the Finch appointments and at that time the continuation of Ruby Martin.

The Panetta victory and some Justice Department suits by Leonard brought the southern GOP chairmen to Washington immediately. The chairmen's pressures were effective and offset in part those generated on Capitol Hill and in the news media by the HEW forces.

The fund-cutoff action Panetta and Veneman pushed on Finch proved costly. The southern reaction was so strong and the White House was so upset that the Finch crowd began losing one battle after another.

There was the Mardian appointment as general counsel at HEW and then the Finch interview in *U.S. News and World Report.* True to his weakness, Finch would talk tough on civil rights with the liberals and soft with the other crowd. The conservative crew at *U.S. News and World Report* "took him to the cleaners." The interview was so good I sent 55,000 copies South.

The southern chairmen left town after their second postinaugural visit to Washington feeling better about our desegregation action, but seriously questioning the sweet talk of the Nixon Administration and the sour actions at HEW, and in part, at the Justice department.

The chairmen felt good about the Mardian appointment. Some remembered him from the Goldwater campaign of 1964. I had talked at length with Mardian, and I knew he was seeking a reasonable approach. He briefed me on his interpretation of the *Green* case of 1968, which had severely restricted freedom-of-choice plans and had decreed desegregation now — all according to HEW interpretation and implementation through the guidelines drawn up before the *Green* decision.

Mardian's idea was to clarify the guidelines quietly and apply the clarified guidelines. He interpreted the *Green* case to mean that desegregation must begin now, not that it must be completed now, which was virtually impossible, anyway.

Panetta reveals Leonard's view at that time in the Panetta book. He quotes Leonard in a meeting to try to arrive at a policy for the president as saying (pages 112 and 113):

> This South . . . the South, I'm so goddamned tired of hearing about the South. When is somebody going to start worrying about the North? That's where the votes are to begin with. Instead, we're fighting over the law in order to give something to a bunch of racists.

> Well the President *did* give the Southerners the clear impression something would change in this area, Mardian responded.

> [deleted], I've looked over the President's campaign statements and they say nothing, and besides, his press conference was tough on the issue.

This is an example of the attitudes of the chief enforcer for Nixon at the Justice Department. The same attitude, except more so, prevailed at HEW. Yet neither Leonard nor Panetta reflected the views of the president or the statements he made in the campaign.

Back at HEW, the crises continued. And Panetta and Veneman continued to influence Finch. Here Panetta describes a favorite tactic he and Veneman used on Finch (page 117):

> I had begun to learn that the quickest reaction from the Secretary usually came under the threat of a bad story or editorial. I had seen Jack use this tactic successfully several times and had employed it myself. Finch was basically a political animal, and the "bad story" was his greatest fear; facts about the deprivation of black children or the bitter consequences of discrimination never quite had the same impact.

At HEW, Finch jumped from one crisis to another. Each seemed to be handled with inconsistency because HEW officials were pulling him in one direction and the White House in another direction.

Nixon was convinced the application of reason was the answer at HEW. Why couldn't those people at HEW see this and end his problems over school desegregation? The president once offered to go to South Carolina and personally negotiate a problem with 21 school districts.

The Nixon offer to negotiate the South Carolina cases sent shock waves through HEW. This had much to do with causing Finch to circumvent his staff on this and settle for less than Panetta was demanding. The deadline dates were moved to September 1970. The news media chalked up another loss for HEW and a victory for the South.

While all this was going on more crises were in the works for HEW. There was the effort to desegregate blood in Louisiana hospitals. As Finch remarked privately, writes Panetta, "Now we're going after blood."

In Charleston, South Carolina, the Medical University of South Carolina came up with an equal-employment opportunity problem. The question posed was whether the medical university and its hospital would lose $12 million in federal aid.

What complicated the situation was a grievance problem with 12 employees at the hospital resulting in a strike by more than 400 employees. The 12 had been fired for leaving their positions of work at the hospital when they were needed and "without good cause."

This situation was also inspired and directed by the Reverend Ralph Abernathy and his Southern Christian Leadership Conference. Abernathy and his forces came to Charleston demonstrating for union recognition, higher wages, equal opportunity, and grievance procedures.

HEW was demanding that William McCord, university president, adopt a series of positive-action programs, including the rehiring of the 12. McCord said no. He was backed up by Democrat Governor Robert McNair, the general assembly, and U.S. House Armed Services Committee Chairman L. Mendel Rivers, and Senator Thurmond.

Working separately, Rivers and Thurmond both claimed they got promises from Finch that the rehiring proposal would be considered further. It was one thing for HEW to cut off funds for school lunches, but now it was talking about funds for the sick.

I became concerned because the impact of a fund cutoff in Charleston for the medical university's hospital would never be understood in South Carolina. Also, HEW was taking sides with a labor union and with Abernathy.

Things got worse when Abernathy, in demonstrating on June 21, was arrested with the Reverend Hosea Williams of Atlanta. The strike and demonstrations had been going on for weeks. When things got out of hand and a riot resulted, the Charleston police took control of the situation. Passions were then at a fever pitch.

The Nixon Administration kept a close watch on the situation from the latter part of April onward. Governor McNair had told me that South Carolina could not recognize a union, and the medical university represented the state. The labor union leaders were in constant contact with Panetta's office, and Panetta tried to back the union all the way.

Finch was off vactioning in the Bahamas. This gave the president the opportunity to call in a stronger man with proved coolness and good judgment. Labor Secretary George Shultz was selected to handle the problem. The excuse was that a labor problem was involved.

Shultz dispatched a mediator to assist in Charleston after I arranged with the city's mayor, Palmer Gaillard, to request such assistance. It was important that HEW types or any federal official be kept out of the situation, unless such was requested by the governor or the mayor.

The local officials wanted the Justice Department to take action against Abernathy. The whole affair was crying for a settlement.

Knowing the mediating efforts were getting nowhere, I volunteered to Shultz to call McCord and try to convince him of the national implications and the need for some solution to the rehiring problem. In Charleston, the longshoremen and the garbage collectors were striking with some demonstrators even in the streets in Washington. Nixon determined to keep order, knowing his losses would be big either way.

Once McCord understood the president's concern and the national implications, he agreed to work out a plan for helping the 12 find employment. The 12 did not have to go back to work for McCord, but somewhere in Charleston. The mayor, Senator Thurmond, and others helped with the job problem; the strike was settled after a while, but the big problem it presented was over; the union rebuffed; and no HEW funds were terminated. Most everyone was relieved except the diehards on both sides.

But from all this, Finch had received another setback. The president started bringing Secretary Shultz into the school desegregation picture. This settlement gave the secretary a big boost to his higher posts as budget director and counselor to the president and also as secretary of the treasury. Shultz eventually became one of the most influential men in the Nixon Administration.

Shultz and I formed a friendship and respect that carried forward and through his 1970 role as the desegregation leader and decision maker in the Administration.

Cool, careful, reasonable, persuasive, and possessing sound judgment, Shultz was a most talented and unusual professor.

While Finch wrestled with the problem of an Administration statement on school desegregation, the secretary was becoming ensnared in another whirlpool. This involved not desegregation, but another liberal appointment at HEW.

Supposedly, Finch justified to his HEW cabal the Mardian appointment by calling it a trade-off to get controversial John Knowles of Massachusetts as his medical chief at HEW. Ultimately, it did not work this way. Mardian was finally approved, but Knowles was not.

The American Medical Association (AMA) adamantly opposed Knowles. AMA Washington representatives visited several Republican legislators. They particularly got through to the key GOP political leaders on Capitol Hill: the late Senator Everett Dirksen of Illinois, Senator John Tower, and congressmen Rogers Morton of Maryland and Bob Wilson of California. The leaders all communicated with me, as did the AMA people, saying they had conveyed their feelings about Knowles to Finch, but to no avail. The president had even said at his previous news conference he would nominate Finch's choice. By that time Veneman had leaked to the news media that Knowles was Finch's choice.

On June 24, Mitchell, Finch, Haldeman, Harlow, Ehrlichman, Morton, and I went sailing down the Potomac with the president on the *Sequoia*. The cruise was to dine and discuss politics.

Soon after we got aboard, I brought up the question of the proposed Knowles nomination, which was scheduled to go to the Senate the next day. Finch said the matter was settled. I urged the president not to go forward with the nomination in view of the Capitol Hill opposition. The question was whether to ignore the Capitol Hill leaders. The idea was not to give AMA its choice, but certainly not to force a most unacceptable choice. Harlow supported me, and no one objected except for a mild effort by Finch.

After the discussion, the president told Finch to come up with another choice, so overboard went Knowles.

This was another hard blow for Finch to absorb. The next morning he canceled all meetings, and word went out that Knowles was on "shaky ground." Within two days, Finch flew in Roger Egeberg from Los Angeles to be nominated for the post as assistant secretary for Health and Scientific Affairs. Egeberg was not AMA's choice by any means, but at least he was not Knowles.

The news media and liberals reacted angrily, but none more so than Knowles, who denounced the president and praised Finch for standing by him—albeit ever so weakly.

The Knowles affair was a good example of the damage Finch was doing the president with the liberal appointments Veneman and company pushed on him. Knowles's denunciation showed how little loyalty the president could have expected. James Allen, the commissioner of education, had denounced the school desegregation statement. And the rest of the "Finch Crowd," as they called themselves on HEW buttons they wore, already felt no allegiance to their president or his policies.

After the desegregation policy statement was issued, the Finch crowd moved forward as though the statement meant nothing and changed nothing.

Panetta was subsequently told by John Ehrlichman and Finch to "lie low" and keep quiet on the subject of the statement. However, Panetta was determined to clarify the statement by sending a letter to school superintendents and a memo to his desegregation leaders in the field.

Mitchell shook the Justice Department when he read of the Panetta actions. The attorney general reported all this to the president, and the proposed letter never was dispatched. The fact that the letter was under consideration and then was withdrawn was published in the Washington press, giving another defeat to the "Finch Crowd."

Every HEW problem and act of apostasy made the attorney general think less and less of Finch, and he expressed his feelings to the president, as did others at the White House, including me.

The battle continued, with the "Finch Crowd" winning some small engagements, losing some, and being saddled with compromises in others.

The next big loss Finch's group faced was what to do about 33 school districts in Mississippi. The districts were in court with a deadline date of August 25. HEW was pushing for elimination of the dual-school system.

Senator John Stennis, Democrat of Mississippi, chairman of the Armed Services Committee, and Senator James Eastland, Democrat of Mississippi, and the judiciary committee chairman, wanted more time for their school districts. They communicated their concerns to Mitchell and the White House, especially Senator Stennis.

One weekend while I was in South Carolina, John Mitchell called from San Clemente asking me to find Senator Eastland in Mississippi and let him know the Administration was going to side with Mississippi in requesting more time for the 33 districts.

Finch wrote a letter to the Fifth Circuit Court of Appeals asking for an extension of time to submit the proposed plans not later than December 1, 1969. When the U.S. government appeared in court, for the first time the

Department of Justice was seated at the same table with the South rather than with the NAACP.

The Fifth Circuit granted the delay, but on appeal the U.S. Supreme Court overruled the Fifth Circuit and ordered immediate termination of the dual-school system in the 33 school districts.

The southern reaction was one of placing the blame on the court and recognizing that Nixon had tried to be helpful.

The Finch era ended as it began, with indecision, confusion, and grief. Ultimately, the grief was Finch's, for not only did Panetta get fired over Finch's head, but Finch himself followed suit a few weeks thereafter.

The fights with HEW were not without their effects on me. After the president made me political liaison chief in the late spring, I found myself working from 7 A.M. to sometimes 1 and 2 A.M. the following day. I tried to handle all the telephone calls I got from all over the country. South Carolinians especially called on me to help with various personal problems. State GOP leaders from all over did, too. And I saw anyone who asked to see me. My door was wide open.

Then, too, I represented the president at various meetings, even at the meeting of the black elected officials. In fact I memoed every Cabinet member and urged their attendance and cooperation. This baffled some of the liberals.

The fact is black groups got as much or more cooperation from my office as from anyone. Bob Brown, an assistant in the White House, and I formed a group of black administration appointees and also the White House Staff Prayer Breakfast Group. And the black press had signaled out me favorably when Simeon Booker, Washington correspondent for *Ebony* and *Jet* magazines did an article on me in 1969.

Nonetheless, I became a target of some of the liberals on Capitol Hill and in the White House. The Washington reporters for various publications were touting my influence and impact in the summer of 1969.

The news media also played up my use of Tom Reed, a former Reagan staffer, as a temporary assistant. This especially disturbed Finch whose No. 1 rival was Governor Reagan. In addition to my other jobs, I was liaison with GOP governors and thus attended all governors' conferences, where I renewed my friendship with Governor Reagan, even though I had helped block him at the 1968 convention.

The Reagan people were sensitive to every pro-Finch act in the Administration. The problem was that Finch was trying to control patronage in California and Reagan was governor. Being the president's home state,

California was getting the lion's share of appointments; and Reagan felt too many were liberal Finchites. Thus I became the Reagan advocate in the White House, which is what the president wanted.

After the harrowing experiences of wrestling with the HEW and Justice Department zealots on school desegregation throughout 1969, President Nixon wanted a better way in 1970 to bring some order from this complex, emotional issue. He was therefore receptive in January 1970 to anyone with a common sense approach that would meet his basic idea of conciliation in place of coercion. The president wanted to display the helping hand to southern school districts faced with the Court requirement "to eliminate the last vestiges of the dual school system."

One point was certain from the past year's experience—one centralized policy-making group was needed to insure a consistent policy and coordinate HEW and Justice Department implementation programs. I suggested that in addition citizens' advisory groups should be set up throughout the affected states in an effort to win cooperation from black and white community leaders in meeting the August 1970 deadline to end the dual-school system. I also suggested creation of a Cabinet-level committee to be headed by the South's friend, Vice President Spiro Agnew, as the centralized coordinating group in the administration.

Strangely, liberal Len Garment, a desegregation advocate, and I agreed on the basic concept. We both saw the need for a coordinated program of cooperation rather than coercion.

Garment and I worked through Ehrlichman since this was a domestic matter, but coordinated the idea through Mitchell. Garment worked the idea through Finch and HEW, where it was not as well received. I do not believe Finch objected—he wanted some relief from the pressures—but the others at HEW felt this was another "segregation sellout."

The president appointed the committee in February 1970. The chairman was the vice-president, and the vice-chairman was then-Secretary of Labor George Shultz. Other members of the Cabinet-Level committee were Finch; Mitchell; Postmaster General Winton (Red) Blount; and counselors Don Rumsfeld, Bryce Harlow, and Daniel Moynihan. Working as subordinates to the committee were Garment; Peter Flanigan, a key presidential assistant from New York; and I, since we did not hold Cabinet rank.

From this group would come one of the president's prime achievements and one for which he has received little credit. This group and its subsequently appointed staff operation, in coordination with local southern assistance and advice, implemented elimination of the dual-school system without tensions, bayonets, and bullets. It instead combined intentions of goodwill with a sensitive understanding of the situation, along with full federal fundings, and used these as its tools to alleviate problems caused by this gigantic upheaval in the public school systems of many southern states.

The program was successful largely because of the personal attention and direction given it by the president himself. The president was active in many meetings with southern leaders, who were inspired to give their best efforts to the project because of his special concern, his reasonable attitude, and his firm determination to get the job done with goodwill on the part of blacks and whites in the affected areas. "Had they been recording all the President's words then," Shultz told me in late 1975, "they would have a proud record of some of the President's finest moments of leadership in addressing our state committees."

The committee became the Shultz Committee because the vice-president was not appreciative of the assignment as the "Number One Integrator of the South" in the Nixon Administration. Also, the president realized the possible adverse effects this committee might have on his 1972 running mate in an area where they proclaimed, "Spiro Is My Hero." (Bo Callaway printed up thousands of such bumper stickers and had them well distributed in Dixie.)

Thus the vice-president was unofficially relieved of his duties, and the vice-chairman gradually took command. At first, I had mixed emotions about the change. I was concerned Finch, Garment, Moynihan, and Rumsfeld would run the committee. But everything worked out almost perfectly in the end.

The strategy used by the president through his committee represented a shift both in policy and philosophy from those of previous administrations. Many voices criticized the Nixon Administration for what the critics called a "retreat" on desegregation, when the Administration virtually abandoned the fund-cutoff procedures provided by Title VI of the 1964 Civil Rights Act. The Administration shifted instead to litigation procedures provided under Title IV of the same act.

The fund-cutoff procedure had been the standard approach in the administrations prior to that of President Nixon. But evidence showed clearly that the method was ineffective. To get a cutoff of funds from school districts not in compliance, 13 months—sometimes, two years—were required. Meanwhile, the noncomplying school district remained segregated. In addition, the greatest resistance to school desegregation occurred in those districts with the highest percentages of black pupils. More than 130 districts in this category had had their funds terminated and remained segregated. Under statutory reallotment requirements, the funds were not returned to the federal treasury, but were redistributed to school districts within the state that had not been determined to be out of compliance. The net result was to punish the children in the districts who needed the funds the most, while favoring districts that needed the money the least.

President Nixon rejected this heavy-handed, ineffective method of school desegregation, favoring one of firmness tempered with conciliation. Before initiating lawsuits, the president told southern school districts: "Desegregation is required by law. I am duty bound to enforce the law. You are in the best position to fomulate and implement your own desegregation plans. If you choose to do so in good faith and within Constitutional limits, we will accept your plans. If you fail to do so, the Federal Government will be required to devise a plan and require you to implement it by court action." Thus the president's initial step was to demonstrate the attitude of conciliation, by indicating willingness to rely on the "good faith" of the school districts.

In this conciliatory frame, the president wanted to extend a helping hand to the school districts being asked to make the intensive transition to desegregation. He ordered his Cabinet Committee on Education to seek to coordinate federal resources that might be used to help the districts fulfill their mandate. In addition, the president named seven state advisory committees, made up of private citizens of diverse ethnic and ideological strains, to work with the Cabinet committee in supporting public education through the transition period and beyond.

Then the president pledged the Administration to seek $1.5 billion from Congress to help fund the desegregation process.

These conciliatory efforts made, the president left little doubt about his intention to enforce the law firmly. He moved swiftly to initiate multidistrict and statewide lawsuits in all the states resisting the constitutional mandate to desegregate their schools.

The background on which these new policies were implemented was one of growing divisiveness between the races. The widening gap between the races presented a dangerous and subtle problem. The possibility existed that as blacks entered previously all-white schools, the whites would flee to alternative educational establishments, such as private segregation academies. "Resegregation" would occur. Washington, D.C., was a case in point. By 1970, the district's schools were more than 90 percent black, although operating on a theoretically integrated basis.

Somehow, the president realized, a drastic effort would have to be made to assure that public education was operating at such a level that no pupil would want to withdraw from the public schools over loss of quality. He hoped that the Cabinet committee and the state advisory committees, working for support of public education, plus the funds he was seeking, would help to make the public schools strong—that quality education could be maintained in the process of total desegregation.

The basic tool in this program was President Nixon's basically centrist position. The president recognized that, in electing him, Americans were rejecting extremism. But the president also knew that much of the nation's character lay in her diversity. He knew that a politics of consensus was not the answer for the country's problems. Consensus was an unreal goal. The solution, thought the president, rested in the principle of accomodation. It would not be possible—or even desirable—to have all Americans agree in all things. But it would be possible to have all Americans accommodating their differences in order to work for common goals and concerns.

The accommodation principle opened a new possibility for the United States and the world. Perhaps it would now be possible to move history from an era of confrontation to one of negotiation—at home as well as abroad. President Nixon had expressed this goal in his Miami acceptance speech. On school desegregation, he hoped that citizens would accommodate their personal racial views to the more urgent concern for maintaining good public schools for all children.

The concept of the New Federalism, with its stress on partnership, was another crucial aspect of Nixon's philosophy of government. It would come to provide the foundation for a major part of the president's strategy on school desegregation. Through the New Federalism, President Nixon envisioned a government in which citizens had a genuine share of responsibility and, to some degree, power in running the nation. In undergirding this concept, the president had traveled about the country, conferring with leaders in their own communities and states. He had proposed a system of revenue sharing, whereby the states would get back portions of the money that came to the federal government. The linchpin of the New Federalism would be partnership between citizens and the federal government they had placed in office.

Accommodation, negotiation, partnership—these three principles formed the basis of the president's new policy on school desegregation. One by one, the principles were placed in action as Nixon prepared to enforce the constitutional mandate and extend a helping hand to local school districts to help them carry out their responsibility before the law.

At the first meeting of the Cabinet committee, on February 3, 1970, it was agreed to form the state advisory committees. Fortunately for the Cabinet committee, Bob Mardian, who had resigned in frustration as HEW general counsel; and Pat Gray, who had also left HEW, were both available to assist it. Mardian was made executive director. Later, when Gray became available, he was used as a special consultant.

On March 24, President Nixon issued what some commentators called the most comprehensive statement ever made by a president on school desegregation. The 8000-word statement on the sociological issue still unresolved by the Supreme Court was unprecedented in American political history. In setting clear policies, the president established the Cabinet committee's parameters and gave it specific roles.

The statement stressed, at the beginning and end, the president's concept of federal-community leadership and partnership, which would be foundational in establishing the state advisory committees. The school desegregation issue, President Nixon said, is neither partisan nor sectional. "It is an American issue, of direct and immediate concern to every citizen," he noted.

Then with regard to his concern for partnership, Nixon said: "In those communities facing desegregation orders, the leaders of communities will be encouraged to lead—not in defiance, but in smoothing the way for compliance. One clear lesson of experience is that local leadership is a fundamental factor in determining success or failure. Where leadership has been present, where it has been mobilized, where it has been effective, many districts have found that they could, after all, desegregate their schools successfully. Where local leadership has failed, the community has failed—and the schools and the children have borne the brunt of that failure."

The statement left no doubt, but that Nixon's chief concern was for the preservation of quality public education for all children. "In achieving desegregation we must proceed with the least possible disruption of the education of the Nation's children," the president stated.

The president reiterated his opposition to compulsory busing out of normal geographic zones to achieve racial balance. But it was obvious that his opposition was based on the greater concern for good public schools. Nixon said: "I am dedicated to continued progress toward a fully desegregated public school system. But, considering the always heavy demands for more school operating funds, I believe it is preferable, when we have to make the choice, to use limited financial resources for the improvement of education—for better teaching facilities, better teaching methods, and advanced educational materials—and for the upgrading of the disadvantaged areas in the community rather than buying buses, tires and gasoline to transport young children miles away from their neighborhood schools."*

The president announced, in the statement, his intention of asking Congress to divert $500 million from his previous domestic budget requests for fiscal 1971, to be used in programs designed to help school districts meet problems growing from court-ordered desegregation. He was ordering $1 billion for fiscal 1972, to be used for the same purpose, the president said. "I have asked the Vice President's Cabinet Committee on School Desegregation (the name was later changed to the Cabinet Committee on Education), together with the Secretary of Health, Education, and Welfare, to consult with experts in and out of government and prepare a set of recommended criteria for the allocation of these funds," said Nixon.

Reaction to the statement was immediate and mostly favorable. The *Philadelphia Evening Bulletin* called the statement a "masterly summation of the law on the subject."

The president's detailed statement of his Administration's school desegregation policies could be the most significant public document of his years in the White House," said the *Columbia State* in an editorial. "Indeed," continued the newspaper, "considering the fundamental importance of the problem and the opportunities for good present in this realistic approach to education, it could be the most historic domestic development since the 1954 Supreme Court school decision." The editorial was headlined, "Nixon Seeks the Middle Road on Desegregation."

The *Wall Street Journal* recorded: "We agree with the President that the call for equal educational opportunity is in the American tradition and that the opportunity unquestionably can be extended at the same time that the quality of education is being upgraded. But the process preeminently requires wisdom, the kind of basic common sense the President's statement reflects."

The *Washington Post,* on the other hand, called the statement "chary, matter of fact, and a bit on the bloodless side" and accused the president of

---

*Justice Hugo Black, during arguments on racial balance and busing, before the Supreme Court the week of October 12 told an NAACP lawyer, "I think there's something to the concept of neighborhood schools that's worthy of consideration in this Court."

"shifting the responsibility for both policy direction and enforcement back to the courts."

The *New York Times* joined the *Washington Post* in its criticism.

The Cabinet committee began work immediately carrying out charges the president had given it in the March 24 statement. The cabinet committee would perform two primary functions, the president had said: With the secretary of HEW it would consult with experts in and out of government and prepare a set of recommended criteria for the allocation of the emergency funds the president was requesting for the desegregating school districts; and it would amass information on the methods of desegregation, making the information available to communities in need of assistance.

On May 21, following completion of several committee work sessions, the president presented to Congress the proposed Emergency School Aid Act. In the bill, he requested $1.5 billion in emergency money for desegregating school districts through fiscal 1972. In presenting the bill, Nixon emphasized the need for its urgent disposal. He hoped that money would be made available during the summer, so that school districts could begin the imperative business of advance planning. The president asked for $150 million in start-up money to be made available in the fall of 1970. Congress slashed this request in half.

In addition, Congress succeeded in sidelining the larger bill requesting $1.5 billion, despite the undergirding of public support, as exemplified by editorials in liberal and conservative publications.

Among the earliest of the resource-information packages was a compendium of federal programs compiled by George Baffa, then deputy director of the Cabinet committee. The compendium sought to provide "an inventory of Federal resources and programs presently available under existing legislation that could be used to help local school systems and communities cope with the problems of racial isolation."

The compendium separated the resources into nine functional groups, including construction, curriculum and instruction, staff training, vocational education, administration, health and food services, community services, research and development, and communications.

The compendium would provide the foundation for the most massive set of data the Cabinet committee would seek to assemble—the "toolbox," as called by Vice Chairman Shultz. Essentially, the toolbox would seek to catalog virtually every federal resource available to communities undertaking an assault on racial isolation.

Developing the toolbox became an important information-building process, since representatives of the Cabinet committee established contact with the staffs of the various programs that would have a "shelf" in it.

The purpose of the emergency funds requested by Nixon was to deal with the emerging problems in developing unitary-school systems. It was obvious that for the funds to be administered effectively knowledge was needed of the kinds of problems that might emerge. The Cabinet Committee on Education, in conjunction with HEW, amassed this information. A nongovernment agency was contracted with to collect and report on the existing knowledge of school desegregation and to perform a survey of the literature dealing with the topic.

From the reports, two groups planned to develop a manual to guide federal officials in making funding decisions under the Emergency School Aid Act. The Cabinet committee also hoped the studies would lead to a clear guide for school and community officials in treating the problem of racial isolation through education.

Not long after its formation, the Cabinet committee began disseminating information it had at that point through a series of personal contacts. The contacts also launched implementation of the partnership concept called for by the president and ultimately to the formation of the state advisory committees.

In late February, Mardian and various members of the Cabinet committee met with a number of southern governors. In general, they presented the governors with copies of Nixon's statement on school desegregation, which also listed the appointment of the Cabinet committee.

Governor Lester Maddox of Georgia, was the first of these contacts. He indicated on February 24 that "he would give his support to geographical zoning if the Courts would permit it in his State." Governor Maddox also indicated to Mardian and Rumsfeld that he would be willing to set up meetings with a cross section of affected people in Georgia and the Cabinet committee staff, if that were desired.

Mardian and Rumsfeld also conferred that same day with Governor Robert E. McNair of South Carolina. Governor McNair expressed concern that there were conflicting interpretations of the president's statements on school desegregation and that the varying interpretations were creating confusion in the public mind.

The next meeting was with Governor John Bell Williams of Mississippi on February 25. Governor Williams detailed the problem of white flight in

Mississippi and expressed concern over the disparity of achievement levels of children being integrated in common classes.

Mardian and Harlow met later that day with Florida's Governor Claude R. Kirk Jr. The discussion covered busing, manpower training, and the problem of the ghetto.

On February 26, Mardian and Harlow met with Louisiana Governor John J. McKeithen. After receiving the president's statement, the conversation centered on the neighborhood school concept. Governor McKeithen also suggested the possibility of the Cabinet committee, or at least some of its members, coming to Louisiana to discuss with a biracial group of the state's leaders problems facing certain parishes.

On February 26, Governor Robert W. Scott of North Carolina was consulted. He expressed concern over the public's lack of understanding of the relationship between the president and the courts.

In the late spring of 1970, Nixon dispatched Mardian, Leonard, and J. Stanley Pottinger of HEW to a series of meetings with southern educational leaders, which the press dubbed "the Traveling Road Show." The team's message was that southern school districts had to be in compliance with desegregation orders by September 1970. "That means not starting, not thinking of a plan, not negotiating, but that the plan must be implemented before you open your school next fall," Leonard told one group.

Time magazine pinpointed what it called the administration's "effective four-front strategy." First, the team would meet with local and federal officials to present the Administration position on school desegregation, as defined in President Nixon's March 24 statement. Then it would hold an off-the-record conference with local news media. State and local school officials would then meet with the team and receive the "no-nonsense" message. All the while, the Cabinet committee was moving toward formation of the state advisory committees.

The whole process stressed local responsibility. The funds-cutoff procedure had placed the burden on the federal government. But under the immediate litigation process, the local districts themselves had to assume the responsibility of making desegregation work. This was the reason for the broad range of local contacts and partnerships Mardian and his team were seeking to establish.

"Our predecessors had no game plan, and we did," explained Leonard, as he gave the road show's threefold plan: (1) Get voluntary compliance from the school districts, (2) minimize the potential for criminal interference, and

(3) leave no doubt that the Nixon Administration would enforce the law with a fair and even hand.

In addition to the team circuit, Mardian conducted a series of press sessions throughout the nation during the spring and summer for the purpose of providing background information. A sensitive topic like school desegregation required the most accurate treatment the press could give. Yet the stories would often indicate a lack of understanding of some of the code words of desegregation, sometimes failing to distinguish the particulars of urban and rural problems. It was also apparent that many reporters lacked clear knowledge of some of the key cases in school desegregation.

From the beginning, the Cabinet committee was aware of the need for citizen groups in the states to be affected by the transition from dual-to unitary-school systems. As the Cabinet committee refined its role, it recognized it was ready to form the state groups.

"As a result of the advisory committees being set up, we are going to find that in many districts the transition will be orderly and peaceful, whereas otherwise it could have been the other way. And the credit will go to these outstanding Southern leaders . . ." So predicted President Nixon on August 14, 1970. He had just spent an afternoon with chairmen and co-chairmen of the seven state advisory committees he had appointed to work with the Cabinet Committee on Education in assuring that the transition from dual- to unitary-school systems in the South would be orderly and without harm to the public school system.

In making the prediction, Nixon was setting the example of good faith. Although the task ahead was monumental, he would trust the citizen groups to fulfill a partnership with him.

The president had noted earlier that if 16 years of seeking to desegregate schools had taught nothing else, it was clear that Southerners would not accept the leadership of Northerners in implementing the Supreme Court ruling against de jure segregation in the public schools.

The seed idea for establishing a federal-state relationship was expressed by the president in his February 16 statement announcing formation of the Cabinet Committee on Education. Said the president: "The Courts have spoken; many schools throughout the country need help. The nation urgently needs the civic statesmanship and levelheadedness of thousands of private citizens and public officials who must work together in their towns and cities to carry out the law and at the same time preserve educational opportunity. This Administration will work with them."

1964—Goldwater campaigning in Columbia, South Carolina, on Saturday, November 2, three days before the general election. This was the only southwide rally held during the campaign. In the background are Republican leaders from across the South. Standing with Goldwater is the late James F. Byrnes, former governor of South Carolina, secretary of state under Truman, Supreme Court justice, and "Assistant President" under Franklin D. Roosevelt. Courtesy of Victor K. Tutte, Chief Photographer, *The State*, Columbia, SC.

1967—California Governor Ronald Reagan making his first political visit to the South to help State GOP Chairman Harry S. Dent (right) clear up party campaign debts.

1968—Candidate Richard Nixon meets with southern strategists Strom Thurmond, left; and Harry Dent, right, in Atlanta at the Marriott Motel after pledging to support key southern positions if nominated and elected president in 1968. Others are Betty Dent and J. Drake Edens Jr., also of South Carolina.

THE STATE AND THE COLUMBIA RECORD—
Columbia, S. C., Sunday, July 14, 1968   5

Philip Grose

Governmental Affairs
Editor

The Studied Silence
Of The S.C. Democrats

The increasing likelihood that former Alabama Gov. George C. Wallace is going to be a major factor in the November presidential election is raising some interesting speculation among political leaders in South Carolina.

While no one is advancing the specific theory, circumstantial evidence could be so interpreted as to indicate that the Democratic Party is training more of its guns on maintaining their slim Congressional majority than trying to get their presidential candidate elected by a plurality in November.

If the polls continue to follow the present trends, and a Humphrey-Nixon-Wallace race does develop in November, the likelihood of a standoff appears to be better than average at this stage.

In such an event, the presidency would go to the party which held the edge in the House of Representatives, a fact of political life of which the party professionals are only too well aware.

Thus, the November presidential contest would be only a preliminary to the House fight in February. Should Nixon and Humphrey run so close in the electoral vote that Wallace could deadlock the issue by carrying several southern or border states, then it would matter little who actually led the November election. The House of Representatives would choose the president.

Thus, the real contest would be decided on the basis of how well the two major parties fared in winning House elections, and Republicans are making it clear they have definite designs on gaining a majority this year.

The growing silence of South Carolina Democrats would seem to bear out such a theory that the best way they can help the national party is to protect their edge in South Carolina. While the state's eight electoral votes constitute only a small fraction of the total of 538, in the House election, South Carolina's one vote would speak as loudly as New York or California.

'In '68 I Plan To Cut This Vote In Half! That'll Fix Lyndon Baines Johnson!'

THIS IS A NEW BUMPER STICKER BEING USED IN FLORIDA

TWO PARTIES   ÷   GEORGE WALLACE   =   HUBERT HORATIO HUMPHREY

1968—Cartoon used by Nixon's southern campaign, Thurmond Speaks for Nixon-Agnew, to show southern voters how "a vote for Wallace would be a vote for Humphrey."

"...THE WINNER!..."

1968—*Atlanta* (Georgia) *Constitution* cartoon by Baldy showing Thurmond and Dent hailing Nixon's 1968 victory with their policies in hand—the Republican Southern Strategy. By Baldy, courtesy of *The Atlanta Constitution*, Atlanta, Ga.

1968—Dent, center; and J. Fred Buzhardt Jr., who later became Watergate counsel to Nixon, both congratulate Thurmond on his 1968 successful work for Nixon's nomination and election. Both former Thurmond aides played key roles in the campaign and later became Nixon aides.

1968—Cartoon showing Dent riding the GOP elephant to Washington when he was appointed as the "Voice of the South" in Nixon's White House. By Walt Lardner, courtesy of *The State*, Columbia, SC.

Dwight Chapin

H. R. Haldeman

Henry Kissinger

Arthur F. Burns

Daniel P. Moynihan

Harry S. Dent

John D. Ehrlichman

Bryce N. Harlow

Herb Klein

John Mitchell

Robert Finch

Associated Press Release ---- August 17, 1969

Nixon's Inner Circle
has set up smooth machine

1969—Associated Press feature reporting Nixon's inner circle has set up a smooth machine.

1969—8 A.M. meeting of Nixon's senior White House staff. The author is seated second from the left with famous Nixon aides Ehrlichman, Kissinger, Moynihan, Haldeman, Harlow, Burns, Butterfield, Rosemary Woods, Chapin, and others.

1969—The author arranges a surprise party for President and Mrs. Nixon on the first anniversary of Nixon's 1968 nomination. Joining in the celebration were, on the left, southern leaders James Holshouser, Howard (Bo) Callaway, and Clarke Reed. Also present were Rogers Morton, Jerry Ford, the late Senator Everett Dirksen, and John Mitchell.

1970—Nixon discusses Republican party strategy for the 1970 elections with Dent, far left, and Republican National Committee leaders Rogers Morton, Elly Petersen, Jerry Milbank, and Jim Allison.

1970—Nixon, Kissinger, and Dent (center foreground) explain progress on textile protection efforts with textile manufacturers and Senators Bill Brock (right of Dent) and Strom Thurmond and other textile-state congressmen.

To my very good friend Harry Dent, in appreciation and with warmest best wishes.

Jerry Ford

1975—The author discusses with President Ford how to avoid a Reagan challenge at the 1976 GOP Convention.

1976—Ford chief of staff, Dick Cheney (left), and the author greet the much-wooed Mississippi and southern GOP chairman Clarke Reed in a Mississippi delegation meeting in Jackson in July 1976 before Ford visited the delegation. Courtesy of United Press International.

1976—In his Kansas City oval office, Ford welcomes key Mississippi delegates for a massaging session prior to winning the delegation's full 30 votes on the first vote of the convention.

1976—President Ford thanks the author in his Kansas City presidential and campaign office for turning around the key Mississippi delegate votes.

1976— As a member of Ford's general election steering committee, the author gives his ideas on campaign strategy at a White House dinner.

Photos by R. Norman Matheny, staff photographer, except Harry Dent (AP)

By Courtney R. Sheldon
Staff correspondent of
The Christian Science Monitor

Washington

Nixon's inner circle

Haldeman: 'lean, loyal, powerful . . .'

Ehrlichman: '. . . up to his chin in the campaign!'

MacGregor: 'talks fast, thinks faster, thinks hard . . .'

Colson: in the rough and tumble of politics

How is the President's inner circle of advisers performing? Is the smooth facade of well-oiled efficiency the whole story? Who are these keepers of the door of power?

A look at the men — and woman — around George McGovern appeared on this page yesterday.

IN 1972, MORE THAN EVER BE-fore, Richard M. Nixon's campaign recipe comes from his own orderly testing kitchen.

The assistant chefs may suggest a little spice or sugar. But mostly, they are there to learn from the master.

One might ask whether President Nixon — who has survived political dungeons to live in palaces — need ask advice. Mirror, mirror on the wall, who already knows the most of all?

Those who see Mr. Nixon often, however, report he is a poised and practiced listener. His acquisitive mind stores up ideas for action. His memory bank of politics rivals the computer marvels of the day.

Then, sometimes quickly, sometimes laboriously, he sorts out the options. Ultimately, it is Mr. Nixon's intuition that advises him most.

In his last oval gallop for votes, the incumbent President draws heavily on the resources of the vast federal bureaucracy for

purrs evidently, but his mind is checking up on infinite details of the White House operation.

Out of sight, he sits in a commanding position near the President's office. He is in the direct line of fire on political decisions. To execute them smartly is his responsibility.

Little philosophical bent

His is not the job of town philosopher. If it were, he is bred of the same Middle America conservatism of his mentor. A former Los Angeles advertising executive, he now has the country's biggest account, the selling of Richard Nixon.

He does it through efficient organization, anticipating the President's need for facts and advice, and being chief policeman, fireman, and arbiter of the White House staff.

Out front where the political backdrop suggests a gregarious man with owlish glasses and a hunger for politicking, Clark MacGregor, chairman of the Committee for the Re-election of the President.

He talks fast, thinks faster, hits hard, and still stays within the political norms as a former member of the House of Representatives before he was appointed Chief Counsel to the President for Congressional Relations, he tackled the right target with Congress.

may prove the most important diversion of his life.

His is to lead the charge, and most of the routine and humdrum of the campaign is left to others at the committee.

In the inner circle, John D. Ehrlichman, a Seattle lawyer and longtime friend of Mr. Nixon . . .

trouble to research issues thoroughly and intelligently. That is one of the strengths he himself offers Mr. Nixon.

Mr. Nixon has not surrounded himself with men itching to revamp traditional American ways. They do, they explain, seek practical progress. And politics is usually very practical business. Getting campaign chores done successfully is easier for them than dealing with an alternately unruly and liberal Democratic Congress.

Gone but not forgotten

Mr. Mitchell is late in sight these days. He is not forgotten. He is as near as a finger and a telephone dial. He was, after all, Mr. Nixon's first choice to head his re-election committee.

His critics may be led Mr. Nixon down some dubious trails, that his advice to both the 1968 and 1970 campaigns was beyond reproach to the Republicans, and that his recommendations for the first two Supreme Court appointments were political disasters.

Mr. Nixon still thinks well of his no-nonsense, orthodox conservative former Attorney General and onetime partner in a New York law firm. He is the same urge to take the offensive against the opposition that Mr. Nixon

feed selective bits of information to the President and have the President's respect.

There is Ronald L. Ziegler, Press Secretary to the President; Herbert G. Klein, Director of Communications for the Executive Branch; Robert H. Finch, Counselor to the President; Harry S. Dent, Special Counsel to the President; Patrick J. Buchanan, Special assistant to the President for Congressional Relations; Donald Rumsfeld, Counselor to the President. And there are many others.

The President's speech writers make their contributions, both in ideas and crystallization of thought. And who knows what Bebe Rebozo, Florida businessman and frequent companion to the President, has to say, or the other friends Mr. Nixon has in the world of business and high finance?

Stans is vocal, too

Maurice R. Stans, former secretary of commerce and now finance director for the Nixon campaign, can hardly be expected to raise millions and then say nothing to Mr. Nixon about the campaign.

John Connally, former secretary of the treasury, and now head of a committee of Democrats devoted to Mr. Nixon's re-election, was never shy about sharing his inner feelings with the President. And at the time of supportive tacts and statements.

An idle hand there isn't

Some on his personal staff in the White House are 99 percent engaged in the politics of re-election. An idle hand, in some offices, is almost disloyal. Some of Mr. Nixon's assistants and advisers are more in the open than he is, some not.

The list has to start with a lean, loyal, powerful White House executive with the deceptive title of "assistant to the President." **H. R. (Bob) Haldeman** keeps the political freight moving — and any other baggage that shows up at the White House door addressed to Mr. Nixon. He is mild-mannered, though intense. When he is relaxed, his smile is friendly.

Wherever the President is, there he'll be. On the campaign trail, his candid camera

Replacement for Mitchell

He leaped into the shoes of **John N. Mitchell**, former chairman of the committee, as if they were his own comfortable bedroom slippers.

A big-bear, athletic type who front-dipped into Miami Beach pools, he is the most outgoing and accessible man among top Republicans.

He doesn't have to hang on Mr. Haldeman's door to see the President; he is always welcome in the political back shop of the White House and is there regularly. When Mr. MacGregor tells what is on the President's mind, it is because he knows.

He landed on the team as a consolation prize for having lost the Minnesota senatorial race to Sen. Hubert H. Humphrey in 1970. It

Haldeman's, seems more vague and influential at Mr. Nixon's first term ends.

Kissinger's opposite number

An Assistant to the President for Domestic Affairs, he is the counterpart of foreign-affairs adviser **Henry A. Kissinger**. But Mr. Ehrlichman, because domestic matters are more politicized and contained by the Democratic Congress, is up to his chin in the campaign.

His normal role is to spread options on domestic issues before the President. His personal convictions are strong and they parallel those of the President.

As a political operative, his experience was limited when he arrived at the White House. He can treat Congress and the press with a tart legality.

He has respect for those who take the

The name of **Charles W. Colson** is controversial. It has been associated with some of the rough and tumble of Washington politics — from complicity with harsh political advertisements to being the man responsible for the work of two of the accused Watergate burglars at the time when they worked temporarily in the White House.

He would agree with the part of his image that credits him with getting things done. In one published memo to his own staff, he said that he "would walk over my grandmother if necessary."

Several others on hand

The list of influential assistants and advisers to the President could stretch on to another half-dozen names easily. There are numerous White House aides and friends who

his resignation, he was a very close confidant.

Sen. **Bob Dole**, chairman of the Republican National Committee, sometimes appears to be on the outside looking in. But his word is heard in the Oval Office more when he raises his voice.

The President is finding more and more time for all his political operatives.

And lastly and not to be mistaken for the least is the man who could sometimes be president himself, Vice-President **Spiro T. Agnew**.

By the nature of his job, his staff operates independently. His campaign assignments are coordinated and Mr. Agnew is said to be characteristically frank with the President.

Then, as with everyone else, the President retires to his own thoughts and takes his own best advice.

Klein: communicates on communications

Mitchell: less visible, but not forgotten

Dent: man for the South

Connally: shares inner feelings with President

1972—Nixon's campaign inner circle as portrayed in the *Christian Science Monitor* of September 13, 1972.

1969—The author strolling into his office in the East Wing of the Nixon White House.

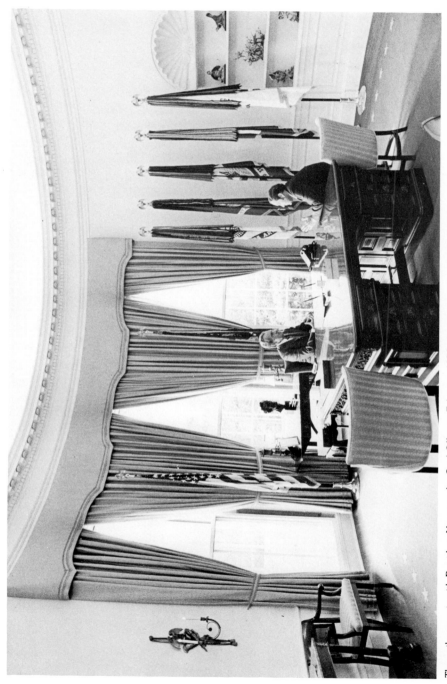

The author meets with President Nixon in the Oval Office in February 1973 after the author had returned home to South Carolina and Nixon had made a well-received address to the South Carolina Legislature thanking the legislators for their support of his Vietnam War policies.

A cartoon in the Columbia (South Carolina) State newspaper depicts the author being dispatched by President Nixon to mend the fences in the Republican Party. The cartoon is by Walt Lardner.

Posting the 1970 Congressional election returns for the president at the Western White House at San Clemente, California, are Harry Dent, seated left, Dent's secretary Rose Smith, and Dent's assistant Tom Lias.

The top of the power in Washington poses for a picture on the steps of the White House on March 24, 1970. This group of Congressional and Executive Leaders had breakfast with the president to discuss Nixon's plan for implementing Court decisions on school desegregation. In the picture are, left to right, first row: House Speaker Carl Albert, Representative Les Arends, Senator Robert Griffin, President Richard Nixon, Senator Margaret Chase Smith, Congressman Daniel Rostenkowski, Senator Milton Young; second row: Representative Hale Boggs, Senator Gordon Allott, Senator Hugh Scott, Vice President Spiro Agnew, former Speaker John McCormick, Senator Mike Mansfield; third row: Attorney General John Mitchell, Representative John Rhodes, Representative Jerry Ford, Representative Richard Poff, Senator Edward Kennedy, Senator Robert Byrd, Nixon aide William Timmons; fourth row: Nixon aide Donald Rumsfeld, Nixon aide Robert Mardian, Assistant Attorney General Jerry Leonard, Nixon aide George Shultz, Postmaster General Winton Blount, Nixon aide Harry Dent; fifth row: Nixon aide John Ehrlichman, Nixon aide Leonard Garment, Nixon aide Patrick Buchanan, HEW Assistant Stanley Pottinger, Nixon aide Herbert Klein, and Nixon aide Kenneth Belieu.

"It was obvious to all of us that we had to have people outside the official channels to be in contact with on a continuing basis from local communities affected by desegregation," recalls Cabinet committee vice-chairman, George Shultz. "Also," he continued, "given the idea that we wanted to work with people in solving problems, we had to have people to work with."

As the Cabinet committee worked through the early spring in refining its role, shaping legislation, and amassing information, it was also giving considered thought to the makeup of an advisory body from the South. It was decided that a chief function of such a committee would be to enlist support for public education, so that "resegregation," caused by pupils leaving the public schools, could be dealt with effectively. To encourage such support would demand leadership from every section of the southern community— black and white. A citizens' group, composed of a mixture of community life might best elicit the widest public support.

The Cabinet committee mindful of the admonition of the Supreme Court in its 1954 *Brown* v. *Board of Education* case also realized that the problems of desegregation varied. What might emerge as a problem in one community might not be trouble in another area, and success in one locale might not spell success in another. To get to the core of all manifestations of the problem, the Cabinet committee recognized the need of having advisory committees in several states, rather than one committee representing the entire South.

Some of the Cabinet committee's most intense discussions were over whether the governors of the states should establish and appoint committees in their states. Those who favored such a strategy argued that it would guarantee support of the governors for the state committees. Those who opposed such a plan argued that it might give the committees a partisan tone.

The Cabinet committee, therefore, decided that the state committees should be completely nonpolitical so that full concentration could be given to the common concern of maintaining good public schools and order.

The committees could only be effective, the Cabinet committee recognized, if they reflected all sides of the school desegregation issue. They must be comprised of citizens committed to desegregation, as well as those opposed to it. Only then could the state advisory committees speak to the many factions of their states with the message on which they had personally united: Let us obey the law and desegregate our schools in a peaceful manner, without injury to the system of public education. The mere existence of such a biracial, bipartisan group would provide graphic evidence that men of varying opinions could reason together, could unite on a common goal. Perhaps it would inspire others to seek accommodation in the spirit of President Nixon's hope for the nation and world.

In the summer of 1970, after some of the advisory committees had been established, Mardian was conducting one of his press background sessions in Los Angeles. A reporter for the *New York Times* signaled he wanted to ask Mardian a question.

"Is it true you have a member of the Klu Klux Klan on the Mississippi State Advisory Committee?" asked the reporter, sure he had centered on a hot story.

"I don't know," responded Mardian, "I've heard there are five. I certainly hope so."

The reporter was ready to sink into the exchange, when Mardian said, "You can report that if you also report that the Vice Chairman of the Committee is President of the Biloxi NAACP chapter." Then Mardian explained that the objectives of the state advisory committees could be met only as they had contact with all segments of the state. This, he stressed, was possible only through having broad representation on the committees.

On May 11, the Cabinet committee began work on the first and hardest state committee to form—Mississippi. The meeting was in Mississippi, making more than 50 individual contacts pursuing the possibility of a state advisory committee.

After much exploratory work, Pat Gray and his assistant, Jim Clawson, asked: Is it feasible to have such a committee in Mississippi? One of the responses, recalls Gray, was typical of virtually all the others. "We've tried everything else," said the Mississippian. "We must take this step because there is nothing left if we are to save the public school system."

After much sorting and study the committee on June 13 sent telegrams to each of the individuals who had agreed to serve on the Mississippi committee, inviting the Mississippians to meet in Washington on June 24 with the president. The first hurdle had been negotiated. Now the question was whether the carefully laid plan would work or explode.

On the morning of June 24, nine white and six black Mississippians, the first of the seven state advisory committees, were chauffered to the West Wing of the White House. Those members included Warren A. Hood, an industrialist from Jackson; Gilbert Mason, a physician and NAACP chapter president from Biloxi; Paul McMullen, a banker in Hattiesburg and Biloxi; Rev. T. B. Brown, pastor of Mt. Halm Baptist Church and president of Mississippi Baptist Seminary, Jackson; Sylvester A. Moorhead, dean of the

School of Education at the University of Mississippi, Oxford; Jack A. Young, attorney and president of the Jackson Chapter of the NAACP; Alvin Fielder Jr., Meridian druggist; J. Herman Hines, banker and chairman of a biracial committee working with the Jackson City schools' case; L. Owen Cooper, industrialist, Yazoo City; Rowan Taylor, insurance executive and chairman of the Jackson Chamber of Commerce Education Committee; Henry Self, banker, Marks; Leslie Lampton, petroleum industrialist, Jackson; Walter Williams, insurance executive, Jackson; Douglas Connor, physician, Starkville; and Gilbert Carmichael, automobile dealer in Meridian. *

Rarely had such a wide cross section of the ethnic and ideological leadership of one state been gathered under such an auspicious roof. Asked later what he felt to be the most effective approach of the Administration in dealing with school desegregation, one of the black Mississippians replied, "The creation of the Committee itself."

For more than an hour, the Mississippians met in the Roosevelt Room—just across from the president's Oval Office—with the Cabinet committee. Also present was Mississippi Republican Chairman Clarke Reed.

It was clear from the outset that the tenor of the meeting would be argumentative. The Mississippians were uncertain about whether they could trust one another or the federal government. The tact of the Cabinet committee members would be attaining basic symphonic harmony from the discord. George Shultz, as vice-chairman, presided over the meeting. Delicately, he orchestrated the issues and problems raised by the State Advisory Committee members with the responses of Cabinet committee members—particularly Attorney General Mitchell and Postmaster General Blount. A problem would be raised, and Shultz would refer it to one of the cabinet officers, who would try to answer it. Through this careful procedure, the tensions failed to impair seriously the discussions.

Shultz opened the session with a reiteration of the president's message in transmitting to Congress the Emergency School Aid Act of 1970. The president, Shultz recalled, had stated: "Nothing in this Act is intended either to punish or reward. Rather it recognizes that a time of transition, during which local districts bring their practices into accord with national policy, is a time when a special partnership is needed between the federal government and the districts most directly affected. It also recognizes that doing a better job of

---

*Later, R.B. Lampton, a Jackson banker, was added to the Committee.

overcoming the adverse educational effects of racial isolation, wherever it exists, benefits not only the community but the nation."

Shultz emphasized the "special partnership" aspect of the president's message and stressed the role of the State Advisory Committee as integral to the partnership. He urged that the State Advisory Committee be in direct contact with the Cabinet committee and stated that the Cabinet committee wanted the advice and recommendation of the State Advisory Committee. He also expressed hope that the State Advisory Committee would enlist the support and assistance of paraeducational groups in its state.

Shultz emphasized that the state advisory committee would not be involved in the development of desegregation plans and would in no way function to interfere with the actions of federal courts, HEW, or the Department of Justice.

Blount talked with the Mississippi committee about its functions. He suggested that the committee provide leadership in support of local school boards and school administrators charged by the law to establish unitary-school systems in Mississippi. Another function of the State Advisory Committee, suggested Blount, would be to provide an early warning alert system to identify school districts that might experience unusual difficulty and to make sure all available resources—local, state, and federal—were concentrated there.

Hope was expressed that the Mississippi committee would establish an office in its state. Mardian indicated that some operating funds would be available for such a purpose and to pay for committee travel, when the Emergency School Assistance Program was cleared by Congress. Each state advisory committee was funded for operating purposes on a temporary basis when Congress approved the $75 million.

Then came the meeting with President Nixon. At about 12:30 P.M., the Mississippians were ushered into the Oval Office. The president received each member of the advisory committee, and the members were photographed with the president individually. The formation of the Mississippi State Advisory Committee, said President Nixon, marked the inauguration of a historic partnership between the federal government and the people of Mississippi in a matter of extreme public importance. The president expressed hope that the relationship would prove of great benefit to the state of Mississippi, and, because of its landmark role in the new partnership, the entire nation.

President Nixon's meeting with the group and its individual members eased tensions that might have proved disastrous. Alvin Fielder, a militant black member from Meridian, expressed feelings of distrust. In the Cabinet session, he asked Mitchell what the Justice Department would do about the fact that there were no blacks on school boards in Mississippi. The attorney general explained that such positions were elective and that the federal government could not constitutionally interfere with the electoral process.

But the harm had been done. A white member of the committee pulled aside James Clawson. He told Clawson that his understanding of the State Advisory Committee's role did not include such matters as that raised by Fielder. If it did, the white member said, he would return to Mississippi at that moment. Clawson referred the man to Mitchell, who calmed his concern. But it was evident that if Fielder pursued such a course in subsequent conversations that day, the committee might disintergrate.

Fielder and President Nixon had met in southern Mississippi just after the 1969 Hurricane Camille disaster. When the president and Fielder shook hands in the Oval Office, the president greeted him by name. "You're the druggist from Meridian," the president said. Then they chatted about their previous meeting. Fielder, having been personally remembered by the president of the United States, forgot his earlier antagonism. His mood through the crucial discussions following that afternoon was considerably different from what it had been that morning before meeting the president.

Following the session with the president, a luncheon had been arranged in the Jefferson Room of the State Department. Shultz had invited Mississippi's two senators and five congressmen to the luncheon: Senators Eastland and Stennis and Representatives Thomas G. Abernathy, Jamie L. Whitten, Charles H. Griffin, G.V. Montgomery, and William M. Colmer. None accepted the invitation. One told Mardian, "You've been around long enough to know I'm against desegregation, and most of all against eating with niggers."

Throughout the meeting with the Mississippians, the cabinet committee members were conscious of the crucial nature of the meeting. Most of those who had finally agreed to serve were at first dubious about entering into the relationship with the federal government, Mardian reported to the president before the Mississipians arrived in Washington. The whites, Mardian said, were reluctant to be associated with school desegregation efforts and were particularly concerned about the name of the Cabinet group at that time—the Cabinet Committee on School Desegregation. Black members feared the advisory committee would prove a sham. "These persons consented to serve only after being assured that the Administration is firmly committed both to achieving a unitary school system in Mississippi and to insuring that the transition occurs peacefully and without detriment to public education," said Mardian in his report to the president.

Apparently, what consent had been won was tenuous. Any extreme incident might cause the advisory committee to break apart. Throughout lunch, members of the Cabinet committee talked intently to individual Mississippians about the potential of their committee and the urgency of the role they were being asked to fill.

The labor-negotiating techniques at which Shultz had great experience would come to be vital before the luncheon was over. Warren Hood, the industrialist and president of the Mississippi Manufacturers Association, had been asked to serve as chairman. The Cabinet committee had asked Gilbert Mason, the black physician from Biloxi and president of that city's NAACP chapter, to be vice-chairman. If these two men could be brought together in the common bond of leadership, it might cement the whole committee. If they refused, the whole effort—with the possibilities for advisory committees in other states—could be lost.

Neither wanted to serve in the leadership roles. Hood protested that he would be in Africa on a hunting expedition throughout much of August. Mason, citing the demands of his occupation and community responsibilities, said he would be too busy.

Shultz and Mardian were dining at the table with Hood and Mason. As they ate, Shultz talked to them. Both Hood and Mason had great credibility with differing factions in the state and on the advisory committee. If they would agree to serve together, it would enhance vastly the credibility of the advisory committee itself. Just as it appeared the zenith had been reached in the conversation, which Shultz had orchestrated, Shultz left the table. He motioned for Mardian to follow. Mardian left reluctantly.

"Why are we leaving?" Mardian asked Shultz. "They're ready to come to an agreement."

"I learned long ago in labor negotiations," replied Shultz, "that when parties get that close to a decision, there is only one way they can complete it—by themselves."

At the table, Mason was telling Hood, "If you and I can't do this, nobody else in Mississippi can. We're probably the only black and white men in the state who can get together on something like this."

This said, Hood and Mason shook hands.

This handshake, so deftly wrought by Shultz, sealed, secured, and delivered the Mississippi State Advisory Committee. Not only that, it was the signal that the advisory committee concept was viable and that the weeks of labor by Gray, Clawson, Fred LaRue, and many other officials were not in vain. The Cabinet committee knew it could move on the formation of other state advisory committees.

The late David Lawrence discussed formation of the Mississippi State Advisory Committee in a subsequent news column: "Probably the most important development in the whole desegregation controversy took place a few days ago here in Washington at the White House. The event, indeed, proved to be far more significant than was indicated by the formal statement issued afterwards."

Work or planning was soon underway that would lead to the establishment of advisory committees in South Carolina, North Carolina, Georgia, Arkansas, Louisiana, and Alabama. Each group would follow the same basic procedure and meet with many of the same problems as those involved in putting together the toughest group, Mississippi. Each group would meet with the president, who performed at his persuasive best in each meeting.

The meetings of each state advisory committee were most memorable and impressive. The exchange between the president and Chairman Robert Davis of South Carolina set a new tone. Rather than talking about whether desegregation was going to happen, the conversation centered on what can be done to work through problems as it happened.

The state advisory committees represented a positive step toward the hope to "bring us together," if only, at first, in one section of the country.

The president's remarks to each state advisory committee varied. But they reflected the philosophy he held of the presidency and the relationship of citizens to the federal government. He lifted the advisory committee members to see their duty in a historical context, rather than a provincialism of time, by citing the possible effects of present activity on future generations. He assailed sectionalism by citing northern "hypocrisy" on southern race relations. More than anything else, he asserted his confidence in the principle of local leadership in partnership with a sympathetic representation.

A major concern with the Southerners, black and white, was what they felt to be a sectional treatment of desegregation. The South, some of them thought, was not being given fair treatment. Later, in their sessions with the president, the commander in chief would assert that the executive policy and desire was not to have uneven treatment.

Each committee, upon its return from Washington, began the process of preparing for the work to which they had committed themselves. But there is a real sense in which, although their foundational work had already begun, the New Orleans meeting of August 14 launched the major efforts of the state advisory committees. Alabama's committee was the only one not announced when the New Orleans session was held. However, the chairman and vice-chairman had been picked, and both were in New Orleans. Four days later, the entire committee met in Washington. Aside from the president going to Louisiana, instead of this state's committee coming to Washington, as had the other states, the president had met with the Louisiana State Advisory Committee in its initial session. The chairmen and vice-chairmen of all seven state advisory committees had been brought to New Orleans. A lengthy session was planned for the afternoon between the president and the leaders of the state advisory committees.

A tight and heavy schedule had been mapped out for the president on the New Orleans trip. He would meet with the Louisiana committee, then be present for the session with other state committee leaders. Next, he would have a press conference and later host a reception for editors, publishers, and electronic media executives. Nixon, however, was so concerned about the progress of the state advisory committees, that he permitted the private meeting with the chairmen and vice-chairmen to last longer than had been planned. For more than two hours, he met behind closed doors with the leaders. The president began by urging that the districts presenting the most severe problems get the earliest attention. It was also suggested that government officials might meet with teachers, school board members and community leaders to attempt to further advise them on actions that should be taken and to assist them in working out their problems. The president suggested the appointment of subcommittees to aid the state advisory committees.

Then the chairmen and/or vice-chairmen of the state advisory committees made individual reports. Most of them had been involved in statewide publicity efforts to inform the citizens of their states.

The president concluded the meeting by telling the state advisory committees' representatives that achieving a "spirit of cooperation, not coercion, an attitude of conciliation, firmness, fairness and obedience to the law" was most important. Nixon said he wanted to be able to look back on 1970 and point out to the country that because of the leadership of the state advisory committees, a good transition was made. He was confident this would be true. "You can have good schools, inferior schools, or no schools," he said, a theme some of the state advisory committees would pick up in their public information campaigns.

Later at a press conference, the president told newsmen that the law would be upheld, but that there were several approaches that could be taken to the laws regarding desegregation. One approach, said the president, would be "to sit back and wait for school to open and trouble to start." But he asserted, "I rejected the approach from the beginning. The real victims in such an approach would be the schoolchildren," the president said.

"The viable approach," continued the president," is that of preventive action." Such was the course the president, in partnership with the state advisory committees, would take.

Several definite results had their origins in the New Orleans meeting. In the president's press conference that afternoon, he had asked the news media to report the success stories of desegregation as well as the problems. At a dinner meeting, media executives and presidential aides discussed this possibility in detail. W.E. Walbridge of Houston, president of the National Association of Broadcasters, later sent a letter to media executives throughout the South, asking for their cooperation in meeting the president's request. Charles Crutchfield of Charlotte, head of Jefferson Standard Broadcasting Co., would later provide major assistance in helping edit and distribute a set of videotapes featuring Billy Graham in an appeal for order and support for public education during the desegregation process.

Nixon, after the first September school openings, praised the media for its contributions to the peaceful transition. In Mobile, a major television network had even removed its camera rather than run the risk of adding to the tension. Officials at Mobile's Murphy High School were complaining that the presence of a battery of CBS filming crews might aggravate the already tense situation. Mardian, upon learning of the situation, contacted Leonard Garment. Garment, in turn, phoned CBS President Frank Stanton, who promptly had the crews and camera removed and the tension subsided.

Much of the work on the state advisory committees preceding and during September school openings was centered on getting out information. Everyone recognized that a prime source of violence was fear and that a prime source of fear was rumor based on misinformation.

Tom Haggai, the North Carolina businessman who had helped form that state's advisory committee, produced a series of television spots for the Charlotte City Schools. The series approached the problems of desegregation from different aspects and carried an appeal for restraint and continued support of public education. The videotapes were made available to the state advisory committees.

Late in August, the president went to the Western White House at San Clemente, California. Evangelist Billy Graham visited him. The president asked Graham to record some television appeals for support of public education and the exercise of order and obedience to the law.

The evangelist was scheduled to enter the Mayo Clinic in Rochester, Minnesota, the first week in September, for a routine physical examination. But he agreed to record some videotapes at a Rochester television station. The videotapes were recorded and dispatched all over the South.

The state advisory committees found ready acceptance at most television stations in the South. Walbridge, after the dinner in New Orleans, in his role as president of the National Association of Broadcasters, had written a letter to station managers, asking for their cooperation. The Graham tapes were shown in nearly all the state advisory committee states and in Texas and Florida.

In South Carolina, the state advisory committee had undertaken an intensive media campaign. Through the aid of a Columbia television station, the advisory committee itself produced a series of videotapes and radio tapes. Its messages, heard all over South Carolina, urged, "Keep Your Cool. Support Your School."

Some of the state advisory committees enlisted the aid of local chambers of commerce. Institutional members of the chambers were asked to write letters to their employees, asking for support of public education and urging obedience to the law. Through this procedure, many thousands of citizens were reached in a personal way by other citizens who were demonstrating responsibility. One of the companies even asked its supervisors and department heads to become familiar with local school district's desegregation plans so they could answer the questions of employees and squelch rumors.

One letter asked: "Why would the president of this company write a memorandum regarding the public school system and the new plan under which it will be operated this fall?" And answered: "The progress and growth of this business, as well as all other businesses, depends on the product produced by the public school system."

The state advisory committees knew that associating their names with school desegregation might be risky, given the controversy of the subject. But repeatedly, they took the risks through availing themselves for exposure in the public media. Some of the advisory committee members had never had experience in dealing with the press, but they resolutely consented to interviews and press conferences to get their message of leadership heard.

In Alabama, the state advisory committee held its initial meeting, and Governor Albert Brewer met with the members. For more than an hour, the governor gave this group complete information of where his law enforcement groups were expecting trouble. The advisory committee pledged its support to the governor, and he in turn endorsed its efforts.

Following that meeting, a press conference was held. All over Alabama, citizens saw fellow Alabamians stand with the governor of the state, and together, and commit their energies to a peaceful transition and upholding of quality public schools. And the Alabamians heard Craig Smith, Alabama's representative on the national advisory committee, as he said, "Our only clients are the white and black schoolchildren of this state."

The state advisory committees were effective.

Still, another prime task of the advisory committee would not draw such attention: negotiation. Most of this work was done by individual members on local and regional levels and some behind closed doors. Charlotte, North Carolina; and Mobile, Alabama, both under extensive and highly unpopular busing orders, carried all the ingredients for major violence. Ample evidence shows that without the private work of the individual state advisory committee members, whose total efforts cannot be chronicled for personal reasons in these two areas, major tragedy could have occurred.

Observed John L. Stickley, a Charlotte textile executive serving on the North Carolina State Advisory Committee, "Had it not been for the work of our committee, this community (Charlotte) would have erupted in violence and bloodshed to such an extent it would have been necessary to have called in outside police officers."

The state advisory committees, in addition to their information and negotiation roles, were also busy in the advisory function. As the Justice Department contemplated action in such areas as Mobile, advice of the advisory committee members was sought and followed. In Mobile, for example, about 1000 pupils were sitting in at schools other than the ones to which they were assigned. The Justice Department was urged to send in marshals to remove the pupils and parents. Advisory committee members warned that such action might incite a major disturbance and that the "non-conformists," as the pupils were called, would eventually find their proper slot.

After the September school openings were completed, with more than

90 percent of the minority children in unitary schools, the Cabinet committee and the state advisory committees began looking closely at their long-range tasks. But no matter what future roles the state advisory committees would come to play, they had penned their names in history. President Nixon had stated in his March 24 statement that one of the purposes of the committees was "to place the question of school desegregation in its larger context, as part of America's historic commitment to the achievement of a free and open society." What had been affirmed by the state advisory committees was the president's contention that such a historic commitment, requiring massive change, could only be carried out in the spirit of cooperation and partnership. History was indeed written by local citizens as well as by national leaders.

Accommodation, negotiation, partnership—the foundational philosophies that Richard Nixon brought to the White House thus provided the undergirding for one of the most widesweeping—and successful—social transitions in American history.

7

Watching Wallace and Wooing the Blacks

L ike most politicians, Richard Nixon did not hesitate to work for the votes on both sides of even such an emotional issue as the race question. On the white side it was necessary to have good peripheral vision on the right to keep an eye on Governor George Wallace who could take away more Nixon votes in 1972 than Democrat votes as a presidential candidate. Nixon also kept an eye cut to the left for the favor of at least a portion of the black vote.

If somehow Wallace could be convinced to forego the honor of another presidential race in 1972 everyone understood Nixon would stand a better chance to be reelected. While the fiesty Alabamian proved to be a pain to national Democrats in their presidential primaries and national conventions, he could only win electoral votes in the general election below the Mason-Dixon line at the expense of the GOP nominee. Thus he was more a problem for the Republicans.

In a December 9, 1970, breakfast meeting with Washington reporters, Wallace claimed he would have thrown his 1968 electoral votes to Nixon had he succeeded in deadlocking the 1968 Electoral College. However, the Alabama governor specified he would have required Nixon to make a national TV address reiterating his campaign statements on school desegregation. He referred to Nixon's TV statement in Charlotte, North Carolina, in mid-September. (See chapter 5). The *Washington Post* reported on December 10 that Wallace said if he won South Carolina, Tennessee, and North Carolina, in addition to the five states he carried, he could have been in a position to bargain with Nixon. What he was saying again was that southern strategy had done him in. He confided to friends as the returns were coming into his 1968 campaign headquarters that "but for Thurmond we'd have made it."

While Wallace was a problem for the southern GOP, he was also a boon. Without Wallace, the Dixie Republicans would have had no boogeyman to use for scare purposes at the GOP hierarchy. Wallace served as the catalyst that convinced Nixon he needed to heavily woo the South in 1968 and 1972.

I believe LBJ and Wallace had an understanding about Wallace's 1968 candidacy and its potential adverse impact on Nixon. LBJ was that shrewd, and for Wallace it was all to gain and nothing to lose. For the Democrats it was all to gain. The strategy was to beat Nixon in the rest of the country and then let Wallace absorb all or most of the newfound GOP sanctuary in the South. Except for the Nixon Southern Strategy, the LBJ-Wallace plan would have worked.

Harold Martin, editor-publisher of the *Montgomery Advertiser-Journal*, has evidence of LBJ-Wallace conversations on the Wallace role in a possible 1968 LBJ-Nixon race. One of Wallace's strongest critics in the state, the

159

Alabama newsman has been giving consideration to writing a book about the governor. According to the materials he showed one of my assistants in 1971, he has some fascinating reading loaded with personal ancedotes and documented facts. His aim is to produce a political study that will present his view of politically opportunistic actions which have supposedly been detrimental to Alabama in Wallace's rise to and use of political power.

Leading Democrats used materials similar to Martin's when they tried to diminish Wallace's voter appeal in 1975 in Alabama. Congressman Morris Udall of Arizona, one of the many Democratic 1976 presidential contenders, was especially vocal with such statements. However, there is no indication the attacks on Wallace had any impact.

Wallace expressed the fears and frustrations of many citizens whose concerns extend beyond the race question to a variety of issues, such as economic populism, hard-line foreign policy, anticommunism, big government, and intellectual elitism.

Generally, the governor is regarded as an arch conservative, yet many economic conservatives view him as being too liberal with his populist appeals for the lower middle-income voters.

In 1968 Wallace received his best assistance from the many John Birch Society members who helped him win ballot position in states like California, where much individual work was required in little time. The news media neither ever understood nor focused on this underground alliance. The Birch Society has one of the best organized cadres across the country, and the Birchers will work long and hard hours to accomplish their assigned tasks. After Wallace was shot in 1972, the Birchers ran one of their own members, former Congressman John Schmitz of California as the third-party candidate for president, polling 1,098,635 votes.

Our watch on Wallace began soon after wc entered the White House. The project was mine as southern strategist. Initially, the task consisted of reading the Wallace newsletters and passing on the pertinent points to the president, Haldeman, and Mitchell.

The thrust of many of *The George C. Wallace Newsletter* reports was against the Nixon Administration. In his issue dated January 1970, Wallace sought to establish a "credibility gap" between the Nixon Administration and conservative voters. He accused Vice President Agnew of being strong on "conservative talk," while the Administration was pursuing liberal policies. In an article on the Nixon Southern Strategy, the governor claimed the strategy was "backfiring" on Nixon by "causing more and more people to realize that he (Wallace) was right all along on the issues in the 1968 campaign and those facing our nation today." He cited a Harris poll showing a three-point gain in popularity for him since August 1969.

Wallace concluded by describing the strategy as taking "the form of a great deal of words but little action . . . (it is) a deceptive and false effort based upon words and not deeds."

While many other Wallace watchers were ruling the former governor out of the 1972 presidential contest soon after he failed to achieve his goal in 1968, I was confident and fearful he could be our prime obstacle again in 1972. I knew the key to his 1972 candidacy lay in his decision to regain the governorship in 1970. Wallace had lost his grip on the top job in Alabama when his wife Lurleen died of cancer on May 7, 1968. She held the title of governor while her husband held the reins of power.

Wallace surprised almost everyone in 1966 when he, in effect, elected his wife governor to get around the Alabama law prohibiting a governor from succeeding himself. Elected lieutenant governor with Lurleen Wallace was a Wallace protegé named Albert Brewer. When Mrs. Wallace died, she was succeeded by Brewer. Instead of serving as a stand-in for George Wallace, Brewer decided to be his own man and to run to continue in office in 1970. In the meantime, Alabama had changed its gubernatorial succession law to "not more than two successive terms." So the prize became even more valuable for Brewer.

Many political observers believed Wallace either would not or could not run against his hand-picked successor for Lurleen. Likewise, many felt Brewer would never defy Wallace and try to hold onto the job.

However, Brewer soon made his intentions clear, but Wallace held off until several months before the 1970 Democratic primary.

I knew the key to Wallace's 1972 intentions would be his decision about the governorship. In the summer of 1969 I met with Grover Hall, a syndicated columnist from Alabama and a man in whom Wallace would confide. He told me he had recently visited with Wallace and that he was writing a column about the Wallace gubernatorial intentions. When I received the July 14, 1969, column I dispatched it to the Nixon hierarchy.

In his first three paragraphs and the final one, Hall told the sad story we hoped would not be the case.

Washington—The signs abound that George C. Wallace has decided to repossess the Alabama governor's chair from his protegé, Gov. Albert Brewer. This would be no more than a move to firm his footing for the 1972 presidential race.

The outcome of the race will be a matter of great moment to President Nixon, because the signs now are that the electoral college will not be reformed by 1972 and once again there might be the threat that the election would be thrown into the House of Representatives.

The one thing that could lead Wallace to abandon his 1972 presidential candidacy would be a defeat next year in the May primary by Gov. Brewer, who had accepted the challenge. But there lies Postmaster General Winton (Red) Blount's chance to become the hero of the Nixon Cabinet.

Wallace, I anticipate, won't take much notice of Brewer. He will talk about Nixon and Washington guideline writers. He won't make any bones of the fact that the race for governor is the prelude to another presidential race, and ask for a mandate to carry that on to keep Nixon straight.

Hall was correct. He knew his friend and his aims.

Postmaster General Winton (Red) Blount did use every resource at his command to stop Wallace and be the "hero of the Nixon Cabinet." The man who supposedly abolished politics in the Post Office department applied the rule everywhere except to himself.

One of my most memorable moments at the White House was one day in 1969 when the president and I had Blount over to the White House to discuss Blount's recently announced policy of abolishing all politics in the very political Post Office department. Most Republican leaders were protesting this new policy, especially after eight years of waiting on postmaster and especially rural letter carrier appointments. This was the best patronage available for grass-roots political workers.

Blount had passed the idea by Nixon one day when he was in a "going along" mood. Now Nixon had second thoughts, particularly at my urging.

When the president broached the subject of retreating, Blount "talked back" to the president in what I considered to be an impolite and impolitic manner. The only other person I saw do that was Senator Barry Goldwater in an Oval Office meeting in 1970. (See Chapter 8.)

Blount helped raise money and was one of Brewer's prime advisers on his campaign. The Senate Watergate hearing revealed that $400,000 in cash was funneled into the Brewer campaign via Bob Haldeman. I did not know about this contribution, but I did favor the overall effort to help repel the Wallace campaign effort. I knew this could mean the vital difference for 1972. Someone else realized this also—President Nixon. Because of his intense interest, I briefed the president periodically on the primary runoff elections.

At the conclusion of the first race, Brewer was leading Wallace by two percent. However, lesser candidates forced a runoff for June 2, four weeks after the first primary. Never before had the top man in the first race lost the runoff.

The president was on the phone to me on both election nights getting hour-to-hour election returns. He called me at 10 P.M. and told me to get him the returns in Jefferson County (the Birmingham area). He would be able to project the winner based on that count and then he could go on to bed. He enjoyed getting the results on key precincts and then figuring the outcome in advance. I always had the final returns on his desk at 7 A.M. the following morning and then he could score himself on his demographic knowledge of the key voting boxes. He fancied himself as being at his best in the game of politics. Only foreign policy was a rival.

Getting the specific returns the president desired was not possible between 10 P.M. and 11 P.M. However, I finally received the information at 11:25 P.M. Even though he had told me to call by 11 P.M. with the results, since he was going to retire for the night, I decided to ask the operator to check and see if he was still in his office. She replied that he had gone to his bedroom. So she connected me with the usher's office. The usher on duty said the president had gone to bed. I asked him to check and see if the lights were on. He looked and said the lights were out. Then he said, "OK, now it's your move, do I wake him?"

This was the toughest decision of my life. He wanted the results, I had been delayed in getting them, and now he, the president, had gone to bed. Do I wake up the president of the United States to give him some results that didn't even constitute the final score?

Well, I passed and headed on to my apartment. As I was walking in the phone was ringing. The operator said, "One moment, please, for the President." I thought I was in for the verbal thrashing of my life. Then on the line came the president asking, "Harry, did you get those results?"

I said, "Yes, sir, Mr. President, I'm sorry for the delay, but I decided not to awaken the president."

He replied, "Oh, just call me anytime. I only half sleep most of the time."

Was I relieved. When he got the partial results he pronounced Wallace the winner and a 1972 contender. Then he said, "Get some sleep, and have a full report on my desk by 7 A.M."

Sure enough, Wallace upset the Alabama runoff tradition and won by 51.5 percent to 48.5 percent. So now the question was how to handle the upcoming Wallace challenge. We knew this time he would be running against us, since we were in the White House and had the desegregation responsibilities.

I made several recommendations to the president in a June 16 analysis of the new Wallace problem.

First, our school desegregation policy was set. (Nixon and Mitchell decided to get the desegregation job out of the way as soon as possible.)

Second, I suggested we ignore Wallace statements and challenges.

Third, I proposed "many visits (to the South), Southern representation on the Supreme Court, equal treatment and attention with no apologies, and a well-planned pro-Nixon-Agnew-Mitchell PR campaign throughout Dixie."

Fourth, use of ex-Judge G. Harrold Carswell as a campaigner.

Fifth, I said, "Beware of any Little Rocks come fall." (Others were suggesting creation of a Little Rock.)

After several more months of Wallace watching, I finally ran into the newly elected governor at the funeral of the late Congressman Mendel Rivers in Charleston in January 1971. Wallace told me he would not see a national Democrat in the White House.

Meanwhile, we had launched a busy visitation program for the vice-president and Cabinet members to tour through Dixie. Each Cabinet member was committed to at least two visits there per year.

The vice-president was sent to Birmingham in October soon after the Wallace primary victory. It was suggested he talk about virtually anything but George Wallace, as the general election was then underway.

The president, who had already visited most southern states in 1969 and 1970, decided to travel to Alabama in May 1971. We planned visits to Mobile for a ribbon-cutting ceremony, which would officially mean work could start on building the Tennessee-Tombigbee water travel project; and to Birmingham to hold an editors' briefing and answer session on domestic policies.

When we arrived in Mobile the morning of May 25, we were pleased and amazed to find a tremendous turnout of cheering Alabamians. "King George" was in second place on this occasion, but he was on hand, extending every courtesy.

Then the question arose during the president's speech about whether we were going to take Wallace with us on the *Air Force One* to Birmingham. The Wallace aides stressed his interest in accompanying the president. We made a quick decision to invite Wallace, but not him alone, lest the plane ride be played up by the newsmen as a "secret deal" trip. So we included all the visiting governors in the invitation. Accepting were Governors Reuben Askew of Florida and Louie Nunn of Kentucky.

When we boarded the plane, the three governors and I were seated in the lounge for the president. Nixon was seated in his private quarters behind the lounge area.

Approximately midway the flight, the president came out and joined us for a chat. We had him sit between Nunn and Wallace. The conversation turned around some small talk and the need to get a more conservative Congress.

Columnist Jack Anderson has reported a few times that a "secret deal" was struck in the trip. But there never was any conversation between Nixon and Wallace about the presidency. All the conversation was audible to Askew and Nunn.

When we arrived in Birmingham, the crowds were even larger—100,000 strong. They stretched out for miles between the airport and downtown. It was the first visit by a president in 50 years for Birmingham. In front of the Parliament Hotel, the Nixon advance men hastily set up a speaking stand, and Nixon and Wallace mounted it. When the president was presented, he received the larger ovation, much to his delight, and mine. I made certain the reporters caught and recorded the point.

Inside the hotel, the president performed magnificently. Before he talked, we had HUD Secretary George Romney, Labor Secretary James D. Hodgson, Economic Adviser Herb Stein, Domestic Chief John Ehrlichman, and Press Aide Herb Klein brief the editors from all over the South. Then Nixon "put them all in the shade." He covered the entire domestic spectrum and part of his foreign policy without notes.

When the president came to the subject of the South and desegregation, he scored strongly with the editors, saying:

> Two specific points that I would like to mention. I would say this in
> the North if I were speaking there, I say it in the South. I know the

difficult problems most of you in the southern States have had on the school desegregation problem. I went to school in the South, and so, therefore, I am more familiar with how Southerners feel about the problem than others. Also, I went to school in the North, or the West, I should say, and I have nothing but utter contempt for the double hypocritical standard of Northerners who look at the South and point the finger and say, "Why don't those Southerners do something about their race problem?"

Let's look at the facts. In the past year, two years, there has been a peaceful, relatively quiet, very significant revolution. Oh, it is not over, there are problems—there was one in Chattanooga the last couple days I understand, there will be more. But look at what has happened in the South. Today 38 percent of all black children in the South go to majority white schools. Today only 28 percent of all black children in the North go to majority white schools. There has been no progress in the North in the past three years in that respect. There has been significant progress in the South.

How did it come about? It came about because farsighted leaders in the South, black and white, some of whom I am sure did not agree with the opinions handed down by the Supreme Court which were the law of the land, recognized as law abiding citizens that they had a responsibility to meet that law of the land and they have dealt with the problem—not completely, there is more yet to be done. The recent decision of the Supreme Court presents some more problems, but I have confidence that over a period of time those problems will also be handled in a peaceful and orderly way for the most part.

But let's look at the deeper significance of this. As I speak today in what is called the Heart of Dixie, I realize that America at this time needs to become one country. Too long we have been divided. It has been North versus South versus West. Wall Street versus the country and the country versus the city and the rest. That does not mean we don't have differences and will not continue to have them, but those regional differences, it seems to me, must go. Presidents of the United States should come to Alabama and Mississippi and Georgia and Louisiana more often than once in 50 years or 100 years, as the case might be with some other cities and they should come because this is one nation, and we must speak as one nation, we must work as one nation.

Second, and here this is difficult, we have made enormous progress and we are going to make more. The problems of race can be and must be solved. They must be solved in an orderly way recognizing that we will continue to have differences, but recognizing that unless they are solved, this destructive force, this division over an issue of this type is going to weaken this part of the country in a way that could be very, very detrimental to the national interest and weaken other parts of the country where there are also racial problems.

What I am simply suggesting is this: I am suggesting that we are at a period in our country when America needs to be strong militarily, it must be strong economically, and it must be strong in its spirit, strong in its heart. I think the South traditionally has contributed to the military strength of this country. More Southerners voluntarily serve in the armed forces than any other part of the country. I think the New South has a greater contribution to make in terms of economic growth than perhaps any other section of the country, because the South starts from a lower base and now is moving up, not evenly, but moving up very significantly and will continue to.

So, you have a great role to play in that respect. I think, too, that this part of the country has a very significant role to play insofar as the spirit of this country is concerned. I speak of such square things as patriotism; I think of such things as religious faith. I also speak of such things as respect for law, even those laws that you don't like. And if this great and powerful and vibrant and dynamic part of the country can make the contribution of which it is capable, then America will have a better chance to meet the responsibility that it must meet in the world to be strong militarily, economically together with the ideological and spiritual strength which will enable us to meet our challenges.

Nixon knew how to speak to Southerners because he understood their feelings and shared in them considerably. He understood the southern mind.

In the meantime, there was press speculation that the Wallace forces were seeking a deal with Nixon. Some of this revolved around indications I had received that Wallace's good friend, Alabama House Speaker Sage Lyons, wanted to establish a good line of communications with us. Lyons was a college classmate of Gordon Gooch, executive director of the Federal Power Commission and an effective Nixon worker in the 1968 campaign. I communicated this to Mitchell. Later, Rowland Evans of the Evans-Novak column learned of all this from Lyons on a summer visit with Wallace and his top advisers.

During all this time Wallace was exploiting the busing problem to the hilt. In May 1971, he told a news conference he would bus no one in the fall of 1971 regardless of what the courts might order.

What would it take to keep Wallace from running in 1972? Here is what he told a Birmingham news reporter in late June 1971: "If President Nixon would end the war in Viet-Nam, settle the economy, take care of unemployment, and straighten out this school mess." Tall order!

Could Nixon buy Wallace off with a political appointment? His reply: "I'd rather sell razor blades in Barbour County before I would sell out like that . . ."

While Wallace was telling reporters he would be running in all 50 states, Clarke Reed was running a public opinion poll in Mississippi. The results on a three-way race for president were like so:

Nixon	36%
Wallace	33%
Muskie	15%

The same pollster had shown Nixon with 13 percent support in 1968 and 26 percent (10 points below Wallace) in 1970. So despite all the cries of anguish from our southern GOP leaders, we seemed to be making steady progress in the Deep South. We were encouraged.

Meanwhile, in Alabama, Governor Wallace was having problems with his legislature and his friendly lieutenant governor, Jere Beasley. We were beginning to believe that Wallace, the invincible, was suddenly becoming vulnerable in his own home base. We certainly hoped so.

In October 1971, the *Montgomery Advertiser* published a poll showing that only 36 percent of those polled wanted the governor to be a candidate for president in 1972. The same people gave a 52 percent approval rating to President Nixon. What really appealed to us was a poll answer indicating 29 percent disapproved of Wallace's performance as governor, while only 22 percent disapproved of the Nixon performance.

Indeed, we seemed to be making progress against Wallace in his home base.

By the end of 1971, Wallace and his aides were debating the question of whether he would run only in the 1972 Democratic primaries or go all the way to the general election. This decision by Wallace was important to us because a Wallace decision to go only in the Democratic primaries would be the best possible decision from our standpoint, whereas a decision to run in the general election would be the worst decision from our standpoint. Thus we monitored this decision-making process as best we could—but only from "informed sources."

Ultimately, Governor Wallace decided to do both—run in the Democratic primaries and the general election—the worst decision for both major parties. However, on May 15, 1972, a mentally unstable young man named Arthur Bremer, after stalking both President Nixon and Governor Wallace, finally decided to shoot Wallace at Laurel, Maryland, while Wallace was campaigning in the Maryland Democratic presidential primary. That one bullet altered the presidential race considerably and confined Wallace to a wheelchair. At the same time, it made George Corley Wallace respectable on the national scene for the first time. Overnight, Wallace became a national hero, especially as the nation's news media showed the pictures of his second wife, Cornelia, lying across his body to protect him from more bullets. Strangely, Wallace was temporarily in the martyred category of John and Robert Kennedy and his No. 1 enemy, Martin Luther King.

Every national political figure of any significance rushed to his hospital bedside in Laurel, Maryland, to have his picture made with the new martyr, including President Nixon.

Tom Turnipseed, the departed former key aide to Wallace was recruited by South Carolina's former governor, Robert McNair, and present governor, John C. West, to escort them to the Wallace bedside. The Nixon political leaders in Washington were, from a political standpoint, both concerned and relieved. We were concerned that Wallace might run from his wheelchair and relieved that he might not run at all. Wallace kept everyone on edge as he made a courageous effort to affect the Democratic National Convention (DNC) in Miami from his wheelchair. However, he was, in effect, voted down by the McGovernites, so he wheeled out of the convention and right into what we feared would be a general election position on a thrid-party ticket. From a wheelchair, Wallace could do us even more damage in the general election. So naturally, I became concerned, as the Wallace watcher, about the outcome of this vital decision by the martyred—and now respectable— Alabama governor.

In the meantime, ex-Wallace aide Tom Turnipseed, now a South Carolina state senator, had become convinced that he had received a mandate from the new Mrs. Wallace—and the ailing governor—at the close of the National Democratic Convention to launch a third-party movement for Wallace. Turnipseed told me of this, and with his friend, Peter Beter, of Cape Cod, Massachusetts, he demanded a meeting with John Mitchell and Harry Dent to discuss a role for himself in the 1972 Nixon campaign. Turnipseed could bring in all the Wallace people since he had organized them in 1968. So Mitchell and I met Turnipseed and Beter at the Mayflower Hotel in August 1972. Our aim was to learn whether Wallace, the martyr, would be a general election candidate. Their aim was to bargain for some type deal they would supposedly broker with Wallace and his chief spokesman at this time, the new Mrs. Cornelia Wallace. Turnipseed and Beter indicated their authority sprang from Cornelia, who in the presence of George at the close of the Democratic convention, had commissioned the two of them to put together a draft-Wallace movement at the forthcoming convention of American Political party (APR) delegates at Louisville, Kentucky. Mitchell intently puffed on his pipe as he listened to their grandiose plans. Then he walked away unbelieving and wondering whether Harry Dent was as smart as he (Mitchell) had previously figured.

From the Mayflower Hotel, Turnipseed moved on to Louisville, where he was manhandled by the APR delegates because he was tabbed as a "Harry Dent stooge!" Unfortunately for Turnipseed he had revealed his Mitchell-Dent meeting at a news conference in Washington. He should have known from all his dealings with John Birchers that they would be very suspicious of any such meeting. To top it all, Wallace, when called by APR leaders from the convention, declined their nomination, making Turnipseed indeed appear to be a false prophet if not an outright Nixon agent in their midst. The truth of the matter is that Turnipseed was a Turnipseed agent bent on his own plans for Wallace with some encouragement from Cornelia Wallace. In the end, the Birchers at the Louisville convention were determined to do "their own ideological thing," and they did, despite Turnipseed. They nominated former Congressman John Schmitz, one of their own, and down the drain went our worst concern, a third-party candidacy for martyred Governor George Wallace.

While Wallace's third-party race was now out of the question and we only had to be concerned with Schmitz, one-fifth the problem in terms of votes, Wallace got his revenge on the Nixon administration. He helped veteran Democratic Senator John Sparkman sink former Postmaster General Red Blount by thousands of votes in the general election of 1972. The top

Nixon leaders were not too displeased as Harlow reminded us that a Sparkman loss would put maverick liberal Senator William Proxmire in command of the U.S. Senate's Banking and Currency Committee.

Soon after the question of a Wallace candidacy was settled, the president made another visit to the South. He rode down Atlanta's famous Peachtree Street with more confetti falling and more people looking on than ever before in Atlanta—more than one-half million people. At the Regency Hyatt House, as these excerpts substantiate, the president gave his enthusiastic southern supporters his best Dixie message to date:

For Immediate Release   **OCTOBER 12, 1972**
Office of the White House Press Secretary
(Atlanta, Georgia)

The White House
Remarks of the President
To Southern Regional Reception
Hanover Room
Regency Hyatt House

2:25 P.M. EDT

. . . Now, to all of you ladies and gentlemen, and to the ladies and gentlemen of the press who are here from the Washington Press Corps and from all over the South, let me direct my remarks to this campaign—what it means to the South, what it means to the Nation.

This election marks the beginning of a new era in the political alignment of the South and of the Nation. For 100 years, one party took the South for granted and the other party, as a matter of fact, wrote it off. Now that is entirely changed. Neither party is going to take the South for granted, and neither party can afford to write it off.

This is going to be good for the South. It is going to be good for the Nation. I have seen this develop. This is not the first time that we have had a motorcade in Atlanta; the first was in 1960. It was one of the most exciting motorcades of the entire campaign. It was a huge crowd, an enthusiastic crowd; not as big as today, but big.

Afterwards, some members of the press said, "Why did you go; you know you are not going to carry Georgia?" I said, "I am quite aware of that." But I went to all 50 states in 1960, and then in 1968 I visited almost all of the States, and many, many States in the South. As President of the United States, I have visited every one of the 50 states, and in the next four years I am planning, to the extent that my schedule will permit, to visit every one of the 50 States.

There is a reason for that. I do not believe in dividing this Nation—region against region, young versus old, black versus white, race versus race, religion versus religion. I believe this is one country. I believe this is one Nation. And I believe that while we are all proud of our backgrounds—some are Western, some are Southerners, some are Northerners, some are black, some are white, some of Italian background, some are American stock, as they call it—but whatever we may be and whatever our background may be, we are Americans first, and that is what we must remember.

Now it has been suggested that by campaigning the South in 1960, and then again in 1968, and now again in 1972, means that we have, I have, a so-called Southern strategy. It is not a Southern strategy; it is an American strategy. That is what it is and that is what the South believes in and that is what America believes in.

. . . That is why we seek what I call a new American majority. Let me talk about that majority, if I can, in terms of the South. Many Southerners will be part of that majority. They will be part of it for reasons that their fathers and grandfathers could never have accepted.

There was a time in the South—and this is still true among some, as it is in some Northern parts with regard to Republicans—but there was a time in the South when any Southerner would vote for any Democrat and never vote for a Republican.

What this new political development is that we see in this election, and I think will be reflected in this election in Georgia and throughout the Southern States, is that that is no longer going to be true. Candidates of either party are going to have to seek support not on the basis of the party lable, but on the basis of what they believe, and people of the South are going to vote for the man or the woman, rather than the party.

Now let me come right down to the issues. What are the so-called Southern issues? This answer is going to surprise you. They are the same here as they are in America.

Now, getting that issue out of the way, let me tell you what the number one issues, based on the polls that we have seen, national polls—Gallup, Harris, all the rest, they all come out the same—the number one issues in the South and the number one issues in the Nation, these are the issues that make most southerners potential members of what we call the new American majority.

First, they want this country to be strong.

The second issue, and this is true of the South and it is true of the nation, is that you want peace, you want it now, you want it in the future, but you want peace with honor.

The third issue: It is a southern issue, it is a national issue. The people of the South want an opportunity for good jobs, high wages and cost of living kept under control so that you are not on a treadmill.

Issue Number 4: Most southerners and most Americans, East, West, North and South, want respect for law, respect for order, and they want justice, justice to all people.

Issue Number 5: People of the South are just like the rest of the country in wanting progress.

. . . One other point that I would make before concluding is that sometimes there is a tendency to speak of the South as being sort of the Bible Belt, and that is said by some in a complimentary way and by some in, shall we say, a rather derogatory way.

I would only suggest I would put it in a broader sense. There is, in this part of the country, a deep religious faith. There is a great respect for moral values. There is a great devotion to what we call character. But let me say that in that religious faith and in that devotion to moral values and in that respect for character, while it exists in the South, it exists throughout this nation.

My Indiana mother and Ohio father put it in me just as your mothers and fathers put it in you. I see it, for example, when I visit an Italian picnic and I see new people, first generation Americans, who are proud of their national background with deep religious ties, who have faith in this country, faith in their God and who believe in moral virtues.

Oh, you can call them old-fashioned, but the day America loses its moral values, its dedication to idealism and religion, this will cease to be a great country. We are not going to let that happen.

. . . I want to say to all of you, from all over the South, some of you are Democrats, some of you are Republicans, all of you are Americans. All that I ask is as you go back to your States, take this message showing the new American majority. Join it not as region against region or party against party or class against class, but join it in order to build a better, freer America for every person in this country.

From Atlanta on, Richard Nixon rode triumphantly to the biggest election victory any Republican presidential candidate had ever scored in Dixie—an average vote of 70 percent in all the old confederate states.

With McGovern as Nixon's Democratic opponent, even the wounded Wallace was applauding in his wheelchair. George Meany of organized labor was also tickled on the evening of November 6, 1972, as were 47 million other American people as a personally unpopular Republican president garnered the biggest majority vote ever cast in America.

□ □ □ □ □ □ □ □

The Grand Old Party had been born in the throes of the question of emancipation under the leadership of Abraham Lincoln. It was thus for many years the home of most Negroes who voted in the United States. It continued that way until President Franklin D. Roosevelt started his welfare state programs and his successor, President Harry S. Truman, initiated civil rights legislation. From there the Democrats increased their grip on black voter loyalty until the actions of the Kennedy and Johnson administrations—in social welfare, voting rights, and civil rights legislation—secured most of the black vote for the Democratic party.

As vice president under President Dwight Eisenhower, Richard Nixon had been the civil rights leader in an Administration that took only mild initiatives toward social welfare and civil rights legislation.

Yet Vice President Nixon had earned his civil rights spurs as the chief enforcer for equal employment opportunities in government contracting. Also, ae presiding officer of the U.S. Senate, Nixon had helped liberalize the Senate rules so that it was made easier to shut off debate on southern anti-civil rights filibusters.

The Southerners in Congress looked askew at Nixon because of his pro-civil rights positions. However, they liked President Eisenhower because of his popularity in the South and his rather neutral position on civil rights. Eisenhower lost some of his luster in the South when he sent in federal troops to carry out a desegregation order in Little Rock, Arkansas, in 1957.

Thus when Vice President Nixon took on the challenge of Senator John F. Kennedy in 1960, he naturally expected to get a majority of black votes in his first quest for the presidency. However, the Kennedy telephone call to Martin Luther King Jr. in an Atlanta jail seemed to change all that. Instead of a majority vote, Nixon won only 32 percent of the black vote.

In his second and successful try for the White House in 1968, Nixon won with a southern strategy that maximized white votes in Dixie and may have helped minimize black votes. I say "may have" because by 1968 the Johnson-Humphrey Administration following on the popularity of the short-lived Kennedy era and martyrdom had made it unlikely that Nixon would win any more than a minimal black vote. This was evident from the beginning of the 1968 campaign. Thus Nixon was virtually forced—as he would say—"to hunt where the ducks are."

Having won with the southern strategy label dripping all over him, President Nixon was faced with the toughest part of school desegregation enforcement. The only way he could have pleased most of the black vote would have been to continue the policy of force used by LBJ's desegregators. However, Nixon was committed not to pursue a policy of force, which personally displeased him.

While Democratic leaders and many newsmen pictured President Nixon as being anti-black and anti-civil rights, they were wrong. Yet they did fashion an image on him that was difficult to overcome with blacks.

Pat Buchanan, the fiery conservative Nixon speech writer and adviser, lamented the Nixon record in favor of blacks in his 1975 book *Conservative Votes, Liberal Majorities*. Buchanan gives an assessment of Nixon's favoritism toward the black community (pages 49 and 50):

> With the lone exception of Lyndon Johnson's, no Administration so consciously tilted policy toward black America as did Richard Nixon's.

> Carl Rowan and the Black Caucus may not leave that statement undisputed. Yet, it contains more truth than error. Though Mr. Nixon's government shorted the civil rights community on rhetoric,

it was not short on delivery. And though John Newton Mitchell does not seem destined to become a revered figure in black America, there was truth as well as irony in his retort, "Watch what we do, not what we say."

Consider. In Mr. Nixon's first four years:

- The civil rights enforcement budget rose 800 percent to more than $600 million.
- Record numbers of blacks were appointed to federal posts. In executive positions with salaries above $20,000, there was an increase of 37 percent. The day the President resigned, blacks, who constitute 10 or 11 percent of the population, held 16 percent of all federal jobs.
- The "Philadelphia Plan," forcing open union training programs and job lists was devised and imposed. Quotas for black academicians, poorly disguised as "goals and timetables," were imposed upon college and university faculties.
- In fulfillment of the candidate's 1968 commitment to "black capitalism," the Office of Minority Business Enterprise was created, and funded to the level of $63 million a year.
- Federal purchases from minority enterprises rose from $9 million to $153 million.
- Small business loans to minorities increased over 1,000 percent from $41 million to $435 million.
- U.S. aid to black colleges more than doubled.
- U.S. deposits in minority-owned banks rose from $2 million to $80 million.
- More school integration was achieved in four years than in the previous fifteen since *Brown v. Board of Education,* without violence, and without troops. "It has been only since 1968 that substantial reduction of racial segregation has taken place in the South," declared the U.S. Commission on Civil Rights in March of 1975.

Leonard Garment, a Nixon law partner, was brought into the Nixon White House to be the civil rights advocate. Also, Robert J. Brown of North Carolina, was installed as the top black aide in the White House.

Garment is a very decent and able person. Although we bumped into each other many times on policy issues, we respected each other. The same was true of Bob Brown. Bob and I worked together closely. We were both southern boys, albeit black and white. But we understood our Southland and the practical problems associated with the race question. Neither Garment nor Brown had been Republicans, but both were Nixonites.

While President Nixon was pursuing a southern strategy he was also putting more blacks in key government positions than ever before. Orders were issued to the personnel recruiters to concentrate on minority appointments. Minority meant not only blacks, but Mexican-Americans, ethnic-Americans, Catholics, Jews, and other groups considered to be minorities in a majority-governing America. By 1972 Nixon had set a new record in making key black appointments—more than Kennedy and Johnson together had appointed.

In Washington the black appointees made their input through Garment, Brown, and their department or agency heads.

In the first two years of the Nixon Administration, many black groups were invited to the White House for meetings. The Small Business Administration's (SBA) minority contract set aside programs—designed to help minorities in getting government work—moved from $20 million annually to more than $200 million. The Office of Minority Business Enterprise in the Commerce Department produced more minority business opportunities and assistance then ever.

However, White House attention to minority concerns increased even more in 1971 and 1972.

On January 9, 1971, I made an unwelcomed talk to the executive committee of the South Carolina Republican party about the need for "a broader based appeal to all people." Later in January the president made a special appeal to the National GOP for an "open door" policy. His remarks were made at the dedication of the Eisenhower Memorial Center on Capitol Hill, this being the new RNC headquarters building. Present for the meeting were Republican leaders from all over the country, including the members of the National Committee. The reaction was very favorable, including that of the southern leaders present.

Shortly thereafter, I attended an Alabama GOP Executive Committee meeting. The state GOP chairman, Dick Bennett, was facing a potentially explosive problem on filling some vacancies on the state committee. Bennett wanted to add two blacks for the first time in many years, and the more conservative forces were determined to reject this base-broadening move. In the course of the meeting I talked to the committee directly on the issue. I did not tell them it was the moral thing to do, I called it "the wise thing to do."

Subsequently, the vote was overwhelming for admitting the two blacks to seats on the committee, and the feared confrontation vanished.

In one southern state after another, GOP conventions, on their own in-
itiative, selected black delegates and alternate delegates to the national convention. The number of black delegates from the southern caucus states increased by 1500 percent over 1968 from 0 to 15. The southern party was
becoming more and more integrated, as had the southern strategy.

The "modified" southern strategy, as I publicly proclaimed it, began
broadening its appeal in early 1971, and particularly after I received the
following memo from the president on May 25, 1971:

THE WHITE HOUSE
Washington

May 25, 1971

Confidential

Memorandum for:	Harry Dent
From:	Jon M. Huntsman
Subject:	GOP Southern Strategy and New South

In the May 21, 1971 Digest of Recent News Comment the following comment by Robert Boyd in 5/7 *Miami Herald* was reported

> The Dem hopefuls have "rediscovered the South." Virtually aban-
> doned in '68, the South is being toured, lectured and courted by
> Dems. But the *Dem strategy, unlike the GOP in '68, is aimed at
> appealing to the liberals and moderates of the "New South"*; they
> are leaving the rural Dems to their own devices. Dems were en-
> couraged by the '70 elections. Muskie recently spoke to black,
> labor and Jewish groups in Georgia; he made no contact with
> Maddox, unlike HHH who embraced the Georgia governor in '68.
> While none of the Dems are writing off the South, they have no il-
> lusion about carrying many of the States against RN or Wallace.
> But the old Confederacy represents 20% of the delegates at the
> Convention.

It was requested that you note the portions underlined above, and that you
recognize that our appeal must *not be* restricted to the old guard southerners.

cc: H.R. Haldeman
      A. Butterfield

On February 11, 1971, I had sent Mitchell a memo pointing to our potential for winning more black votes in the South than elsewhere. I attached a Gallup poll containing pertinent information.

Do you approve or disapprove of the way Nixon is handling his job as President?

The following table shows how blacks and whites rate Nixon at three points in time—when he took office, at a mid-point during his administration and at present. Results are based on combined surveys.

Views of Blacks

	Approve %	Disapprove %	No Opinion %
Jan.-May, '69	40	17	43
Mar.-June '70	26	55	19
Sept., '70- Jan., '71	28	53	19

Views of Whites

	Approve %	Disapprove %	No Opinion %
Jan.-May, '69	64	9	27
Mar.-June, '70	59	29	12
Sept., '70-Jan., '71	57	29	14

Disapproval is most pronounced among better educated and younger blacks and those living outside the South.

The following table shows how various sub-groups in the Negro population rate Nixon:

Views of Blacks by Sub-Groups

	Approve %	Disapprove %	No Opinion %
National	28	53	19
College & High School	22	62	16
Grade School	36	41	23
21-29 years	19	65	16
30-49 years	24	64	12
50 & older	36	41	23
South	42	38	20
Non-south	19	62	19
Men	29	55	16
Women	27	51	22

Various reasons accounted for this potential:

1.   Southern blacks were more conservative minded than the more liberal northern blacks.

2.   More black capitalists were in the South.

3.   Southern blacks had already passed through most of the desegregation crises and were more integrated than their northern friends and without the hostility in the North.

Bob Brown and I decided to go South and tell blacks and the public all the good things Nixon had been doing to improve the lot of blacks. So on October 20, 1971, Brown and I spent a full day in Atlanta talking to 80 blacks, most of whom had been recommended by southern GOP chairmen. The idea here was to make the southern chairmen feel a part of the new strategy.

The *Washington Post* reported what it considered the unusual meeting with this story in its October 23, 1971, issue:

> In the course of a quiet campaign to woo minority voters across the country, the White House has assured Southern black Republicans that Negroes are wanted and needed as active partners in the Southern GOP.

> The message was conveyed by Harry Dent, special counsel to President Nixon, during a sometimes emotional day-long meeting with 80 blacks Wednesday in an Atlanta motel.

> Eugene McLemore, a Black lawyer from Mississippi said some of the younger members of the group let Dent know that the administration would have to do more for Southern blacks if it hopes to win their support.

> "Dent caught real hell sometimes, but he handled it beautifully ," McLemore reported, "I thought he would be a real Southern cracker, but I left impressed with him."

> Today in San Antonio, Dent said he had been "impressed with the comments about the President and the indication of desire by the participants to support the President." Recently, he said, blacks have indicated "a growing measure of confidence" in the President. "The polls show more approval of the President among blacks in the South than in other regions of the country," he said.

Writing in the *Washington Star* of May 17, 1971, Don Bacon picked up the flavor of the new appeal with this report:

> If you talk to Dent today, Nixon's "Southern strategy" of 1969 and early 1970—a much criticized effort to placate Southern resistance to desegregation—seems like something that never happened.
>
> The discussion now focuses not on those remaining white Southerners who hold on to the past, but on those who have accepted desegregation as a fact of life, and on the 25 to 35 percent of the new Southern electorate which is black.
>
> Wherever Dent looks in the South, he finds growing acceptance of desegregation. Three of his own children think nothing of attending integrated Dreher High School in Columbia, S.C., where a Dent girl is a cheerleader for the school's basketball team, which is predominately black.
>
> Dent sees a changing South, filled with political opportunity.
>
> He sees a majority of whites, weary of generations of racial conflict, ready to "accept the fact that desegregation is here."
>
> He sees a growing black electorate, already strong enough, in the Deep South, to defeat segregationist candidates and to demand political rewards from candidates they support.
>
> For the past several months, Dent has been preaching his gospel to Southern Republican leaders. A political party that shuts out the white moderate and the new black electorate philosophical differences within its ranks, he says, in effect is doomed to chronic defeat at the polls.
>
> "I'm a realistic conservative, and I like to win elections," says Dent.

From the Atlanta meeting came many jobs and honorary appointments for southern blacks. We soon put 20 on honorary boards. Another, Sonny Walker, of Arkansas, became regional director for the Office of Economic Opportunity in Atlanta, the first black to hold such a high appointive post in the South. Another, Benjamin Hooks of Memphis, Tennessee, became a member of the Federal Communications Commission. He is now executive director of the NAACP. Another, T.M. Alexander Jr., of Atlanta, was promoted to the number two HUD job in the Southeast. Stan Scott, also of Atlanta, was added to the White House staff and eventually succeeded Brown in his job as special assistant to the president.

The forward momentum of the changing southern strategy continued. Next came the biennial meeting of southern GOP leaders in Memphis, Tennessee, the first weekend in December 1971.

Arthur Fletcher, a black former assistant secretary of labor, was our best speaker. He outshone the vice-president and Julie and David Eisenhower. The articulate black leader received a long standing ovation with his entertaining and eloquent off-the-cuff speech. One of our conference signs spelled out the new theme this way: "The Grand *Open* Party!"

I began in November to push Fletcher for a Cabinet-rank job, but George Meany vetoed him under the table. Imagine that, Harry Dent being for the author of integrating union members and George "integrator" Meany against him. But such is the battle for desegregation—do it everywhere but here! (Fletcher authored and developed the Philadelphia Plan virtually requiring racial quotas while Shultz was secretary of labor.)

The reaction to Fletcher was proof positive that southern strategy was changing its coloration fast.

A week after the southern GOP Conference, I had an opportunity to comment on the black vote position paper CREEP was preparing for Mitchell. The paper read:

December 14, 1971

CONFIDENTIAL

Memorandum For:	Bob Marik
From:	Harry S. Dent
Subject:	*The Black Vote*

I concur in the points made in the draft to the Attorney General on the overall strategy for black voters. I would simply add some additional thoughts, as follows:

1. President Nixon's record in housing is unparalled. Yet, politically, this record has not been exploited. Through Farmer's Home alone, the lives of thousands of rural blacks have been changed. Farmer's Home ownership lending has increased under President Nixon from $268 million annually to $350 million a year. Private agreements negotiated by Farmer's Home have

extended another $400 million of credit to rural people. This is in addition to a record $140 million available for emergency loans. In all, federally subsidized housing for the needy will jump from 150,000 starts in FY 1968 to 650,000 in 1972. Blacks—especially in the South where 52% of them live—are prime beneficiaries of these programs. It is imperative that we focus attention on this.

2. I urge we consider recruiting a black field person for every Congressional district. If this is not possible for the entire country, I think we should at least implement the project.

3. Art Fletcher is our big star from the black community. He is immensely effective, not only among blacks, but among whites as well.

4. Black fraternal organizations have been, with the church, a major forum of power for blacks. Another special group should be formed—"Black Fraternal Officers for Nixon."

5. We will not succeed in recruiting black candidates if there is no specific line of responsibility delineated to someone. Since the black effort will be run through 1701 [CREEP headquarters], perhaps Ed Sexton [a black Republican political leader] should be assigned as his sole or priority duty the recruiting of black candidates.

6. With the large number of special interest groups, there is the danger each will take a too autonomous approach and fragment, rather than consolidate our strength. A coordinating council, composed of chairmen of all the black special interest groups should be set up through 1701.

In an effort to get our potential black leaders together and to honor a good leader in our Administration, blacks put on a Bob Brown Tribute Dinner on January 31, 1972. The dinner overflowed the biggest hotel ballroom at the Washington Hilton with more than 3000 in attendance. It was highlighted by a presidential drop by.

Master of ceremonies Sammy Davis Jr. complimented the president handsomely. At breakfast in the White House staff mess the next morning, Davis pledged to Brown and me he would go all out for RN in the election.

On April 21, I went South to talk to blacks again—this time alone. I addressed the Hungry Club in Atlanta and got a standing ovation. I told the black audience we would double or triple the black vote of 1968 in the 1972 election because "blacks can see the changes brought about in and outside the South to allow them to get a piece of the action."

In talking to the Mississippi and Louisiana state conventions in May, I predicted we would double the black vote and received good applause both places.

Then on June 11, blacks numbering 2500 turned out in Washington for a salute-to-the-president fund raiser. The *New York Times* reported the unusual get-together this way on June 12, "It was a weekend of considerable wonders: President Nixon was compared to Christ, Churchill, Bismarck, and the prophets Isaiah and Amos at one of the sessions, while Senator Strom Thurmond of South Carolina, long a foe of civil rights was honored at the other meeting."

The reporter noted that even southern strategists Harry Dent and John Mitchell were present and speaking on one of the programs. It was more than the *Times* could stomach. But to us, it indicated our new strategy was on the rise.

The strategy culminated in the big black turnout at the August National GOP convention. The highlight of the whole convention was the "around the hips" hug Sammy Davis Jr. gave President Nixon on a national TV show from the convention. Who would have believed that possible in a southern strategy administration!

From there on Bob Brown and Paul Jones, the CREEP minorites leader, put together a smooth operation which gave the president 13 percent of the black vote, 1 percent more than in 1968.

The "new majority was indeed being forged on a fully integrated basis, and the modified southern strategy was a potent force in this new political coalition.

8

Nixon Delivers on Busing, Textiles, the Court, and Vietnam

D espite the good work of the Cabinet Committee on Education, the Nixon Administration had other problems affecting the overall question of desegregation, with busing being a major concern.

Senator Thurmond's tough statement on July 17, 1970, on the Senate floor accusing the president of a "breach of faith" on desegregation policies set things off. The speech concerned the president. Thurmond had in effect threatened defeat for Nixon in 1972 when he thundered out: "I remind the Chief Executive that the presidency is an elective office, and that what the people give, the people can also take away!"

In the *Washington Sunday Star* on July 26, columnist James J. Kilpatrick gave this description of the Thurmond thunderbolt: "Strom Thurmond's short speech had all the characteristics of a good right hook: It was quick, explosive, and squarely on target; it carried conviction; and it left an impression. If the President was bruised, okay, politics is a body contact sport."

Thurmond had strongly admonished the Administration: "I am warning the Nixon Administration—I repeat, I am warning the Nixon Administration today—that the people of the South and the people of the Nation will not support such unreasonable policies."

What was wrong with Thurmond? The president asked me to find out. I suggested we set up a private meeting with Thurmond and other conservative GOP leaders to hear them out since I knew Thurmond's concerns were shared by many others.

What had primarily upset Thurmond was the Internal Revenue Service (IRS) decision to deny tax-exempt status to private schools that supposedly fail to meet IRS open admissions standards and a statement by Jerry Leonard that he was sending what the press called "mixing marshals," or "vigilante teams," to the South to monitor desegregation. There were other matters too.

The president agreed to set a meeting for August 6. The meeting, which ran from 5:20 P.M. to 7:30 P.M., was remarkable and subsequently caused the president to try harder to please the Southerners.

This abbreviated account of my record of the meeting follows:

> The meeting was opened with a statement by Senator Gurney who spoke of the concern among many Southern Republican leaders about what he described as a change within the past thirty days of Administration policies toward the South and the overall question of school desegregation. He mentioned the recent news story about U.S. Attorneys and Marshals going South to assist with desegregation, IRS tax-exempt status decision on private schools,

and the current law suits being instituted by the Justice Department in a number of Southern states. He specifically recommended that Jerris Leonard be fired as Assistant Attorney General for Civil Rights. Leonard was described as being arrogant and politically harmful to the President. Gurney complained also that there had been no indication of any change in attitude or actions on the part of the leadership in the Department of Health, Education and Welfare. It appeared he was referring to the change in Administrations to Secretary Richardson from Secretary Finch.

Senator Tower spoke next saying he concurred in the comments of Senator Gurney and expressed extreme concern about the political damage being done to the President.

□   □   □

The President then addressed the meeting, stating that the Ripon Society does not represent the President. He spoke of the thin gray line which helped him win the convention and the election and that what is needed in the South is a good strong base for the future. He emphasized his interest in the South and his strong feeling for the Southern people whom he said have been saving the nation, particularly in the area of national security. The President made a distinction between desegregation and integration, saying the former represented his policy.

The President asked Senator Goldwater to speak next, and he did so in a very candid manner. He said he was going to be "brutally frank." He stated he had told the President in early 1969 that unless he was going to be able to get hold of the government by May of that year that he would never get control of the government. He described the Administration as being in the "same fix" as President Eisenhower when he didn't remove 18,000 Democrats that he should have fired. He spoke briefly about what apparently was an OEO legal assistance program for the Navajo Indians in Arizona. Goldwater described the Program as silly in comparison to their needs in another area which would cost much less. He told the President he thought that instead of removing the Secretary of HEW he should have fired 300 employees who were giving the Secretary such a difficult time. He said they won't follow the President's policies. He suggested further that key career government employees be rotated every five years among the departments and agencies.

Senator Goldwater insisted in strong terms that the President had not changed the policies of this government in accord with the mandate that was given in the 1968 election. He was particularly critical of an article published by the National Institutes of Health. He said the article made fun of the President. He indicated other such actions have been taken within the government and that people who engage in such activities should be severed immediately from government service and publicly so. The Senator particularly stressed the embarrassment to the President "eventually of every left wing Riponer the President appoints." Extreme comments by Negro leaders and the Heard report on student unrest were particularly cited by Goldwater. He said Dr. Heard made the President "look silly." He advocated getting rid of government employees who do not carry out the President's will, starting with Cabinet members and going on down to the bottom. He complained that he had not seen the President since August 28 of last year, commenting in a joking manner that the Coast Guard would not let him within 3 miles of the President's home at San Clemente.

As he was closing his remarks, the Senator exhorted the President to "quit wooing Meany." He said we could win without Meany and that we could go over Meany's head and those of other union leaders directly to the hardhats and blue collar workers.

The President then addressed himself to the IRS ruling, assuring the group that IRS would not be operated as an HEW. He said the program would be administered in the right way, and that there had been a meeting on this subject earlier in the week with the Secretary of the Treasury, the Secretary of HEW, the Attorney General, and the Vice President. The President said the most important thing we have to do is to get the U.S. Supreme Court balanced as soon as possible. He indicated that on the next appointment he thought he would be able to send up a nominee whose name could not be turned down by the U.S. Senate. He described as his most significant action the effort to change the Supreme Court, pointing out that the President has taken considerable heat on this subject.

At this point Senator Goldwater broke in to ask how hard the President was going to work for Senator Charles Goodell of New York. The President responded by saying this is one race in which nothing will be done because there is so much confusion. All laughed and agreed with the comment.

The President then referred back to the IRS matter again saying that the Administration is now working on a questionnaire. The Attorney General interjected a comment that the implementation of this policy change would not hurt the South but that there would be a PR effect. The President commented again saying that neither the OEO tuition grant or legal assistance programs would be used to harass private schools.

The President spoke next, pointing out that he must carry out court orders. He added that his busing stand will be adhered to by this Administration and that a man has been assigned the job of seeing that this is carried out. The President conceded that there is a question as to how long the school matter will continue to hang around as a political problem. He forecast rocky roads ahead, emphasizing that he would like to get rid of any image that would classify this Administration as being militantly integrationist. He then stressed that there will be no lawyers sent to the South for purposes of coercion and that there will be no command posts or offices established in the South this fall.

The Attorney General agreed with the President's statement.

Again the President referred to the previous meeting with the Secretary of Treasury, the Attorney General, and the Vice President. He pointed out that he realizes that there are many people in the woodwork at HEW, Justice, and other departments and agencies. Then he turned to the subject of efforts recently made to have him grant amnesty to United States deserters in Canada and Sweden. He responded that 2½ million Americans had chosen to serve their country in the Vietnam war and that 40,000 had died. He said that the hundreds that desert will never get amnesty from this President. The President then emphasized that the Vice President and Attorney General are very much on the side of the South and many of the points that had been made in the meeting. He said that Harlow can stay as long as he will.

The President addressed himself next to Senator Goldwater, saying that the problem with the bureaucracy is the fact that so many civil servants have been frozen into their positions since the Truman Administration. He said that President Johnson seemed to be even more violently concerned than Senator Goldwater about this subject. Then he made reference to the O'Donnell comments and a statement made to President Nixon by former President Johnson to the effect that "the Kennedy people cut my throat." The President indicated that more aggressive efforts would be made in at least transferring uncooperative civil servants who are frozen into their civil service status. He pointed to the dismissals of Panetta and Allen.

Congressman Ben Blackburn of Georgia was the next speaker. He said the IRS should start probing labor unions on their tax-exempt status. He said the union leaders are buying the votes of the rank and file union members with their own money. He indicated Randolph Thrower commissioner of the IRS from Atlanta thought that such investigations "were none of his business." The President then made some nice comments about the construction trades and the hardhats.

Blackburn stated that in this Administration the Republican Party had two places to gain more votes—the suburbs and the South. Then he strongly criticized Secretary Romney for his efforts to integrate the suburbs of Atlanta and Detroit through housing programs.

The President responded that this was not the policy of this Administration and will not be the policy of this Administration.

□ □ □

Senator Goldwater asked to be excused because of a previous engagement. He suggested that the President go fishing with him sometime soon since he (Goldwater) had not been able to see the

President since August 28. The President then suggested that Goldwater come to see him and call him at San Clemente on the President's next visit there. The President indicated he was not much of a fisherman because he always throws up when he goes fishing. Senator Goldwater said, however, that fishing is so good that he would like to go fishing and throw up anyway. Someone made the comment that when Senator Goldwater left the room, he should go to the *right* to get out. This comment was made after the President tried to guide the Senator with his hands to the door. This exchange with Goldwater drew laughter.

The President asked several times for Senator Thurmond to express himself. At this point, Thurmond finally agreed to do so. His first comment was to the effect that every time he talks to the President he is encouraged but when he (Thurmond) leaves, he gets very discouraged based on the lack of execution of the President's orders by others in the Administration. He emphasized the importance of schools and textiles to the South. He said the Administration would not today carry South Carolina, Florida, Georgia, or North Carolina. He proposed that the President advocate a freedom of choice Constitutional amendment. He also urged very strongly that the President send no one to the South to assist with school desegregation this fall. He asked the question why should they go at all even if they are not to be sent for purposes of coercion. He pointed to all the regional attorneys, U.S. Attorneys, Assistant U.S. Attorneys, U.S. Marshals and their assistants already in the South.

Senator Thurmond next turned his comments to HEW. He said HEW had done tremendous political damage to the President. He referred to Bob Finch as a man who talks one way when he is with Thurmond and another way when he is with someone on the other side of the question. He urged the President to clean out HEW. He said people cannot believe the President cannot get rid of these people in HEW. He said that they just do not understand why the President of the United States with all his power cannot get this job done. The Senator then said that he has not been at all encouraged by Secretary Richardson as a replacement for Finch.

The Senator said that the President's orders appear good on the surface but they are not carried out.

□   □   □

The Senator then pointed to the D.C. school situation which he said now has 95% black students. All the South wants, he said, is equal treatment. He next referred to the Voting Rights Act and the need to have the law apply to every state, not just to the South. He indicated to the President that someone must be influencing you because the Senator does not believe these actions represent the President's thinking.

The President asked the Vice President if he had any comments to make. The Vice President told the President that these are his good friends and are sincerely motivated, pointing out that this is shown by the very candid manner in which they had addressed themselves and their problems to the President. He told the group that the President has tremendous sectional pressures on him and other such pressures which were sometimes in conflict with their own desires. He pointed out that the President has to represent the entire country. He recognized that implementing the court decision was tough and concurred in Senator Tower's view that the President's instincts and philosophy are very good. He expressed gratitude for the good "inputs" made in this meeting. He indicated that the President would not be able to implement all the suggestions made in this meeting but that they would all be given very serious consideration. He said the Administration is very glad to have the support of what the President had termed the thin gray line.

The President interjected here to predict that he would win at least three more Senate seats this year and that this should give the Administration philosophical control over the Senate.

The President then made references to Don Rumsfeld and his tough administration of the VISTA program. He said the only people who seemed to have demonstrated against him (the President) on his last world tour were Peace Corps volunteers.

Congressman Leslie Arends then commented that the country is moving right. The President indicated that he hoped so. Then the President gave some statistics on liberal versus conservative thinking in the country. He said that conservatism had become more popular since he had come in office and the Republican Party seems to have gone downhill in popularity.

The final comment was made by the President when he suggested that Republicans stress on their bumper stickers to vote conservative rather then Republican.

The excerpts from my memo cannot effectively illustrate the sparks caused by Goldwater's acid attitude toward the president and the fire that danced back and forth between Thurmond and Mitchell.

The conservatives had their impact. They never had to come back in that fashion.

The busing problem did not disappear too easily. The Supreme Court and lower federal courts inched closer and closer to requiring busing plans to be drawn by the Nixon Administration. This would mean continued problems for a president who had declared in his 1968 campaign and repeatedly since his opposition to forced busing.

And the president's appointees to the Court did not make it any easier for him. In a decision written by Chief Justice Warren Burger, on April 20, 1971, the U.S. Supreme Court ruled in a unanimous decision that busing, gerrymandering school districts, and shifting students between schools that "may be on opposite ends of the city"—as the Court put it—are legitimate ways of ending government-imposed school segregation. This was the case of *Swann* v. *Charlotte—Mecklenberg Board of Education,* which voiced the key decision on the unpopular question of busing.

The *Swann* case challenged every public opinion poll. All the national polls showed the public to be against busing by approximately 2, 3, or 4 to 1, depending on the proximity of the busing. Even blacks favoring forced busing were recorded as being in a minority position in their own race.

In June 1971, I reported on a Tennessee poll showing 85 percent opposition to busing. Whites registered only 5 percent approval of busing, while only 39 percent of the blacks expressed favor with busing.

In November 1971, I sent Nixon a Gallup poll showing 76 percent opposition to busing. At the same time, my memo cited the action of the liberal Michigan legislature against busing. Each memo was advocating the Administration's action to favor a constitutional amendment outlawing busing.

Fortunately for the president, the public had the correct perception on his opposition to busing. The Court was getting the blame or acclaim for the *Swann* decision; and I informed the president of this saying that "the point has been made on the front pages of most southern newspapers that the decision is against the position taken by the president last March and also before the Court in Justice arguments. There is resentment against the decision, but it seems to fall on the Court."

However, in a later memo I told of a deteriorating political picture caused by the busing problem.

The president became concerned enough about the overall problem that he assigned one of John Ehrlichman's top assistants, Ed Morgan of Arizona, to report directly to the president on the busing and other desegregation problems. Morgan had been working with Secretary Shultz on the Cabinet Committee on Education. However, by mid-1971 the cabinet committee was virtually in limbo as its major task of 1970 was completed. The president, however, continued to use Shultz as a key adviser on school questions. Yet the day-to-day action was shifted to Morgan. Neither the Justice Department nor HEW was to move without checking with Morgan.

Morgan had orders from the president to carry out Nixon's public statements. The statements were for minimum busing. For instance, if a judge in Texas ordered HEW to draw a busing plan—and judges were issuing such orders in Texas, Tennessee, North Carolina, and elsewhere—then Morgan was to see that the local school officials received maximum cooperation from Administration people and that the minimum amount of busing required by the judge's order would be the guideline for the HEW plan writers. Morgan found it much easier to work with Stan Pottinger than with Pottinger's predecessor Leon Panetta. However, some of the judges almost seemed determined to write the toughest type orders possible. In Tennessee, a judge recommended by Senator Howard Baker and appointed by Nixon totally disrupted the school system in Memphis by reordering more desegregation busing. Where communities would get settled in one course of action and then find a judge upsetting the system again, the emotions would run to fever pitch, especially when busing was required by the judge.

Thus as the Nixon Administration entered 1972, the big election year, busing problems were threatening to disrupt its carefully nurtured southern strategy plans to carry a Solid South for reelection.

In March 1972, the president became convinced it was necessary to take additional action. Thus he devised a new set of antibusing proposals, which were dispatched to Congress and televised on March 10. The new program consisted primarily of two proposed new laws: the Student Transportation Moratorium Act of 1972 and the Equal Education Opportunities Act of 1972.

The president basically proposed a halt for one year of all new busing and an indefinite halt to all busing for students below the seventh grade. In lieu of busing, the president advocated large doses of federal aid for schools in segregated inner cities.

Both proposals were difficult to understand and thus were susceptible to being distorted. Indeed they were distorted as a matter of a policy directive by the Democratic National Committee. The idea was to whipsaw Nixon on the proposals. Nixon would be hit in the North for being against busing. Then in the South he would be criticized for being against busing only in the North where it was only beginning to be ordered, while he did nothing to stop the busing that had been ordered in the South much earlier. In other words, Nixon was pictured as being against any new busing that affected the North, but not against the old busing orders that plagued the South.

It was a clever Democratic strategy. Thus off I was sent down through Dixie to try to explain the Democratic ruse and the Republican antibusing proposals. Others followed me on what press assistant Ken Clawson referred to as "the Busing Road Show."

Prior to the scheduled road show, I held a news conference at the Spartanburg-Greenville (South Carolina) airport and made seven points about the programs:

1. The moratorium Act relieves more districts in the South than in any other part of the country. Long-term relief for districts already busing comes under the Equal Education Opportunities Act proposed in addition to the Moratorium.

2. The EEOA proposes to limit busing for the elementary grades to that which was being done prior to the issuance of massive busing orders, and school districts would be able to reopen cases to comply with that provision.

3. All educational agencies operating under court orders or desegregation plans under Title VI may have their cases reopened and modified under the provisions of the act.

4. All new or existing busing orders terminate five years from entry or passage, whichever is later, unless the educational agency has denied equal opportunity or protection.

5. All desegregation orders terminate 10 years from entry or passage, whichever is later, unless the educational agency has denied equal opportunity or protection.

6. District lines can't be ignored or altered unless it can be proved they were drawn for segregation.

7. Additionally, the act stipulates that racial balance is not required and affirms and establishes the priority of pupils being assigned to schools closest to their residences.

The president himself got into the road show. At a GOP congressional leadership breakfast meeting at the White House in late March, he pounded the table to let the Capitol Hill leaders know he wanted to roll back busing in the North and South alike.

More than two-thirds of the meeting was concerned with the busing proposals. The moratorium seemed to be all right, but the part serving as a southern sweetener did not fare well because of the opposition of House Judiciary Chairman Emanuel Celler, the champion anti-South activist in the House.

The question of a constitutional amendment, the only way to stop the judicial decisions, was ruled out in the meeting because, while antibusing advocates could muster a majority, they could not get a two-thirds vote in both houses of Congress. In the end, only the money came through.

On the subject of busing columnist Kevin Phillips reported on April 4, 1972: "In sum, White House aides make it very clear that President Nixon himself had become the driving force behind the Administration's campaign to halt busing and restore the neighborhood school."

Through all the busing furore, Nixon seemed to win the acclaim of the opponents—much in the majority—while the courts received the blame. As the buses rolled to school, Nixon rolled up the biggest presidential vote in history in 1972.

Since then the Nixon position in opposition to busing was adopted by his successor, President Gerald Ford; and even some of the most notable busing advocates—such as University of Chicago sociologist James S. Coleman—have come to recognize the validity of the Nixon position. Coleman in 1975 reversed his field after writing a report in 1966 giving the prime impetus to busing. Others have followed, including black columnist William Rasbury of the *Washington Post;* California's black superintendent of public instruction, Wilson Riles; and even *Time* magazine made this point in its September 15, 1975, issue: "Busing as a means of achieving racial balance in the schools may well be the most unpopular institution imposed on Americans since Prohibition."

□ □ □ □ □ □ □ □ □

To the Southeast, textiles means jobs, money, and establishment power. In southern politics, it has been difficult for a politician to have the support of the textile mill owner and his management staff and also the support of the mill worker and his family.

The mill and worker share one big "enemy": low-wage textile imports, especially from the Far East. When the imports take up more of the domestic market, they likewise cut back on both salary and profits.

Thus the southern political leader in the states from Virginia to Alabama who fights "Jap textiles" is a winner on the side of management and labor— the best of both possible worlds.

When the textile industry is humming in South Carolina, virtually everyone is humming, for textiles account for 40 percent of the manufacturing labor force in the state and 29 percent of the total manufacturing output there. The same is true for Virginia, Tennessee, North Carolina, Georgia, and Alabama to a slightly lesser degree.

While textile production is basically centered today in the Southeast (with some still in the Northeast), the total textile industry is ranked among the top industries in the United States. Contributing to the overall textile industry is the garment industry (bigger and located in about every state), the man-made fiber producers such as DuPont; the cotton growers in the Southeast and Southwest and California; and the wool growers in the West. Combine all this and the result is a big clout in jobs, income, and political leverage. When the textile lobby speaks with one voice in Washington on a given issue, it has a big impact. The textile lobby can give any free-trade type legislation a tough battle and usually, at a minimum, win some safeguards along the way, although it is not powerful enough to defeat the overall legislation. On occasion the textile lobby has been able to unite itself and then weld together other industries troubled by imports—such as steel, shoes, and chemicals—and then stop or change some significant trade legislation. However, if the textile lobby were to be excised from the protection lobby, the "house of protectionism" would crumble.

Thus in the Southeast, textile imports are extremely important. Textiles made the major difference in defeating Richard Nixon in 1960 and electing him in 1968. I watched it happen both times; so did Nixon. He did not forget the tragic lesson of 1960.

Thus when I accosted him on the subject in 1968 and he asked for the answer to the question, I was prepared: "Do the same thing Kennedy did to you in 1960—be the first to offer a commitment to provide reasonable protection, as Kennedy did in 1960, and not as you refused to do in 1960."

Later, Nixon readily agreed to make a commitment to help the textile industry.

In the general election campaign, Nixon's textile pledge became a key part of the campaign appeal to attract Wallace voters and other southern voters to Nixon. Those of us campaigning for Nixon had distributed many thousands of handbills on the textile pledge in textile areas.

Textile industry officials united behind the efforts to win southern votes for Nixon in the 1968 general election. Textile workers seemed to do likewise, as is attested to by the 1968 vote in Greenville County, South Carolina, the textile hub of the industry. Here Wallace had a good chance, as did the Democrats, with 18 percent of the total registered vote being black. However, Nixon carried the area on election day with 25,809 to 13,042 for Wallace and 11,838 for Humphrey.

Even next door neighbor Spartanburg County, which never voted Republican, joined the GOP column.

South Carolina and North Carolina, both having voted for Kennedy in 1960, this time pulled into the Nixon column unexpectedly, giving Nixon a comfortable margin. Much of the magic had to do with the textile commitment.

Hubert Humphrey made virtually the same commitment, but he made it after Nixon, which mattered to many textile workers. They felt that not only had Nixon committed first, but his platform generally was better. Still, had Humphrey made the commitment and Nixon had not, the final vote would have ended differently.

In the Nixon White House, the president himself was determined to see that the textile commitment was carried out. Kennedy had executed part one of his commitment in early 1961 by calling in George Ball, the undersecretary of state, and getting him to corral a voluntary cotton textile agreement with Japan, then the major exporter of textile products to the United States. However, he did not finish the job by making the agreements comprehensive enough to cover all fibers—man-made, wool, and cotton—and limiting the textiles by category. Thus the Japanese would flood one category to their advantage, transship to other countries and then into the USA. Most ingeniously of all, they started blending their cotton fibers with man-made and/or woolen fibers, thereby losing the identity of the all-cotton products, which they had agreed to limit.

Well, this time, the American textile leaders were much wiser and more determined. They wanted full protection with no Japanese hocus pocus.

Therefore, in the Nixon commitment, the textile spokesmen had proposed comprehensive agreements covering all fibers, all categories, and all countries shipping textiles into the United States. However, like the Kennedy commitment, the agreements were to be voluntary agreements arrived at on a basis of negotiation with each country. The agreements would eventually be tied together under an international agreement. This would be done to keep a country from being adversely affected by the failure of another to carry out its commitment.

To Richard Nixon the commitment seemed simple enough to implement. Nixon had at least expected a request for mandatory imposition of quotas. However, to the State Department types, the commitment was abominable and had to be ignored; or failing that, the commitment had to be scuttled in the best traditions of the "Fudge Factory of Foggy Bottom."

As soon as the Nixon Administration got in the White House, the battle over textiles began. Robert Ellsworth, one of the president's top assistants, was assigned to coordinate the efforts to get the job accomplished. He was to work with all agencies concerned with the textile question.

Together, Ellsworth and I had worded Nixon's commitment to the textile industry. Ellsworth was a moderate former GOP congressman from Kansas.

Nonetheless, before Ellsworth could get his assignment underway, he was shuffled off to be U.S. ambassador to the North Atlantic Treaty Alliance. This resulted from a struggle with the president's top two assistants, Haldeman and Ehrlichman, known by some as the "Katzenjammer Kids," "The Germans," "the Krauts," or the "leaders of the Beaver Patrol."

Thus a new coordinator of this positive-action program had to be found.

Commerce Secretary Maurice Stans was made interim coordinator. This pleased me because the secretary favored working out the necessary agreements, while all the other top administration officials concerned were either opposed or lukewarm.

Under Stans's leadership, a world trade mission was established for the purpose of trying to increase American exports of farm commodities and to limit the escalating increase in textile imports. I was included on the mission.

Everywhere the mission went, a Japanese was on hand to watch its activities. We later discovered that he or a Japanese associate had preceded us to weaken our position. When we would bring up the subject of textiles, we would be told the same thing: "We practice the belief in free trade and are opposed to any form of protectionism. We suggest you see what you can first do with the Japanese and then come back to see us."

The Japanese had worked their plan well, knowing they were at the end of our trade mission's visits.

The business about practicing free trade was a farce. A big part of the overall mission was to point up all the nontariff trade barriers the various governments were using or were permitting to be used against American exports in their countries.

Nontariff trade barriers are an informal set of regulations placed on imports by governments that would not interfere with formal international agreements (General Agreement on Tariff and Trade). For example, the Japanese government may restrict the licensing of automobile imports by size and weight, because Japanese highways are only equipped to handle a certain size car. In this manner, all American automobile imports are effectively eliminated. Restricing the import of advanced computers of foreign direct investment in the computer industry under the pretext of protecting an "infant" industry would comprise another such barrier. Quota restrictions on the imports of finished textiles from less developed countries would be another nontariff barrier.

In the Far East, we knew the results there would determine the outcome. Here was the problem area. The Japanese were important to America's foreign policy objectives in this vast area of the world. Since World War II, America had reestablished Japan politically and economically as the most rapidly rising commercial nation in the world. It helped the Japanese establish its textile and other postwar industries. Soon thereafter, however, America found its own domestic markets being absorbed considerably with Japanese products—such as steel, auto, electronics, chemicals, and textiles. Now that the Japanese were back on their feet economically, they were moving swiftly to capture every available market which their lower prices made possible. They became great advocates of the principle of free trade, but felt it was a one-way street. This group's domestic markets were virtually impenetrable, except where it felt the need, such as with agricultural products, an area in which the Japanese were one of America's best customers.

The Japanese were all set for our visit. They had been encouraged to stall us off by the attitude of the State Department and the Office of the President's Special Trade Representative against granting any concessions to Secretary Stans.

For years, Mike Daniels, a Washington, D.C., lobbyist, had represented Japanese textile interests. He kept advising against any action at all, for the Nixon Administration would not press the issue seriously.

The real lesson in one-upmanship, however, was when the Japanese Diet unanimously passed a resolution preceding our arrival protesting against any action on our textile requests. This gave the late Prime Minister Eisaku

Sato all the answers he needed to stall Secretary Stans and the prime ministers.

The Japanese had thus made good on their pledge to the other countries we had visited, having said, in effect, "Leave Uncle Sam to us; we'll handle him when he comes to us hat in hand." Sato did just that.

Back in Washington, we concluded that our task was a game of persistence, taking a hard line and sticking to it. We also realized we were being undermined by our own officials in the State Department and in the Office of the President's Special Trade Representative, who kept pressing for weak solutions, which were being written in Tokyo and/or the office of Japanese lobbyist Mike Daniels. The solutions both proposed reflected ignorance of the Administration's policy and determination.

We realized, however, that any agreement had to be fudge proof, or like the Kennedy cotton textile agreement of 1961, it would be woven around and through to the point where it would have only limited effect.

Peter Flanigan of the White House staff took over the world trade mission as coordinator, since the president pushed again in fall 1969 to get the matter behind him.

Realizing the prime minister of Japan would be coming to visit the president in November 1969 to take home his right to bring Okinawa and the Ryukyu Islands back under Japanese control, Nixon moved to get the matter concluded by using this big quo to assure the small quid he was seeking, knowing that once he got Japan on board everything else would follow.

The president did his job masterfully. In his private meetings with Sato, they reached an understanding that since the president was helping Sato through his upcoming election, Sato would see to it that the president would get his textile agreement soon after the election and in a form acceptable to our desires.

John Mitchell told me of the super secret understanding. The president thus became convinced the problem would now be settled in a reasonable matter of time.

Time passed on into 1970 and still no action. Meanwhile, the protection lobbies in Washington were moving to amend the pending trade legislation with amendments put on mandatory import quotas for textiles and shoes.

Meanwhile, I attended the annual convention of textile leaders in San Francisco in March 1970 and later reported to the president the reaction of the textile people to our failure to successfully carry out the commitment. The consensus was to end further negotiations with Japan and the other countries and to get legislation enacted that would impose "effective, comprehensive, quantitative limitations on imports into this country of all textile articles."

This information was followed up by a further report to the attorney general, Harlow, and Flanigan on a meeting Secretary Stans had the first of April with Henry Kissinger and Alexis Johnson, the man handling the textile problem for the State Department. Subsequently Stans, Johnson, and Kissinger had a meeting in which the issue was to try to wind up the textile matter through executive action, or if this were impossible, have the Administration support the concept of reasonable legislative action in order to carry out the 1968 campaign commitment.

On April 16, Treasury Secretary David Kennedy delivered to the president messages from the prime minister of Japan and his finance minister on the subject of textiles.

Sato expressed his regrets for not having been able to resolve the textile issue in the time he had planned. However, he expected to keep his secret pact with the president to reach an understanding between the two governments and have that understanding accepted by the Japanese textile industry. Sato and the finance minister, Fukuda, both expressed their gratitude for Nixon's cooperation on the return of Okinawa to Japan, which they both felt to be primarily responsible for their great success in the recent Japanese election.

In other words, the two Japanese leaders understood a summit quid pro quo.

In the fall, the issue of textiles became a political football in textile states. The Democrats in South Carolina used the issue effectively against Congressman Albert Watson in his race for the governorship. Congressman William Brock of Tennessee complained about the harmful effects in the close races in Tennessee.

The real political heat, however, was brought on by a Democratic effort to amend the trade bill so the president would have to veto the bill with relief contained therein for textiles. To get around this, members of Nixon's staff advised him to say he would go along with a "textiles only" amendment, but no more. However, the textile amendment could not be successful without shoes included; and with shoes in, the president, in answer to a question about the prospects of vetoing the proposed trade bill, said on July 20, 1970: "I would certainly veto it, if it contains the provisions which I did not recommend. Speaking in general terms, first, quota legislation, *mandatory* quota legislation, is not in the interest of the United States."

The president went on to say that textiles were an exception to this general proposition and that the approach of the bill for "textiles only" was acceptable.

The crisis of having to veto the trade legislation never became a reality, fortunately. The textile issue continued without a solution on into 1971.

Meanwhile, the Japanese lobbyist, Mike Daniels, got together with Congressman Wilbur Mills on a Japanese voluntary approach to textiles. This approach caught everyone off guard, especially since it had the blessing of the most powerful man on Capitol Hill on the subject of trade. The Japanese government announced that since the Japanese Textile Federation had come forward with its voluntary program, its government was breaking off negotiations with the U.S. government.

When the president learned of this effort by Mills and the Japanese to outflank him, he immediately issued a statement denouncing the plan and calling for congressional passage of a bill setting mandatory textile import quotas and establishing a system to monitor textile imports into this country.

The Mills plan got nowhere and was denounced by even many of his own House colleagues. The informal Textile Committee labeled the congressman's approach "totally unacceptable."

"In one fell swoop," declared the committee, the approach "destroys the concepts of categories and government-to-government agreements, concepts which have been built up so carefully and over such a long period of time among 30 nations involved in the GATT cotton textile agreement (which regulates international trade and tariffs). This unilateral declaration thus sets back by 10 years the whole concept of orderly international trade in textiles."

The Japanese government leaders were shocked at the reaction in the United States against their plan, especially the sharp blast of the president, who felt he had been personally betrayed, based on the November 1969 Sato commitment. The Japanese had been led by their U.S.-based lobbyist to believe that the Administration, especially the president, would welcome this way out of the textile dilemma. After all, they had been assured that the State Department and the president's special trade representative were sympathetic to their position.

Becoming restless about the continuing problem, the president turned the task over to Peter Peterson, his new assistant to the president for foreign economic problems.

Peterson soon made a determination that we would somehow get the matter successfully concluded in 1971, and he finally did. (Although Flanigan wanted the commitment out of the way, he was biased in handling it, because he sympathized more with his friend Don Kendall of Pepsico, who kept trying to get the problem solved satisfactorily for the Japanese.) However, the solution required a tough line with the Japanese; Peterson understood this.

Peterson called me in one day to inquire who could get the negotiating job done with the foreign countries, particularly Japan. I recommended Special Ambassador David Kennedy and his deputy Tony Jurich in light of their extensive experience and acceptance in the Far East.

Peterson accepted the suggestion; and soon Ambassador Kennedy, former treasury secretary, was given the responsibility and was off on a special presidential mission with advance billing from the president.

More problems ensued, but Ambassador Kennedy, Jurich, and Peterson persisted despite all the undercutting some were convinced was coming from the State Department, the special trade representative, and Kissinger's shop at the White House.

Ambassador Kennedy and Jurich embarked on this mission in a high level of secrecy, since in each of the countries they, too, had their political problems. The negotiations with these countries were started at the highest levels to establish the U.S. position and to work with the approach that would be successful. This mission was to take a number of trips to each of these countries before the agreements were finally concluded.

Ambassador Kennedy finally became bogged down with the Far East negotiations during a visit to Japan in early August. The Japanese, who continued to be the key to the successful negotiations for all the countries, kept having difficulty with timing. Something was needed as a stimulus to the Japanese for immediate action.

After considerable study Peterson finally concluded that strong action had to be taken, because the matter had now moved far beyond a political commitment to a question of the president's credibility and strength in Japan, other Far Eastern countries, China, and the rest of the diplomatic capitals in the world.

Thus he began drawing together legal opinions on the various authorities the president might have for invoking tough presidential action on textiles. His work centered on the national security clause of the Trade Act, section 232(b). This clause permits the president "to adjust the imports of such articles and their derivatives so that such imports will not threaten to impair the national security." It authorizes the president to act on recommendation of a finding by the director of the Office of Emergency Planning.

The four smaller Far Eastern countries learned that consideration was being given at the highest level to invoking the national security clause against them and then proceed against Japan by using another law to bring Japan in.

Section 204 of the Agricultural Act of 1956 authorizes the president to impose limits on textile imports of another country *if* (1) the agreement is multilateral and (2) it accounts for a "significant" part of world trade in textiles. Fear of imposition of the national security clause would get the four smaller nations involved to cooperate and effectively arm Nixon with section 204 of the Agriculture Act as a possible weapon against Japan.

Just as the White House was preparing for a presidential decision on the use of the national security clause, the president struck with his tough and bold economic policy of August 15, 1971. These policy actions—closing the U.S. window on exchanging gold for dollars accumulated by other countries, establishing wage and price controls, and placing a surcharge on imports— provided the leverage, proof of determination, and shock action our side needed to conclude the textile agreements within the next 60 days.

I was at home in Columbia on that weekend when I got a call from Haldeman's office to return to Washington immediately for a Sunday morning meeting, which was being held to help with preparation for the notifications and distribution of the upcoming August 15 bombshell involving the gold window, controls, and the imposition of the import surcharge. When I saw what the president was preparing to do I knew textiles would not be far behind.

As Paul Clancey reported in the *Philadelphia Inquirer* on October 21, 1971: "The textile agreement sharply cutting Far East exports to the U.S. was one of the greatest single political strokes for Richard Nixon in the South since he landed in the White House."

The successful conclusion of the textile agreements did further strengthen Nixon abroad, particularly following his August 15 actions. At home the president was helped also, and especially down South.

The textile agreements had positive effects on the 1972 election in the textile states. In 1968 the promise of relief had been crucial in the southeastern states. Now, in 1972, the relief had arrived, and with the relief there was not only restoration of jobs lost or curtailed, but new jobs were created.

As Thurmond said, "The president kept his commitment," and the voters kept theirs, with an overwhelming margin at textile-mill voting boxes.

One of the most appealing points Candidate Nixon made in 1968 was his pledge to put conservatives on the U.S. Supreme Court. The pledge was not just political with Nixon, for nothing concerned him more than the left-ward tilt of the Supreme Court.

In his 1968 campaign for the GOP nomination, Nixon's Supreme Court statement made the biggest impact on southern Republican chairmen and Senator Thurmond. When I called the senator to come to the Marriott Motel in Atlanta on June 1, 1968, to give Nixon and his team our pledge of support, the point which assured Thurmond the most was the pledge "to appoint Supreme Court Justices who will respect the Constitution rather than rewrite it." When he heard Nixon make that statement, Thurmond said, "That does it, Harry, let's go ahead and commit."

At the convention and in the general election a "new Supreme Court" was one of the foremost points.

As a candidate and later as president, Nixon said: "I'll never make a liberal appointment to the Supreme Court. It'll take every appointment I can make just to get a balanced Court." He felt that "balancing the Supreme Court is the most important and lasting effect I can have on government while I am president, and I intend to have that effect." When the president made this comment to a Delaware audience in 1971, he drew strong and sustained applause, for his conviction showed.

Then in May 1969, when Chief Justice Earl Warren announced his retirement, Nixon had his first chance to make good on his Supreme Court pledge. On that evening, he invited most members of Congress and other Washington leaders to the East Room of the White House to dramatically introduce his choice to succeed Warren, Chief Judge Warren Burger of the U.S. Court of Appeals for the District of Columbia. The selection was popular. Burger had the credentials, the right philosophy, and he looked just like a chief justice.

The secret of the selection was well kept. The senior White House staffers were called in by Haldeman and given assignments of people to call before the presentation of Burger. However, we were not provided with the name, only the message that "you'll like the appointment, I assure you."

A few days later in a memo to the attorney general, I presented the name of Chief Judge Clement Haynsworth of the Fourth Circuit Court of Appeals for another Supreme Court vacancy. I repeated the suggestion in a subsequent memo.

These efforts were directed toward putting a Southerner in the place left vacant by the Johnson administration's failure to win confirmation for liberal D.C. attorney and LBJ confidant Abe Fortas in 1968. Senators Thurmond and Robert Griffin of Michigan had led the fight that stopped Fortas. During the time of the Nixon transition, LBJ tried to send up a name to replace Fortas on what was considered the Jewish seat on the Court. LBJ had an arrangement with his old ally on the other side, the late Senator Everett Dirksen, GOP leader. However, Thurmond influenced enough Senate GOP conservatives to stop Dirksen and thus save the vacancy for the new president to make. Thurmond and I duly reported the results directly to Nixon and Mitchell in New York in December 1968. Thus twice Thurmond was instrumental in saving the Court seat for a Republican president to fill.

When Haynsworth was finally nominated in September, some question arose about whether he was Thurmond's choice or that of the junior senator from South Carolina, Ernest Hollings. The Haynsworth name came from me, and it went over well with the president and the attorney general. Thurmond preferred South Carolina District Judge Donald Russell, but Russell was older than the age limits set by the president in private conversations. Yet Thurmond did not see why it could not be done. Russell had served briefly in the Senate with Thurmond, and although rivals earlier, Thurmond had come to respect Russell and his abilities. (Thurmond and I did later get Russell promoted to the Fourth Circuit Court of Appeals.)

Hollings learned that Haynsworth was receiving serious consideration. So he jumped out ahead of Thurmond and publicly proposed Haynsworth's name. Thurmond proposed Russell publicly. Haynsworth was selected.

Thurmond favored both, and when he finally accepted that Russell's age was a bar, he supported Haynsworth strongly.

I realized it was not in Haynsworth's interest to have him tabbed as Thurmond's man. This would be played as a "deal" and give the impression Thurmond was dictating Supreme Court choices. This would be good for Thurmond, but not Nixon. So I suggeeted that the senator continue to stand by his real first choice, Russell, and let the press draw their own conclusions. And initially, this plan worked.

The Haynsworth nomination upset many liberals on Capitol Hill, the news media, organized labor, civil rights groups, and anywhere two or more liberals assembled.

One result was a demand by Republican liberals in the Senate that Bryce Harlow bring the top White House staff—and especially Harry Dent—to two luncheon "chewing out" sessions the last week in September.

Although Haynsworth had the endorsement of the American Bar Association's judge selection committee and had been previously approved by the Senate when President Eisenhower nominated him for the appeals court, the liberal leadership turned against him, with the biggest being non-supporter George Meany and organized labor. Meany felt Haynsworth was not prounion, and in fact, might be antiunion. Aside from all the arguments used, this, plus his southern background, was the prime reason for Haynsworth's eventual rejection.

At the White House and the Department of Justice, an all-out effort was made to put the judge on top and it looked possible—until Meany moved forcefully into the battle. Then things began to change.

Haldeman organized efforts at the White House, and Deputy Attorney General Richard Kleindienst headed the efforts at the Justice Department.

Haldeman pressed hard to get the maximum lobbying leverage applied. The other side was working even harder to stop Haynsworth. The president prepared for an all-out fight. At a Republican congressional leader's breakfast on October 14, he said he would never withdraw Haynsworth's nomination and would keep fighting for him if "he only got one Senate vote."

Vice President Agnew pledged his vote if the Senate vote should be a tie.

The president told the GOP leaders—two of whom, Senator Griffin and Senator Margaret Chase Smith, had declared against Haynsworth—that "I would never be a party to ruining a good man like Haynsworth." Special Counsel Clark Mollenhoff gave a point-by-point refutation of charges against Haynsworth. He admitted only one technical mistake by Haynsworth. This was the judge's purchase of a thousand shares of Brunswick Corporation stock after taking part in ruling on a case involving the company.

The Haynsworth fight raged for all of October and most of November before he was rejected 55–45 on November 21, after having won approval in the Judiciary Committee 10–7.

In its November 28, 1969, issue *Time* magazine analyzed the pressures applied by both sides and the effects for and against. Bryce Harlow, Clark Mollenhoff, and I were credited with hard lobbying, which *Time* said won some votes and may have cost others. As *Time* concluded:

Haynsworth, to some extent, was a victim of history. Had he been nominated a decade ago, there is little doubt he would have been confirmed swiftly. But the court has become increasingly involved in all aspects of National life. This, and the revelations that led to the resignation of Abe Fortas from the Supreme Court, dictate closer scrutiny and higher standards for Justices than in the past.

Nixon reacted strongly against the rejection of Haynsworth. He called the rejection an "anti-South" action and vowed to give the U.S. Senate another southern judge to consider after the first of the year. Thus reaction in favor of Nixon and Haynsworth was overwhelmingly good among Southerners and conservatives everywhere.

The president called me in to commiserate over the Haynsworth defeat. He was very upset. We both agreed there was still anti-South bias in the liberal establishment, especially because of newly won political powers by the South. He said, "Harry, I want you to go out and this time find a good federal judge farther down South and further to the right."

Out I went in search of that person.

I wasn't sure whether the Nixon sentiment was anger and frustration of the moment or whether he would still feel the same a few weeks later. I assumed what I wanted to assume. And I found the man: "farther down South and further to the right." He was Judge G. Harrold Carswell of Florida. A recently promoted and Senate-confirmed member of the Fifth Circuit Court of Appeals, Carswell had been appointed by President Eisenhower. And he had easily won Senate confirmation. Subsequently, I recommended the judge to the attorney general in a memo.

While commuting from South Carolina to Washington, I roomed with several friends who were also commuting. One was my old friend Bill Murfin, the former Florida GOP chairman who had helped nominate Nixon in 1968. Murfin then was one of the top executives at the Small Business Administration. He had pushed Carswell at me when Haynsworth was being considered for nomination. He told me, "Here's a man twice confirmed by the Senate, the last time being this year." At first, the nomination seemed secure. Then the liberal establishment and George Meany went to work again.

This time, after a ten-week battle, the nomination followed much the same course as the Haynsworth fight, except the vote centered not on a weak claim of conflict of interest in one case, but rather on the question of whether Judge Carswell was a "mediocre" judge. On April 8, the Senate voted 45 to 51 to deny Carswell the nomination.

The real issue now was whether a liberal U.S. Senate would ever confirm a southern federal judge on the court right below the Supreme Court. These two circuit court judges—one a chief judge—had followed the same fate of North Carolina Judge John J. Parker, the chief judge of the same fourth circuit as Haynsworth, in 1930, when President Herbert Hoover nominated Parker for the U.S. Supreme Court. As soon as the Carswell rejection was voted, the president called and asked me to come over.

When I got there he said, "Here, Harry, read this and let me know what you think." It was to be the president's statement on the Senate's defeat of the second southern judge in a row:

> I have reluctantly concluded—with the Senate presently constituted—I cannot successfully nominate to the Supreme Court any Federal Appellate Judge from the South who believes as I do in the strict construction of the Constitution. Judges Carswell and Haynsworth have endured with admirable dignity vicious assaults on their intelligence, their honesty and their character. They have been falsely charged with being racist. But when all the hypocrisy is stripped away, the real issue was their philosophy of strict construction of the Constitution—a philosophy that I share and the fact that they had the misfortune of being born in the South. After the rejection of Judge Carswell and Judge Haynsworth, this conclusion is inescapable.

☐ ☐ ☐

> As long as the Senate is constituted the way it is today, I will not nominate another Southerner and let him be subjected to the kind of malicious character assassination accorded both Judge Haynsworth and Carswell. However, my next nomination will be made in the very near future; a President should not leave that vacancy on the Court when it can be filled. My next nominee will be from outside the South and he will fulfill the criteria of a strict constructionist with judicial experience either from a Federal bench or on a State Appeals Court.

> I understand the bitter feeling of millions of Americans who live in the South about the act of regional discrimination that took place in the Senate yesterday. They have my assurance that the day will come when men like Judges Carswell and Haynsworth can and will sit on the High Court.

As I read the statement I was shocked and pleased.

As I was finishing the statement, Ron Zeigler, the press secretary, walked in and said, "Mr. President, the TV cameras are ready." The president jumped up and said, "What do you think, Harry?"

I said, "Mr. President, it's great! Are you going to say this?" (I thought he wanted me to find someone to give the statement.)

"Your're right! The people might as well know what a bunch of bigots there are in the Senate."

I tried to give the president his statement to read before the cameras, but he stalked off without anything in his hand. I followed him to the press room and stood amazed as he gave the statement virtually verbatim, except for one slight misstatement near the end.

The president had a photographic memory. He could look at suggested remarks prepared by his speech writing staff and walk out to the visiting group and give it to them virtually verbatim. I witnessed that marvel many times.

I slipped back in the Oval Office and commended the president for his statement and delivery. We agreed I should make a quick tour of the South to let the southern people know why there would be no third straight southern nomination to the Supreme Court. This was a mission I relished with great satisfaction. Everywhere I went the reaction was great and the headlines very good. Richard Nixon was a hero in the South, and so were Judges Haynsworth and Carswell.

No action by the president did more to cement the sinews of the southern strategy, although Nixon never meant to have his southern nominess assassinated by the U.S. Senate. The outcome may have strained some congressional relations and peeved the liberal establishment, but it considerably improved the president's standing with southerners and conservatives.

Judge Haynsworth decided to maintain his position as chief judge of the fourth circuit. However, Carswell elected to give up his seat on the fifth circuit and return to the practice of law in Florida.

Judge Haynsworth is today highly regarded as chief judge. Even the national consensus appears to support the view that a good judge may have been wronged by the U.S. Senate in an ideological and regional fracas with overtones of the Fortas fight.

Judge Carswell, probably because he resigned and lost in a U.S. Senate primary contest, and has had a problem with the law is considered much less favorably. The idea of mediocrity stuck to some degree, even though not nearly so much in the South.

Carswell probably would have been elected to the U.S. Senate had the Republican party chosen to give him the nomination without a fight. He was a martyr in Florida, and not having the party label all over him, he was a "merchandisable product." The judge was not a natural politician, but that would not have been necessary. What he lacked that did matter was party credentials; and he ran head-on into the man who did, Congressman William Cramer, the first Republican elected to Congress from Florida in many years. Ultimately, Cramer won the primary, but the GOP split cost him the election. Going down to defeat with Cramer was his real enemy, Governor Claude Kirk.

Soon after the Senate's rejection of Carswell, the president moved to nominate a non-Southerner to fill the long-vacant position on the Court: U.S. Circuit Judge Harry Blackmun of Minnesota. He was suggested by Chief Justice Burger, also of Minnesota. Once confirmed the two justices were known as the "Minnesota Twins."

The confirmation of Blackmun seemed to prove the president's point—only non-Southerners need apply at the Supreme Court at this time. I made this point in every speech, and the president loved it.

If there should be any geographical balance on the Supreme Court, then the South has been on the regional short end for many years. Only the late Justice Hugo Black, who died in Nixon's first term, could be said to have come to the Court from the South. Black was a U.S. senator from Alabama when he was named to the Court by President Franklin D. Roosevelt in 1937.

Roosevelt named another southern leader in 1941, when he awarded a seat to the late Senator James F. Byrnes of South Carolina. Byrnes served only briefly, nine months, because of Roosevelt's need of his services as "Assistant President" to run the domestic front during World War II. From that date in 1942 to the present, only one Southerner has been among the nine justices on the Supreme Court.

Black was not considered representative of the conservative South on the High Court. Thus Southerners have felt unrepresented on the Court.

Thus when in May 1969, President Nixon had to fill two more vacancies on the Court, when Warren retired and Fortas resigned, Southerners expected and got one Southerner to fill one of the vacancies. Perhaps this is one explanation for the Senate's refusal to confirm Judges Haynsworth or Carswell—an inner Senate belief that the South deserved no more than one seat on the highest Court in the land.

The honor of filling the southern seat vacated by the death of Justice Black was given to Richmond Attorney Lewis Powell, a former president of the American Bar Association. Although not a man with judicial experience, Powell's qualifications were excellent. He was given none of the problems encountered by Judges Haynsworth and Carswell. The Senate realized two were enough, and the senators had had time to reflect on the previous Nixon criticism of Senate bias against the South.

Powell was submitted in tandem with Assistant Attorney General William Rehnquist. A native of Arizona, Rehnquist was the most conservative man ideologically Nixon had nominated to the Court—even over Haynsworth and Carswell. This combination was a Nixon-Mitchell master stroke. The South stood up and cheered, even though both were relatively unknown to most Southerners. The headlines told the South all it wanted to know: "Two Conservatives Appointed to Supreme Court!" When the press played up Rehnquist's background and it was stated he was more conservative than even Powell in Virginia, this was great news throughout Dixie.

The selections were rapidly made, and the secrecy was well kept. The nominations caught everyone by surprise.

Several of us staffers were called over to Haldeman's office a few hours in advance of the presidential announcement to make selective and secret telephone calls to key people who were to be notified prior to the announcement. While we were in the Haldeman office, Haldeman got Powell on the telephone, and I had a chance to congratulate the new nominee.

To me, this combination was virtually perfect, and it showed Nixon at his best. Haldeman was wild with ecstasy. But he did not lose control of his sense of security, making us do our calling from his office, so we would not let the president be robbed of the valued shock effect of his surprise announcement.

On December 10, 1971, the two nominees were considered and finally confirmed by votes of 89 to 1 (Powell) and 68 to 26 (Rehnquist).

With these confirmations the news media began talking and writing about the "Nixon Court" and no longer the "Warren Court." Nixon had accomplished one of the biggest aims of his presidency, and in grand style. No president ever had as many Court appointments in such a short time. The impact on the nation would be considerable. In an assessment of the Nixon Court on May 23, 1973, the *Washington Star* gave this appraisal of the new Court's move back to the right:

> Over Justice William O. Douglas' protest about "a 'law and order' judicial mood," an apparently dependable "Nixon majority" had formed on the Supreme Court.

The President's desire for a court that would swing the criminal law pendulum back to the conviction side seemed to be fulfilled yesterday in the first real test of the "new" Court's posture.

It happened exactly as the President could have anticipated months ago when he got the chance to name his third and fourth appointees to the high bench.

His four men, each picked precisely because he was "conservative" on the crime issues, formed an alliance and gained the seemingly automatic support (and crucial fifth vote) of Justice Byron R. White.

In less than a full term in the White House, the President thus had delivered on one of his boldest campaign promises, and one of his keenest personal ambitions.

The Nixon, Mitchell, and Kleindienst appointments to lower federal courts helped provide some balance to the federal court system at the lower levels. The Kennedy and Johnson administrations had moved the federal judiciary to the left ideologically, and Nixon had done about all he could at all levels to bring a sense of ideological balance, although philosophy is supposedly muted in court decisions. Yet the powers of the courts have been enhanced to the point now at which even district judges are making rulings that reshape and remold the law of the land.

Originally envisioned by the Founding Fathers as the weakest of the three branches of the central government, the federal court system has come to wield the most power on occasions and questions affecting some of the most vital questions of not only national but local policy as well.

One of the prime attractions Southerners liked about Richard Nixon was his anti-Communist record and his apparent basic sense of patriotism and loyalty to the United States of America. No section of this country is more in love with the old American way of life and all the fundamental principles which undergird the basic fabric of America than the people of the South. This is true of the white population as well as the blacks.

The best evidence is the situs of antiwar demonstrations during the Vietnam War period—very few in Dixie.

More evidence can be perceived in conversations, in voting records of southern members of Congress on national security and foreign policy questions, and the instinctively rightward reaction and voting record of southern voters in supporting presidents executing a hard line for America's defense and foreign policy objectives.

The spirit of anticommunism is strongest in the South, and especially her oldest cities, such as Charleston, South Carolina; and Savannah, Georgia. "Honor" is still a hallowed word in the South. "National honor" is foremost among all the "honors."

The flag is still important in Dixie, as is the National Anthem and any other symbols of patriotism.

In fact, the side of Richard Nixon that most attracted Senator Thurmond to him in 1968 was the patriotic side. Thurmond liked the candidate's words about "balancing the Supreme Court," about "restoring state and local powers of government," "about preserving law and order."

The foremost rallying point for southern Republicans—and most Southerners—however is patriotism, the call to the colors.

Thus the sides of Richard Nixon that repelled many in the Northeast—his anticommunism, his prosecution of Alger Hiss, his stands for strong national security and foreign policy objectives—were his biggest attractions in the South.

In discussing the question of going all out for Nixon, Thurmond told me in 1968: "Harry, this man's a patriot. He understands the Communists and what they're trying to do to our country and the world, and that's what counts the most for America. Reagan does too, but this is the man who can win and can do something about the threats facing America today."

Thus to Thurmond the 1968 convention and general election battles were real crusades to save America. The same was true for other southern GOP leaders.

Nixon's stance in favor of the anti-ballistic missile (ABM) defense system was vital to Thurmond, who had been leading ABM fights in the Senate for several years. The first major issue Nixon faced as president was the appropriation of funds to build the first ABM sites in the USA.

This was our first fight to get support on Capitol Hill by operating a massive public lobbying effort from within the White House. H.R. Haldeman, "Mr. PR" of J. Walter Thompson advertising fame, commanded our task force. We even had special reinforcements brought in to the White House to get the public to lobby Congress. This was in accord with the Nixon credo that "when we win 'em it'll be that close and when we lose 'em it'll be that close." Sure enough, the ABM battle would be a close one.

It was a classic Nixon-Kennedy fight all over again. This time it was President Richard Nixon versus the youngest Kennedy Brother, Senator Ted Kennedy. The winner in another squeaker this time was Richard Nixon.

The ABA battle was the first sure sign Nixon would be a man of his word and was indeed the patriot we had expected.

Then in keeping with his inaugural theme of "an era of negotiation rather than confrontation," the president in the summer of 1969 began announcing troop withdrawals from Vietnam. Yet while bringing American boys home, Nixon was not giving up to the Communists in Southeast Asia. This brought applause from Dixie, but demonstrations elsewhere.

While withdrawing troops from Vietnam, the president was talking tough to the Communists through his speeches. He was attempting to go over the heads of most national newsmen, whom Nixon felt were conveying an impression of a weak national will on Vietnam.

Thus he ordered a tough speech prepared for delivery at the Air Force Academy graduation exercises on June 4, 1969. The purpose was to make "isolationists" out of his critics and to let the Communists in Peking, Moscow, and Hanoi know we weren't going to be run out of Vietnam.

As the demonstrations increased, the president made an appeal to the "silent majority" in a nationwide TV address. If any people felt included in that group it was Southerners. So we enjoyed that speech. Many of the people criticizing Nixon were also in the forefront of those critical of the South.

Even though he continued to withdraw troops from Vietnam, Nixon still could not satisfy the antiwar protestors and writers. He kept referring to "peace with honor," and the word "honor" warmed southern hearts. So whenever the president said it was necessary to take a tough action in Southeast Asia, the national polls might show a loss of support, but not in Dixie.

Thus when the president made his boldest move thus far in Southeast Asia on April 30, 1970, he stirred passions for and against him. On this date he announced on nationwide TV his order to send American and South Vietnamese troops into Cambodia to clean out the Communist sanctuaries being effectively used against South Vietnam and U.S. troops. There was a question whether our dwindling number of U.S. troops could survive as the North

Vietnamese and Viet Cong were threatening to overrun Saigon with their buildup of troops and supplies.

The president contemplated the Cambodian invasion decision for 11 days in April. He knew the decision would particularly provoke the demonstrators. The subject was much on his mind Monday, April 27, when he called me into the Oval Office to discuss politics. He was sitting with his feet propped on the desk. He started by telling me how much he respected and liked the people of the South for their basic sense of patriotism. He had come to know the Southerners while a law student at Duke University in Durham, North Carolina.

Then he told me he was preparing action in Southeast Asia that would stir up the war protestors and Nixon haters. He wanted to know how the southern people would react.

I responded in all sincerity with these words of support, "Mr. President, you can count on the South. We've stood by you on Vietnam, and we'll continue to do so with whatever action you deem necessary to end the war with honor."

I told him his tough and realistic position on the war was as much responsible for his staunch support in Dixie as his Supreme Court appointments.

He concluded by observing that the South might be his only ally in this fight, but it was vital to American lives and his overall plan to get out of Vietnam with honor. Then he told me how important it was that we leave with honor in the eyes of our allies and the rest of the world.

I left that meeting admiring the man more than ever. This was the kind of courage I had come to respect in my former boss, Senator Thurmond.

When the curtain went up in the Cambodian invasion, the antiwar rockets burst all over the White House and in the national news media. At the White House we prepared to fight back with all our resources.

The executive officer in our fortress was again Haldeman. By May 19 it was beginning to look like a wise decision to rational folks. So Haldeman, as these excerpts from two of his memos show, exhorted us to score points for the president's decision.

As the success of the Cambodian operation becomes known, our opposition will be out to distort and play it down.

We need to work on admissions by some of our most skeptical supporters that "perhaps the President was right. It is an obvious success." There are good political reasons for some of those off the reservation now to start adopting this line. Pickings will be slim, most likely, but the rewards are there.

□ □ □

Last week everyone in the media was referring to "Nixon's Gamble." This is a fact that we cannot let them ever lose sight of as the success of the operation develops. Nixon's gamble was a well-calculated decision and the gamble turned out to be a sure bet. We should make reference to "what some considered to be a gamble by the President." This point can be used to counter those who feel the President would have acted short of knowledge or in an ill- advised way. It was a safe bet and the President had the facts.

The Cambodian decision was never accepted by some, but it was generally regarded as a decision which would ultimately accomplish Nixon's aim of shortening the war and keeping the Vietnamization program on schedule. Enemy supplies and equipment were considerably destroyed with the heavy and surprise attacks.

The antiwar reaction at home caused more problems in domestic disorders. There was the Kent State incident and the masses of youngsters trying to invade the White House and its premises.

The growing antiwar sentiment also caused a rash of disloyalty within the ranks of key national security government employees. As Nixon and Kissinger continued the war instead of totally withdrawing, more and more news stories began appearing in the news media revealing top secret papers and plans of the National Security Council. The *Washington Post* and the *New York Times* led the way in publishing the leaks.

These leaks were of much concern to the president and Kissinger. Twice I watched the two explode in anger over the leaks at 1969 senior White House staff meetings. I could understand their concerns. Nixon was sincerely determined to end our involvement in Vietnam also, but in what we at the White House considered to be the only right, realistic, and honorable way. it would take longer, but it would last longer and would serve to preserve our own long-range vital interests in coping with the Communist aims for making Communists of the USA and finally all the world. The difference between "us" and "them" was that we believed there was a Communist aim centered in the Soviet Union to make the world Communist by any practical means whereas "they"—the leakers and demonstrators—believed that all we had to fear was fear itself.

The idea in the White House—which I then shared and still do—was that the president was having to fight the Vietnam War on two fronts—in Southeast Asia and in Washington, D.C. Paranoid or not, this was the correct view. The Communists—wherever they were, in Vietnam, China, the Soviet Union, or Washington—knew we had a soft Achilles' heel at home so they counted on victory in the villages and hamlets of Southeast Asia. Sometimes I was convinced the danger of our losing was more in the streets and news media here than in the jungles and rice paddies of Vietnam.

This concern by Nixon and Kissinger was responsible in large part for the White House decision to set up the infamous plumbers unit to plug WH news leaks and ultimately to blunder into Democratic National Committee headquarters at the Watergate.

On October 23, 1975, Nixon was quoted by the Associated Press as saying at his San Clemente home that other presidents had used the FBI and CIA to do their dirty work.

What he meant, I believe, was that the congressional hearings on the CIA and FBI have now shown how both intelligence units were used by previous presidents to accomplish what the administration leaders deemed to be their essential "black bag" jobs, such as wiretapping, embassy break-ins, and mail surveillance.

When J. Edgar Hoover was in his prime, he performed his "black bag" jobs with skill and without discovery. No one would question the FBI director's actions. So with Hoover there was undercover expertise and security.

However, when Nixon came to the White House the president-Hoover relationship of previous years soon became strained and suspect. One would think the opposite would be true since Nixon and Hoover had for years been staunch anti-Communist allies. However, the problem was with Hoover's aging process, increasing dotage, and his firm determination to hold on to his czarist position atop the powerful and efficient FBI.

One of Hoover's top men, who will remain anonymous, used to complain privately to me that "the director sits in his office and naps for three hours in the middle of the day and nothing of any importance can be decided or ordered during that dotage time." The president and his top aides dealing with the FBI were aware of this problem. Thus the president and the attorney general had tried unsuccessfully to coax the "old bulldog" into retiring. All they had succeeded in doing was stepping on Hoover's ego to the point where they became very suspect in his eyes, and he became very unreliable in theirs.

Hoover's number two man, William Sullivan, had warned the White House that Hoover might blackmail them on the wiretaps and other security surveillance projects.

Thus the ultimate decision was reached to plug the leaks with the plumbers unit led by Gordon Liddy and Howard Hunt.

This was one of the worst decisions made in the Nixon Administration. Liddy was a one-time FBI agent whose views were to the right of Ghengis Khan. He was a daredevil ideologue—a horrible choice, but a loyal one, as America was later to learn. Hunt was another ideologue with much more experience, but with Liddy as his commander and not the top brass at CIA. Sitting on top of Liddy and Hunt were Egil (Bud) Krogh and David Young, two fine young men, and on top of them was Ehrlichman. The problem with this organization was that it was being directed and supervised by rank amateurs in the area of covert activities, except for Hunt.

Had Hoover been in his prime—when there was no dotage problem and the FBI was unassailable, as in the 1950s and early 1960s—the covert activities of the Nixon Administration would have been handled with aplomb and without discovery—as in the previous administrations. This does not mean it would have been right, only that, like his predecessors, Nixon might have survived intact as president. Thus Watergate can rightfully be assessed as having been born from these human frailties: anxiety, fear, egomania, dotage, poor judgment, rank amateurism, and ultimately improper conduct.

In his book, *Before the Fall,* Bill Safire gives a revealing insight into Nixon's feelings about the South. Safire was preparing a speech Nixon expected to give at Stone Mountain, Georgia, but which the vice-president finally delivered.

Safire relates this conversation with the president on the night (May 9) he visited with demonstrating students at the Lincoln Memorial (page 203):

> "All this business up here, it'll work out okay," the President said. "If the crazies try anything, we'll clobber them—relax, whenever I say anything like that, it drives people up the wall, I know. The country's been through a terrible experience this week. We've got to do the right thing, and we will.
>
> "In Cambodia, we had to give an important answer to an important challenge. Oh, it's easy to flyspeck it, and they will, but you've

got to do the right thing. We're trying all we can to bring this war to an end, but what's right is right. What are you doing in Atlanta?" When I reminded him, he said, "You know, my father's grandfather is buried down there. My father's father was born after his father was killed in the Civil War.

"That's a good speech Agnew is giving down there," he said. "I wrote it myself." Puzzled, I looked into the phone. The President chuckled, "You helped. You know, I believe in all this—my mother's grandfather ran an underground railroad. When I was a kid, it was easy to hate Robert E. Lee and Davis and Jackson. For 115 years, most Americans have been taught that all those guys down South were sons of bitches. But Robert E. Lee was the greatest general we ever had, and Jackson the greatest division commander. Davis was not to be compared to Lincoln, but he was a good man.

"In this speech, I was trying to show how we are one people. I'm the goddamndest desegregationist there is, but it has to be done the right way. We mustn't ever give any indication that we don't care about the South, about their feelings. We've got to care.

"This Southern Strategy stuff—all we're doing is treating the South with the same respect as the North. But your friends in New York won't see it that way."

These comments by the president sum up the numerous remarks he made to me about his feelings for the South and its position of being persecuted by the same people who also disliked him.

Another thing Nixon appreciated about the South was the support southern legislators gave him on Capitol Hill in many of his legislative fights, especially on national security, foreign policy, and Vietnam issues. Nothing meant more to Nixon, so he did not forget their support.

On October 20, 1971, I got the following memo from Bob Haldeman:

It should be clearly understood in our political planning for next year that there is to be no Presidential opposition to any of the House Democrats who voted with us on the Mansfield Amendment vote yesterday.

The President wants to be sure that he is not led into doing any thing against any of those people who have supported us on Vietnam. I will ask Clark MacGregor to make up the list of 40-50 that fall into this category.

We should be sure that no commitment is made in any way, shape, or form to any Republican candidate, that is set up to oppose these people. This includes pictures with the President or anything of that sort.

On October 28, 1971, a second memo arrived. It listed 76 Democratic legislators we were to leave "unmolested" in the 1972 election. They were rated according to six Vietnam votes, one in 1970 and five in 1971. The contents read:

Attached is a memo from Bill Timmons which contains the list of House Democrats that voted with us on the Mansfield Amendment. As you can see, there are 76 names—a few more than had been expected—nevertheless, the President wants to be sure that there is no Presidential opposition to any of these Congressmen. No commitments should be made to any Republican candidate that will oppose these people (i.e., picture with the President, meetings with the President, etc.)

We carried out the orders, by and large. Republican leaders around the country did not like Nixon's actions in laying off the Vietnam War friends of the president. However, they did not have to get his Republican programs through to an overwhelmingly Democratic Congress, and they did not have to account to today's population and future generations on the outcome of the Vietnam War and its effects on U.S. standing in the world. To Nixon, the consequences of his Vietnam policies meant almost everything.

The next big event on Vietnam came on May 8, 1972, when the president made one of the toughest decisions any president has ever been called upon to make. The president had been to Red China in the interest of "world peace with honor" and now he was getting ready to go to Russia for the second major summit meeting in 1972. To do anything rash at this point would be considered the height of folly by diplomats, the liberal press, and the ivory tower professors. It was a difficult time for them with "ole anti-commie Tricky Dick" off and running with their ball toward détente with the Communist powers. This was the dirtiest trick of all! Maybe there really and finally was a new Nixon. Could it be? Hardly.

And they were proved right on the night of May 8 when Nixon appeared on national TV, again on the subject of Vietnam. They had grown tired of Nixon's Vietnam addresses—always talking of troop withdrawals and then some type tough action against Communists, like the 1970 incursion into Cambodia, the bombing of North Vietnam, and now this new anti-Communist Nixon action.

On the evening of May 8, President Nixon announced he had taken the audacious—and courageous—action of dropping mines in the Haiphong (North Korea) harbor.

The *Washington Post* screamed editorially that this would mean an end to détente and probably the beginning of the big war. This was one of the harshest denunciations the *Post* had ever put on Nixon.

This set the tone for widespread, vitriolic antiwar reaction to the Nixon action.

The following evening the president called me seeking some political information. Richard Nixon never stood taller with the South and me than on that evening, and I told him so.

When the operator told me the president was calling, I opened the conversation by telling him I considered this the greatest, wisest, and most courageous decision any president had ever made. I repledged my loyalty and gratitude.

Naturally, he was pleased. He told me, "This was a very lonely decision. Only Agnew and Connally favored it. Everyone else was opposed."

The reaction was divided, but the president never flinched, and his bold ploy worked. True to form, the Communists wilted in the face of determination, and the Moscow summit came off as planned. The Nixon determination paid off with the successful exit of American troops soon thereafter—all in an honorable fashion.

Later, in December 1972, the president made another courageous Vietnam decision. He decided to bomb North Vietnam when they backed off their agreement to let us leave with honor. There was hardly anyone on his side at the upper levels of government, but he was right again. After his "wild" decision, American prisoners of war came home in early 1973 singing his praises. He had understood the Reds, and he had gotten his way—an end to American involvement in Vietnam without surrender and with the return of American boys. Richard Nixon rose to a new high in public favor and opinion polls.

In Dixie he ranked higher than he had in November when he won the whole South with an average vote of 70 percent.

This was underscored when the president was given a hero's reception by the public and the South Carolina General Assembly when he visited Columbia, South Carolina, to thank the people of South Carolina for their staunch support of his Vietnam policies. His address to the Democratic legislature was punctuated with strong applause on numerous occasions.

This presidential visit to Dixie to express gratitude for faith in his Vietnam policies pointed up the importance of the South's support to his hard-line Vietnam position.

9

CREEP– From Perfection to Disaster

T he 1972 campaign for reelection of the president of the United States was underway from the time the Nixon team entered the White House in January 1969, unlike the Ford campaign of 1976, Nixon's planning began in earnest in late 1970 and early 1971.

The 1970 election was to set the stage for 1972 by electing to Congress more Republicans with whom the president could work in getting his programs enacted into law. We succeeded only partially, picking up three Senate seats and holding our House losses to twelve, less than the losses normally expected in an off-year election.

The first two years of the Nixon Administration had not seen great progress for the Nixon legislative program. The Congress was controlled by the Democratic leadership, and they wanted the White House back. They yearned for the emoluments of office that had been theirs for seven of the past nine presidential terms of office.

And then, too, when the only Republican president had occupied the Oval Office in that 26-year period from 1932 to 1968, he had been on friendly terms with the late Senate Majority Leader Lyndon Johnson and the late House Speaker Sam Rayburn, both of Texas. This president was Dwight D. Eisenhower also of Texas and an American war hero. This was a lucky break for the Grand Old Party. This too would pass. And in 1960 it did.

To staunch Democrats Nixon was the partisan, feared, and hated Eisenhower veep. They defeated him in a presidential squeaker in the 1960 election. In 1962, the "villain" had been buried even deeper in his political grave with a humiliating gubernatorial drubbing in his home state of California. Nixon had coined his own bitter political epitaph when he told a group of reporters after his loss: "You won't have Richard Nixon to kick around anymore."

The Democratic leaders rejoiced. Only all that changed suddenly in the early morning hours of November 6, 1968, when "Tricky Dick" rose from his political grave and narrowly defeated Vice President Hubert H. Humphrey for the presidency.

Thus when Richard Nixon took the oath of office on January 20, 1969, as the thirty-seventh president he was not just another Republican "imposter" occupying the Democratic White House. Nixon was the "enemy imposter" to some.

Since Watergate, the public has been led to believe that only Nixon and his team were political antagonists with "enemies." Except for most Republicans and a small group of objective Democrats, particularly southern Democrats, Richard Nixon was considered the "enemy," or something approximating that.

Thus President Nixon got short shrift from the Congress, the breeding ground of Democratic presidential hopefuls. Not even Nixon felt secure in his reelection prospects for 1972 until the Democratic convention again bestowed a gigantic favor on their No. 1 GOP enemy. In 1968 all the riots and disarray at the Democratic convention had given Nixon a campaign lead he almost lost, save for the southern strategy. In 1972 the Democratic convention delegates gave Nixon the answer to his prayer—the nomination of Senator George McGovern. *Time* magazine quoted me in its issue of July 10, 1972, as expressing the fond hope this way: "Some of the people here (White House) are about to wee-wee in their pants waiting for him (McGovern) to get the nomination."

So as far as anyone could see in 1969, 1970, and 1971, and for the first half of 1972, Nixon was vulnerable to being a one-term president.

While there had been little thought of unseating the popular Eisenhower in the 1956 election there was more Democratic hope in ousting the less popular Nixon in 1972.

No one realized the limitations of his tenuous hold on public opinion more than Nixon himself. Using his hands, he had told his staff in 1969: "The ones (battles) we'll win will be by that much (very close), and the ones we'll lose will be by that much (very close)."

Thus the outline of the strategy for the 1972 campaign was initiated at Key Biscayne in December 1970.

In response to criticism the White House had received for its extensive involvement in the 1970 congressional election, the White House was to be depoliticized." The late Murray Chotiner had been brought into the White House to help with the 1970 campaign effort. Now he was to go. But I was to stay and keep a low profile on politics. I would continue as liaison with all GOP groups and with special attention to southern strategy.

Colson would now move into Herb Klein's area of communications in order to implement the tough PR job the nice Klein would not handle. Also Colson would dart in and out of my area as well, wherever the hard line might lead, such as injecting a harder line in the Republican National Committee publication, First Monday, or trying to convince the national chairman to make some hard-hitting statement.

Klein and I were not tough enough to deal with the many chores of "rock 'em and sock 'em" politics. Klein chafed under the Colson intrusions because they were many and demeaning. With me, they were less frequent, and these involved the Haldeman-type directives I never liked. Most were what we called "Mickey Mouse fire drills." Many assignments were never carried out, or if they were, they were mainly eyewash to satisfy the hard-line guys, whom I considered to be the president, Haldeman, and Colson.

Some of us would laugh about all the "Keystone Kop" capers and wonder when anyone or all might blow the roof off the White House. These were what I looked upon as "cute" tactics in politics. My years in politics had taught me that "cuteness" was counter productive. I had once been burned with a special edition of a scandal sheet in the 1966 South Carolina election. It was full of "cuteness," and while it may have influenced some votes, it cost others. Most of all, I became personally ashamed of the "cute" sheet.

Everything of this nature I had seen at the White House was not of a criminal nature—just "Mickey Mouse" antics, mostly vindictive in nature, that only served to harass the "enemy" to the amusement of the hard-liners. It constituted a little fudging, retaliation, or public lobbying on various special issues. It was all designed to make that small difference between victory and defeat, or to satisfy a presidential, Haldeman, or Colson desire to punish an enemy or score points.

Much of the "Mickey Mouse" routine was run through Colson's public lobbying shop, through Jeb Magruder, or through the RNC on orders of Colson. Colson naturally received cooperation in his shop and also from Magruder, who knew the real source of all the anxieties, the orders, and the "go get 'em" atmosphere. Magruder was a young man who could create, understand, and exploit opportunities. The way to advance in the Nixon White House was wrapped up in the success of Haldeman and Colson—machismo, show your loyalty by playing hard-ball politics.

I never had any reason to feel the president questioned my loyalty. However, I was never quite certain about Haldeman since I did not gee-gaw fully to the HRH hard line. I felt I was not considered by Haldeman to be fully reliable—that is, an unquestioning loyalist.

However, I felt secure at the White House because of my standing with the president. He complimented me on many occasions in Haldeman's presence. And what Nixon approved was fairly sacred so far as Haldeman was concerned.

Even when I would commit a faux pas the president was most understanding and forgiving of me.

One Sunday afternoon in 1969, the president found me working in my East Wing office. This was immediately following the settlement of the Charleston Hospital strike. He thanked me for my role. I accepted the compliment and then tried to apologize for a bad headline in the *Washington Post* on my first talk to a closed door session of the Republican National Committee. The Republicans were angry about patronage limitations, and Peter Flanigan felt I had done a good job cooling them off with my comments about how political the new president was going to be. So the headline by the eavesdropping *Post* read "Dent Calls Nixon Most Political President Ever."

The president let me know that if the *Post* was down on me I was making points with him. He said, "Forget it. It's just a flash in the pan. Like most bad stories, it'll be forgotten in a few weeks."

Our relationship continued to be good while I was in the White House. We seemed to click together on politics and philosophy, and he was very complimentary on the job I was doing on the side with the South—before and since the 1968 election. He let me know I could get through to him immediately on any sensitive matter affecting the South and politics. But I used discretion lest I kill that good entré.

Haldeman and Ehrlichman knew of my favorable standing with the president, so regardless of their views on Harry Dent, they never gave me a "hard time" as they did others. Of course, I tried not to earn their enmity. But everyone in the White House knew of their clout, and I know of no one who was not affected by knowledge of that clout. Some staffers caught heavy flak from Haldeman and Ehrlichman. A nasty memo was tough to take because all staffers realized "the Germans" spoke for the president.

In a memo dated October 16, 1970, Haldeman made this point to me when he wrote, "Any guidance I ever give . . . comes direct from RN."

I always felt a certain confidence in my tenure not only because I stood in well at the top, but because of the support of Mitchell and Harlow and the fact that I was about the only staffer with a real constituency—the South.

My presence at the White House was fairly well known in the South— thanks to the news media. If Nixon and company kicked me out, many Southerners could come to the conclusion they were kicking out the South. The press would surely play it that way, and gladly so.

However, while I used discretion, I did speak up in meetings and stated my objections even to ideas advanced by "the Germans" when I thought they were unwise or unpolitic. And there was much of that—ideas or actions that did not seem realistic, wise, or politically smart.

To voice objections was not wise either. I lost points from time to time, but I counted on my southern indispensability to keep me afloat in such situations.

When Haldeman would overrule my point, I would fall in line except where I had dire concern about the proposed action. Many of us at the White House questioned instructions where we could. Sometimes we would say "yeah, yeah" and then let it slide.

Unlike most of the others, I had two routes around Haldeman and Ehrlichman: Harlow and Mitchell could make the better connection because no one had better entré to the president than "Big John" except Haldeman. Mitchell would talk to the president during the day and almost every night on the telephone. He was very much a heavyweight with the president.

After I would tell Mitchell about the developing Haldeman problem, it would disappear. He usually handled the problem over the telephone on a nightly chat with the president. The problem would usually arise over some rash order the president might issue in a moment of anger. Haldeman seemingly carried out the order or perceived wish with a strong reaction. He was *very* loyal to the president, and when the president did not like someone or some action, Haldeman seemed to dislike the person or idea even more. He had tunnel vision—he saw things substantially one way—his and Nixon's way. He was not too realistic, and he was dogmatic. On the other hand, the president was the most realistic person I have ever known. Yet he could be very bombastic privately when his ire was stirred. I considered some of that to be a cover-up for a personality deficiency. He was articulate at locker room talk and he seemingly enjoyed the idea of wielding the power of the presidency—not unlike his predecessors. What I saw and learned through other staffers indicated he was not nearly as tough as LBJ. Nixon seemed about normal for a man with so much power.

Clearly, the president realized every battle would be close, and he had made a point of making his staff aware of this.

What this meant to us was that we had to fight every battle with everything we had in order for our chief to win. Haldeman was particularly sensitive to this Nixon concern. Excerpts from this column by the late Stewart Alsop in the April 9, 1974, issue of *Newsweek* sum up Nixon's desire to succeed as I perceived this battlecry:

> The President had, and always has had, one unvarying characteristic—an almost ungovernable impulse to indulge in supererogation. He has a compulsion to go too far, to try too hard, to press as the athletes say, when he ought to hang loose.
>
> In the 1934 Whittier College yearbook there is an easily recognizable photograph of a skinny football player with a ski-jump

nose and a do-or-die expression. Nixon was, by all accounts, a terrible football player—he was used as a sort of animated tackling bag by the better players, and he hardly ever got into a game. When he did, a football lineman who was a Nixon classmate once told me: "I always braced myself for those 5-yard penalties. Dick was so eager he'd be offside just about every play."

The supererogatory impulse that took the young Nixon off side about every play had been a hallmark of the President's career. The "old Nixon" was given to rather sleazy debating tricks ("Isn't it wonderful, finally to have a Secretary of State who isn't taken in by the Communists?"). This sort of thing was not worth a vote to him—in fact, the memory of the "old Nixon" probably elected John Kennedy in 1960. So the things the President said and did in the "rocking, socking" campaigns of his youth seem less a matter of cool calculation than of impulse, of some inner necessity.

These days, the supererogatory impulse takes a somewhat different form. It had repeatedly led him to go too far, to exaggerate each achievement in such a way as to leave him vulnerable later. He called the Apollo 11 flight "the greatest week in the history of the world since the Creation."

He called the Smithsonian agreement (which subsequently collapsed) "the most significant monetary agreement in the history of the world." He had endlessly reiterated that the settlement in Vietnam, a major achievement for which he deserves much credit, is "peace with honor."

A President with a supererogatory impulse attracts around him people with a similar impulse to overdo, to press, to indulge in the superfluous. Charles Colson cannot have helped much with the grandmother vote, when he said that "I would walk over my grandmother if necessary" to insure Nixon's re-election, but the remark was typical enough of a lot of over-eager young men in the Nixon entourage.

□ □ □

There is a sadness here. President Nixon is an intelligent, able, hard-working man who, as Walter Lippman said recently, has "done pretty well" at playing a "disagreeable role . . . imposed upon him by historical necessity." In some ways, he has done better than that. The extrication from Vietnam, the détente with the Communist powers, were great achievements. Yet the big things he had done may all be obscured by a silly, tawdry and purposeless exercise in political supererogation.

This "supererogatory" bent paved the way for the Watergate problems. It was telegraphed down the line from the president through Haldeman to the advance men types. In his book, *Breach of Faith*, Theodore White captures the advance man mentality at the White House and its impact on the Nixon downfall.

There was no higher honor in Nixon's White House than to have been an advance man in the 1968 campaign under Haldeman and Ehrlichman. It was akin but not analogous to being in the OSS of World War II fame or the CIA. These were the daring young men who made things happen on presidential travels so that everything would fall in line and "the Boss" would return home elated over the wildly cheering mobs who greeted him along the way.

They were much like the side show barkers—they drummed up the crowds and stuck the placards in the hands of enthusiastic supporters to be waved before the TV cameras. With them just about anything was justified in the game of advancing the "Big Man's" political fortunes.

These modern-day John the Baptists would roll into a city several days in advance of the presidential or campaign visit and take over direction of all activities and planning. They would rent several motel rooms, install phone banks, and put volunteers to work rousing crowds and preparing leaflets, confetti, and staged demonstrations of enthusiastic support. As an example, when President Nixon paraded through Atlanta in the 1972 campaign tour, advance men had Bo Callaway prepare and dump tons of confetti on thousands of watchers and all over Peachtree Street. At the close of the 1968 campaign, a sharp advance man, "Rally" John Nidecker, put the much publicized Nixon inaugural theme "Bring Us Together" into the hands of young Vickie Cole who gained instant fame from the famous placard.

With Haldeman, only the advance man types were to be substantially trusted. They comprised the secret honor guard, so to speak, and they were sprinkled all through the reelection campaign. To rate at the top with Haldeman, it was vital to have come from southern California and to have been an advance man in the 1968 campaign or at the White House.

Teddy White describes the advance man in this appropriate fashion (pages 87 and 88):

> But "advance men" are the king's lancers, his companions of battle; for them, politics is the bloodless equivalent of war.
>
> Every political system has advance men—perhaps every animal system had advance men, for both animals and men are clusterers. Those who can cluster together in groups survive, while the scattered solitaries die out; and in any human group, the leader, the politician, needs advance men to call people into clusters. In Communist countries, advance men are organized in what they call "agit-prop" brigades. In England's Parliamentary system, the parties have "constituency agents" who call voters to cluster to hear the parties' candidates. Peter the Hermit, who preached at the fairs of medieval France, was the advance man of the Crusades—the recruiting sergeant of an idea. But whatever advance men are called, whether they practice their craft as hobbyists, dedicated advocates or professionals, their function is the same: to race the blood, heat up the consciousness, mobilize emotions so that crowds eventually gather—in some countries to storm the palace, in democracies to pour votes into the polls. And all advance men are wired together into the central purpose of politics—which is the pursuit of power, the control of events. Much has changed in the professionalization of politics in the past twenty years—specialists can organize telephone banks more efficiently than the old party regulars; direct-mail technicians can deliver a message scientifically to precisely sensitive cross-sections better than the old leaflet men; television producers can mold or carve the image of a candidate in thirty- or sixty-second spots better than the old-fashioned two-hour speech. But the advance man remains an anthropologically distinct species, the generator of the direct excitement of an American campaign.
>
> To be an advance man is great fun. Campaign headquarters sometimes attract young businessmen who get three to six months' leave from their corporations; Democrats sometimes enlist young labor leaders who know the proper factory gates and the union halls where workingmen cluster; both parties like young lawyers. For all of these types, politics is the adventure of a season. "It's a once in-a-lifetime deal," said John Whitaker, the most respected of the Nixon advance men. "They burn out. Advance men have to be over twenty-five and under thirty-eight."

White says some advance men of early U.S. political campaigns moved on into the White House themselves, such as James Madison, Martin Van Buren, and Chester A. Arthur (page 91).

Some of us in the White House would wonder together and individually when or if the White House roof would ever blow off with some wild scheme, instruction, or decision to fudge ahead.

We particularly scratched our heads over the entry and rise of Colson in the summer of 1969. Colson, now a different person through his religious conversion, was then a walking political TNT looking for a place to detonate. Advance the "Ole Man" at any price was his credo.

I watched as Colson surpassed me in WH clout based in large part on his hard-ball political machinations. He turned out to be tougher than Nixon's old-time friend and first campaign manager, Murray Chotiner. I discovered this in the 1970 congressional election.

Chotiner was brought into the White House to help with an effort to elect more Republicans to the U.S. Senate to help the president get his programs through the Congress. Almost every Capitol Hill battle was uphill for us because the Democratic majorities predominated so heavily. In addition, the Senate was more liberal than the House, where we could win battles because of the GOP-southern Democratic coalition and more basic conservative composition.

In our efforts to win several more Senate seats, I concentrated on helping the southern and southwestern campaigns and Colson looked after the Northeast.

Word came down through Haldeman that we needed to convince certain GOP Senate candidates to run two sets of campaign ads in support of their campaigns. One set was very negative against the incumbent Democrat and another set was positive, showing the GOP candidate to be in support of Nixon policies.

Colson was selected to handle the project. However, Chotiner and I were consulted by Colson on the ads as drawn by an outside PR group. When Chotiner and I saw the proposed ads we objected that the negative ads would be counterproductive. They were too hard-ball in nature. Our objections were not given consideration by Colson, so I carried my protest to Haldeman, where I was told the ads would be run as drawn and planned. I could tell I was losing points with Haldeman.

Then Chotiner and I were ordered to sell the ads to the candidates. We ran into chilly receptions, even though the candidates were told the outside sponsoring group headed by D.C. Republican leader, Carl Shipley, would provide the funding. I reported back to Colson and Haldeman that the candidate reception was adverse and that they would rather have the ad committee give them the money to use as they might desire.

That evening Colson came over to my office and in effect took over the phone calling and sales project, pushing the ads on various candidates.

Later, after the ads were run, the operation was deemed less than a success, the outside ad committee was traced back to Colson, and I came to the conclusion I had been overtaken in clout by Colson.

Chotiner was returned to the outside world against his wishes, and I was moved from the East Wing of the White House to the Old Executive Office Building.

I am convinced this resistance on my part to hard-ball politics set the judgment in place that Harry Dent was not to be relied upon for hard-ball and/or covert missions. It concerned me at the time, but gave me much consolation during the period from 1973 to 1975.

Mitchell understood the problem at the White House. This was what he meant in the Senate Watergate hearings when he referred time and again to the "White House Horrors." Mitchell forced himself to get along with Haldeman, Ehrlichman, and Colson. However, he got along less well with Ehrlichman, and much less well with Colson. He considered them to be unpolitic and unwise. Yet the three White House heavies respected Mitchell's special clout with the president.

Mitchell had little political experience—only in part of the 1968 campaign—but he possessed sound judgment. This is why Mitchell could be so persuasive with the president. He was *the* senior counselor over all. But he was not the closest aide to the president. This was Haldeman, even over Haldeman's close associate and friend of long standing—Ehrlichman.

A close friend of mine with personal insight observed the inner workings of the Haldeman office for a year. And as he told me:

> The President would dictate his answers to memos and pending decisions and dictate ideas occurring to him in his own private think sessions in the Lincoln Room late in the evening. When Haldeman would visit the President first thing in the morning, he would pick up the tapes for transcription. Once they were transcribed, Haldeman would prepare action or talking papers. If the President wanted the senior staff or any group to get certain instructions, Haldeman would call a meeting and work from his "talking papers." The talking papers would be Nixon's memos over

Haldeman's name and/or from Haldeman's mouth virtually word for word.

Sometimes I would be told in advance exactly what was to be discussed in the meeting. Sure enough, it would turn out that way. I had the additional benefit of knowing that while it was the voice of Haldeman, it was the mind of Nixon. Of course, we all realized Haldeman spoke for the "Big Man." However, few realized how exactly Haldeman spoke for the President."

Haldeman surrounded himself with young men who had no stature except that which he gave them, and "gave them" he did. Gordon Strachan and Larry Higby were good examples. They and other Haldeman troopers were nicknamed "the Beaver Patrol." When they called others of us on the telephone we felt it was like talking to Haldeman because we knew he handed them the instructions to pass out, and they followed orders exactly—or else. It was a joke. Harlow, with all his clout, wisdom, and Washington experience, would chuckle about getting his marching orders from "General" Higby.

Haldeman delegated only to trusted aides and evidently only to those he could order around and dress down with impunity. He was rough on them, but they relished their roles because they knew they were where the action was and were transmitting orders from the major domo.

Higby and Strachan gave some of us inferiority complexes because they often knew more inside information than those of us with bigger jobs and titles. Haldeman was very secretive, and people around him knew only what they had to know. However, the Beaver Patrol saw almost all, and while they had little rank, they carried considerable authority—at least by proximity, which at the White House connotes power.

From the first day in the White House Haldeman stressed his theme of unswerving loyalty to our commander in chief. He told staffers we were fortunate to be working for "the most important man in the world" and that we owed him our "utmost in loyalty or we could find another job now." He said we were the president's personal staff and that we were the only people responsible only to the president. We, he said, were unlike the Cabinet. We were confirmed by no once except the president, thus our loyalty had to be 100 percent.

In that first meeting in 1969, Haldeman also told how to write memos, which would be the principal means of communicating with the top men at the White House and the president. We were told to be concise, but clear, leaving nothing to the imagination and that everything was covered by executive privilege. Then "executive privilege" was explained briefly to us as the right of the president to maintain the secrecy of his communications with his White House aides. This assurance gave us a feeling of security—only to find four years later the privilege was to be ripped away and all our memos and taped conversations were laid bare to the Watergate investigators.

I left the meeting feeling an even greater sense of loyalty, although I already was prepared to give my loyalty to the commander in chief.

I liked all these people—the big and little staffers—and did my best to have good relationships with them. I understood their roles and accepted their authoritarian actions. For instance, many griped about the actions of the so-called "Palace Guard" in limiting access to the president. I knew this was on orders of the president, and I realized the necessity. After all, everyone in Washington and everywhere else for that matter wanted to have access as much as possible. There was something magical about basking in the limelight of the president's presence. Mitchell was the only person I ever heard complain about it, and I never believed him.

Harlow explained to me there had to be a tough traffic cop in Haldeman's position, although the tough cop crowded Harlow, too. Harlow was with President Eisenhower for his two terms, and he is one of the wisest and most likeable people in Washington.

Haldeman did not have time to explain every order and action. He believed in Richard Nixon and his will and welfare. Everything else paled in significance. Perhaps his greatest problem was his intense loyalty and second, his lack of realism. He was not an evil person as has been implied. He was loyal to his family, had good personal habits, and was a very efficient action man. He was a patriotic person with strong convictions about his country. On visiting Haldeman in 1975 I found him to be still convinced his actions in the White House were in the interest of his patriotic cause. His first public show of humility and submission came in 1977 when he was reporting to the federal prison facility at Lompoc, California.

Ehrlichman was much like Haldeman. Both seemed arrogant to many, but their positions and duties dictated a certain amount of authoritarianism. He was more realistic than Haldeman and probably deeper. He was to the left of Haldeman and more flexible ideologically. Ehrlichman was a moderate and would have shown it more in another crowd. Also a Christian Scientist, he was a good family man, with good personal habits. He was a Boy Scout adult leader and also patriotic and loyal to his president.

When I first moved into the White House I was assigned to Ehrlichman's staff.

Under Ehrlichman, one of my assignments was reading FBI reports on people being considered for appointment to Nixon jobs. This was most interesting. The reports pictured the subject as though he were naked in the bathroom with J. Edgar Hoover peeking in. They contained every bit of gossip and innuendo a person's friends and enemies have to say about him. It seemed from the amount of material collected that people evidently feel they must tell everything they suspect.

Many people think erroneously that the FBI decides whether a person is fit for appointment, which is not true. Usually, an assigned White House aide reads all the input on a subject, then determines from the overall picture whether the subject poses any danger if appointed. The FBI director may make some pertinent points in a cover letter, but ultimately, the decision belongs to the appointing authority, the president, or to whomever he delegates the authority.

Of all the White House Watergate characters, Ehrlichman seems to have paid the heaviest price in penal sentences, in loss of family, in legal indebtedness, and in personal shame and humiliation. As he reports, he took himself down to "ground zero" and rethought his philosophy and life. From a ranking Nixon square he turned appearance wise into a lowly hippie type.

In winning a reduction in his prison sentence, along with Haldeman and Mitchell, Ehrlichman made the most candid confession when he told Judge John Sirica: "I abdicated my moral judgments and turned them over to someone else."

Haldeman and Ehrlichman both knew they had to fight tough and hard to win those close battles.

Colson was tough, efficient, and a mite on the ruthless side, and brazenly and openly so. He was considered the "bad guy" and "evil genius." But even Colson was not all that bad. He just fought harder and with more weapons to win. Now he has had a true Christian conversion, and he is gentle as a lamb. I told Colson in 1976 while he was visiting in my home, "Chuck, I'm convinced your born again experience is for real. Watergate is the best thing that ever happened to you." He agreed.

Looking back on the reactions of all the top Nixon associates caught up in the web of Watergate, Colson clearly fared best. I have wondered how Nixon's fate might have been changed had he followed the Colson course and experience. His enemies would never have forgiven him regardless of God's reaction.

Mitchell was not nearly so tough as he was pictured. He was really quite nervous. He was more liberal on some matters than perceived. His strong suit was judgment and caution. He was my friend, and I liked him and worked in part as his eyes and ears at the White House.

I once offered to leave the White House and work for him at Justice. He was the big political man in the Administration, yet he used little political help at Justice, although his deputy, Richard Kleindienst, was experienced in this field. Mitchell used Kleindienst to help administer the department.

Mitchell had four big jobs—attorney general, senior adviser to the president, political boss second only to Nixon (and Haldeman through Nixon), and husband of Martha Mitchell. Had he the proper help, he would not have the problems he has today. The record is clear he turned down Jeb Magruder's entreaties to adopt Gordon Liddy's operational plan twice and apparently, with reluctance, agreed to a scaled-down version on the third conference. He knew better, but he evidently realized the pressures to get that type work accomplished. It proved to be the worst decision of his life, if indeed he did make that decision.

However, he was in poor shape at that time to make such decisions. He was still overseeing Justice to some degree, he was campaign manager for the 1972 campaign, and he had his hands full with Martha Mitchell.

The president told me twice, once in late 1972 and in early 1973, that had "Mitchell not had Martha Mitchell in his hair there would have been no Watergate."

While some may put prime blame on Mitchell, I have felt he was in part the victim, considering his problems, his position, and the strong direction the campaign was getting from the White House.

When I saw Magruder being sent in 1971 from the White House to 1701 Pennsylvania Avenue to be in effect the operating head at CREEP until Mitchell could come aboard in the spring of 1972, I knew Haldeman was putting there a Haldeman "yes" man. Magruder had efficiently tried to implement Haldeman's orders in running Klein's White House public relations shop around Klein.

I could see the same thing coming for my friend Mitchell, and I warned him. His answer was, "But, they've made it clear I'll be the boss for the 1972 campaign."

I responded, "Yes, but the president has cut Bob Haldeman loose from previous duties to handle the big political show and to schedule the president's far-flung flights for world peace in 1972."

In late 1971 the president had called me in to inform me that I should report my political information and actions to Mitchell in 1972. He said he was going to remove himself from politics to "do some big things on the world scene." He did not say what, but I gathered he believed the best politics for reelection would be little political activity by him and big accomplishments by him on the world scene. Even though this meant less basking in the presidential presence for me in 1972, I agreed with the concept.

His political participation in the campaign planning and operations was far less than usual for politically oriented Richard Nixon, who always previously tried to be his own campaign manager and strategist.

However, he wanted Haldeman to supervise Mitchell and get the tough jobs accomplished. He did not trust Mitchell to know all the "ins and outs" of campaigns because of his limited campaign experience. Besides, Nixon usually assigned two people to do the same job. Thus when it came to filling the Magruder post in the campaign, Haldeman had to use his own faithful executor of orders—no questions asked.

I almost was given the Magruder campaign assignment in the 1972 campaign. I have never seen the memo, but I have been told I was passed over by Haldeman to be the deputy campaign manager under Mitchell because I was considered "too Boy Scoutish." I had much more experience in politics and a good background in public relations work and polling. This is what Magruder handled as number two man.

However, my lack of reliability for not being a blind loyalist to Haldeman, my co-establishment of the White House Staff Prayer Breakfast Group, and my friendliness with White House news reporters made me an untrustworthy candidate for the Magruder post. For this I will ever be grateful!

Magruder was the acting director of CREEP for several months before Mitchell finally left Justice to become the full-time campaign director. Even then, Mitchell had to be only part time because of his problems with his wife Martha.

While Mitchell was still at Justice, Magruder was busy setting up the most unusual presidential campaign organization in history. For the first time, a presidential campaign was to be totally self-contained and self-sufficient. An in-house polling and advertising operation was established under Magruder's direction. This was a Haldeman idea to save money, maintain secrecy, and exercise total control over the strategy and image development.

It was determined in mid-1971 that my duties in the 1972 campaign would consist of the following: (1) continue my liaison role with all GOP groups, including the RNC, the Hill campaign committees, the Republican Governor's campaign committee, and all state GOP committees; (2) serve as a surrogate candidate for the president (to speak and hold news conferences, along with most Cabinet members and Herb Klein); (3) head the issues development committee; (4) serve as a member of Magruder's advertising and polling committee; and (5) oversee the southern campaign.

These assignments suited me better than Magruder's job. I had been speaking considerably to GOP and other groups. The 1972 campaign took me into almost every state. I ended up working in Pennsylvania and New Jersey more than the South after McGovern was nominated. However, when I would speak in the South I would proclaim a sweeping GOP victory in the presidential campaign from "the Potomac to the Pedernales" (LBJ's river in Texas).

I learned many things on my speaking tours. What amazed me most was the degree of conservatism I found outside the South in GOP ranks, especially in New England, the Upper Midwest, and in California.

I found that the more conservative I talked and the more I turned up my southern accent, the louder was the applause. Being introduced as a former Thurmond sidekick was a plus. If my introducer failed to mention the relationship, I did in my speech.

When I first entered the White House, there was a serious question whether I should appear anywhere outside the South. Finally, in late 1969, I was sent off to Albany, New York, to assure the Northeast Republican Conference that "there was not no sech a thing as a Southern Strategy in the Nixon White House." The northeastern press had played up southern strategy so much that some of our Yankee Republicans were afraid they were receiving short shrift from the Nixon Administration.

When I got through speaking, the icicles in the auditorium had melted, and I was receiving generous applause. I denied we were pursuing a strategy that put the South above the rest of the country. Rather I told them we were trying to include the South as an equal partner and that we were working toward a national strategy designed to win in all sections of the country. They accepted the idea enthusiastically. But next morning the *Boston Globe* took some wind out of my sails as the *Globe* headline appeared in the president's *Daily News Summary,* "Dent Refuses to Deny Southern Strategy: Only Calls It Winning Strategy."

Nevertheless, from then on I received speaking invitations from all over the country, and I accepted many of them. Also I attended every GOP meeting of any importance and all governors' conferences. I spent much time speaking all over the country in 1971 and especially in 1972.

These travels and visits convinced me the Republicans who do the party work, who attend meetings, who are elected delegates are largely conservatives. In the Democratic party the opposite is true—the workers and delegates are generally liberals everywhere except in the South. Thus at the local level the party workers of both parties are usually poles apart ideologically. This is why a person seeking the GOP presidential nomination must first go RIGHT and then back to the MIDDLE after the convention. This is also why the Democratic candidate must usually first go LEFT and then toward the MIDDLE to win in November. The GREAT MIDDLE is where most Americans are. Actually, they are slightly RIGHT OF CENTER. This is what Goldwater learned in 1964 and McGovern in 1972.

With the Reagan challenge, President Ford needed first to go RIGHT and then toward the MIDDLE in the general election. The proliferation of Democratic candidates in 1976 ran LEFT in the primaries, but Carter ran RIGHT realizing he could win all the conservative Democratic vote while the liberals split the majority liberal vote. Thus he proved the effective exception to the rule in 1976.

In our 1972 campaign operation, Magruder reported to both Mitchell and Haldeman. They, in turn, reported to the president. After Mitchell's exit from the campaign, following the Watergate break-in, Magruder reported to Mitchell's successor, Clark MacGregor, and Haldeman. However, MacGregor was essentially a front man as campaign manager. MacGregor, too, had been told he would be in full command when he was pulled off his White House congressional liaison duties to succeed Mitchell.

Fred Malek, White House personnel recruiter, was initially used at CREEP in a part-time capacity while continuing to be personnel chief at the White House. He had no previous political experience, but he was a management expert. No question, his boss was Haldeman. Also, Malek was from southern California. When Harry Flemming, a Mitchell man, was moved out as director of organization for CREEP, Malek moved in on a full-time basis of equal rank with Magruder. Magruder had a little more political experience than Malek, but not much. Magruder was a PR type, a southern Californian, and a Haldeman man.

Handling the special assignment tasks with Donald Segretti was personable Dwight Chapin, Nixon's appointments secretary. From southern California, Chapin was also a Haldeman man. The same was true of the

CREEP advance men, the advertising men, and almost everyone else in the top or vital CREEP positions of trust and responsibility. The CREEP operation was a Haldeman operation, and Mitchell evidently never realized his real boss was not Nixon directly, but Haldeman, his erstwhile rival.

Mitchell's top men in CREEP were limited to Fred LaRue and Bob Mardian. However, even Mardian was also from southern California.

I point all this out not in condemnation of my friend Haldeman—and I sympathize with him and his family—but rather in the interest of clearing up an unjust picture of Mitchell, also my friend.

Mitchell made mistakes, but like Agnew, he, too, was used unwittingly on his part. I would have expected Haldeman might miscalculate because of his stubborn Prussian mind and manners, but Mitchell was too careful and too wise in his judgments to initiate pranks and risky political ventures. Whatever he got caught up in was not of his own origination in the political arena.

Magruder kept pressing Mitchell on the Gordon Liddy covert budget program. The testimony shows how Mitchell resisted and deferred. Thus I have never believed, as many, based on news reports and opinions, that Mitchell was the cause of Watergate. I believe he was in part one of the victims of Watergate.

Had anyone, even Jean Dixon, told Mitchell and his wife Martha in 1970 that they soon would be divorced, Martha would die shortly thereafter, and Mitchell would be incarcerated in one of his own federal prisons—none of it would have been believable to them and to all others.

The question of Nixon's image as a leader and the potential campaign issues, both pro and con, became matters of rather constant thought and study through 1971 and 1972.

In late 1971 Magruder and I formed a Political Issues Group, consisting of top White House, RNC, and CREEP people. The purpose was twofold: to study and develop issues and to make certain aides feel they were having a part in Haldeman's campaign, even though they were not. The real action was taking place in the Magruder PR, advertising, and poll meetings on Monday evenings, and most of all, in the Mitchell and Haldeman meetings sometimes with and sometimes without the president. The Magruder-Dent meetings sent reports into Mitchell and Haldeman, but they did not lead to decision making generally. However, the Monday night meetings did.

Our Monday meetings consisted primarily of Magruder, his advertising and polling experts, Len Garment, Pat Buchanan, Fred La Rue, Bob Finch, Murray Chotiner, and me. We would have dinner, a briefing session on polling and/or advertising, and then we would discuss strategy in the preprimary and primary periods. In the preprimary and primary time frames we were concerned with soundly trouncing two GOP congressmen with presidential aims. They were Paul N. (Pete) McCloskey Jr., of California and John Ashbrook of Ohio. McCloskey was challenging us from the GOP left and Ashbrook from the GOP far right. This put Nixon right where we wanted him—in the GOP right of center. In the end, they were both good for Nixon. Our aim was to polish off both with a minimal financial outlay while we tested our advertising and polling operation for the fall campaign. For instance, we wanted to maximize use of direct mail in identical swing vote areas of key cities and communities. We also planned to use TV to maximum advantage at the lowest possible outlay. We would aim some TV spots at certain areas and localize other spots in other areas. The same was true for our newspaper advertising. So all this took a certain amount of trial and error.

Thus the primaries were a blessing to Nixon. CREEP scored very well, tested ideas, and expended minimal funds from the biggest political war chest ever raised—thanks to Maurice Stans, Lee Nunn, and the other CREEP finance experts.

In New Hampshire, with the president working solely for world peace, the Nixon campaign took the measure of our two opponents with 69 percent of the vote. In Florida, where Ashbrook should have scored his best, we rolled up 89 percent with no presidential involvement. And the Nixon-Ashbrook battle, plus the busing referendum, helped George Wallace win a big Florida victory. Governor Reuben Askew of Florida accused me of producing the idea of getting the Florida legislature to put the busing referendum on the primary ballot. I only underscored its importance when the idea was bounced off me by Florida GOP legislators. Anyway, it was a grand idea, and it worked to our benefit—on the GOP side and the Democratic side of the primary.

The *National Journal* of April 22, 1972, captured some of the flavor of the Nixon campaign in the midst of the primaries:

> As defined by Harry S. Dent, special counsel to the President for political affairs, Mr. Nixon was alluding to the fact that the Republican Party was not taking any state for granted nor writing off any state as hopeless in the column of the Democratic Party.

> "Like the Bible, we are going all the way from Genesis to Revelations and show the President as a man of peace," Dent said.

Thus, unlike 1968 when Mr. Nixon rode a victory behind the so-called "southern strategy," he will seek to make a broad, national appeal to American voters and present himself as President of all the people. And, in contrast to the 1970 midterm elections, Mr. Nixon will eschew divisive politics; less will be heard about law and order, violence and dissent.

□   □   □

Ready to takeoff: Today, with less than seven months remaining before the Nov. 7 election, the Nixon reelection forces are fully operational, elaborately organized and, according to indications, psychologically primed for battle.

Vice President Spiro T. Agnew told the Republican National Leadership Conference on March 3: "We have the issues. We have the candidate. We have the organization that will turn out the vote."

Yet, as the President himself has said, the issues of today may not be the issues of November.

Strategy: With the political winds rapidly shifting, Nixon aides say it would be impractical at this point in the campaign to develop a grand strategy. "You never hear big strategy as such discussed," Dent said. "If there is any, it is in the minds of Nixon and Mitchell."

Nevertheless, there are several verities that prevail in the Nixon camp:

- Mr. Nixon will remain aloof from partisan politics and leave the campaigning to trusted surrogates until after the Republican convention in San Diego in August.
- Emphasis will be on the President's record and performance rather than on his personality.
- "The selling of the President" will be less blatant in 1972 than in 1968, with more stress on campaign fundamentals (organizing at the grass-roots level, promoting voter registration, and getting out the vote) than on media theatrics.

- Despite the alleged disaffection among the blacks and the young for the Administration, an intensive effort will be made to convert them to Mr. Nixon's side.

☐   ☐   ☐

Surrogates: Although the tone of the Nixon campaign is low-keyed, its size in terms of manpower and available facilities is immense. In addition to using the resources of the White House, the Republican National Committee and the reelection committee, the President relies on non-career appointees in the executive branch and Republican Governors, such as New York's Nelson A. Rockefeller and California's Ronald Reagan, to act as his proxy in making political speeches and raising campaign funds.

During the Florida primary, Shirley Spellerberg, a Republican state committeewoman who worked for the candidacy of Rep. John M. Ashbrook, R-Ohio, said of the Nixon campaign, "This talk of a low-keyed campaign for Nixon is ridiculous. They're coming down here in hordes. If this is low-keyed I'd hate to see what they'd do if it were high-keyed."

Traveling Salesmen: The most popular Administration speakers are Cabinet members and White House staff members, including Herbert G. Klein, director of communications for the executive branch; Robert H. Finch, counselor to the President; and Dent. One unexpectedly effective campaigner for the President is his youngest daughter, Julie Nixon Eisenhower. She has made appearances in several states and is scheduled to be used more frequently.

During one recent week, Dent made nine speeches. Besides making speeches, the Nixon evangelists hold news conferences and appear on local radio and television stations.

Dent on the road: Describing his role as Administration spokesman on the road, Dent, a former aide to Sen. Strom Thurmond, R-S.C., and an architect of the "southern strategy," said: "I go out and sell what the Administration is doing. I localize it, put it in hard, cold political terms and rev them up on the economy, busing, world peace, the whole gamut . . .

"The old conservative Strom Thurmond image which people hang around my neck turns out to be an advantage when you are in the South and running against a guy like Ashbrook. My credentials are good and can help offset Ashbrook.

"I don't decide what I'm going to say until I get there. I kind of case the joint. In almost every instance, they want the hard line. I put a conservative twist to welfare reform and generally translate what the President is doing in conservative terms to meet demands of conservatives around the country."

Dent, who speaks all over the United States, said, "The farther you get out in the field, the more saleable you are."

He added that in speaking to college students he found that "if you tell the truth, not be a false prophet and don't try to pull the wool over their eyes, they'll give you a good reception even if they don't agree with you philosophically."

The Nixon style was always a matter of internal concern. Thus on November 5, 1971, I submitted to Haldeman a memo, excerpted here, on the subject as per the 1972 campaign.

The question of the Presidential campaign style for 1972 depends in part on our situation at campaign time. Harry Truman pulled it out with a "give 'em hell" style. However, the underdog, salty role was best suited for Truman. Eisenhower, the non-politician, could stay above the fray and maintain the political clout of his non-political image. FDR, the wily politician, was too busy running the country to fight with Wilkie or little guys. All these styles proved to be winners.

The one most applicable to this President seems to be the FDR style. It fits this President best with today's crises and the special importance of the President's plans for producing a realistic limited inflation.

Also, the people seem to want this President to be above politics as much as possible—and the old press-created image of being so politically motivated must be dispelled. This was part of LBJ's downfall, shifting for himself. Even the enemies realize this President is a realistic leader bubbling over with expertise and experience, especially in foreign affairs. The reality of bold leadership is now getting through. Let's keep it that way. People now see the President as being more concerned with their welfare than his own—the political risks of the bold, new ventures. This is the best politics by far. They should know the President will give up his job or lose it to pursue courses which he believes will give them and their children peace, stability, safety, and prosperity.

Previously they had begun to become convinced that the press was right—we will shift and straddle for our own political skin. Now they see it differently. Thus, the rise in popularity. We should strive to avoid finger-pointing or political cuteness. And, we should not appear to be winding up our own Democrat assassins, though this job should be done in the right fashion.

We have a record and goals to sell. They can be sold—the President and the family can be sold, positively.

The President should appear to be reasoned, realistic, dignified, and also, bold. The material is available to get this across with surrogates and others speaking across the country—now, and then. We still don't get enough of this done.

TV should be used by the President to give his record, his aims and aspirations for the American people. He does well on TV now, but he is even better behind closed doors. He comes through in the Cabinet Room as knowing his business, being as American as apple pie, and with real sincerity.

The style for 1972 should include moving about the country much as has been done this year—getting out with the people but avoiding crass politics. Isn't this awful coming from me?

The President should wind up with the constructive image of building a better, more stable America. The other side will be forced to carp and criticize. And, likely, they will have little of substance with which to work. So, they'll be destructive, negative, and assassins by their own actions and words and with some assistance.

If the President is a President—cool, calm, reasoned, etc.—not a grabbing politician in the minds of the public, this will add to the campaign theme which I feel should be to give the American people the feeling of security, safety, stability because of this leader. And, this leader must have this unfinished quest—for a realistic and lasting peace and prosperity with limited inflation.

Events could force a Truman style, but not if we can help it. This style doesn't fit this President too well.

In June 1972, Haldeman was still seeking input on the Nixon campaign posture through the convention and also the election. In an "eyes only" memo dated June 12, 1972, he asked four significant questions.

THE WHITE HOUSE
Washington

June 12, 1972

Eyes Only

Memorandum for: Harry Dent
From: H.R. Haldeman

It has been requested that you summarize your views and analysis on the following points:

1.   What should the President's posture be between the Conventions?

2.   What should the President's posture be from the Republican Convention to the election? When should he start campaigning? How much travel should he do, where should he go, what type of activities should he engage in?

3.   Any general thoughts you have as to strategy for the campaign on issues, timing, points of attack, etc.

4.   Your thoughts as to what the opposition strategy will be and how we should meet it.

Please let me have your memorandum by 5:00 p.m. Friday, June 16.

I responded in two memos dated June 16 and 21, respectively.

June 16, 1972

EYES ONLY

Memorandum for: H. R. Haldemam
From: Harry S. Dent
Subject: *1972 Campaign Suggestions*

1.   What should the President's posture be between the Conventions?

The President essentially should continue the present strategy of being a professional President working to solve national and international problems. From now until the GOP convention would be a good time to show personal emphasis on domestic programs and problems. This period might be right for some non-political type travelling to important states not to be visited in the campaign—appearances to big and key groups such as the national Jaycees Convention we just passed up under the post-summit strategy.

Surrogates should begin hammering away on the Demo ticket and the issues.

2.   What should the President's posture be from the Republican convention to the election? When should he start campaigning? How much travel . . . , where . . . , what type . . . ?

The President's posture from the GOP Convention through the election should be much in the Eisenhower style as contrasted with the Truman style. The approach should be one of humility and dignity, with the President ignoring the enemy. Leave him to the surrogates and others. The President should address himself in appearances to his vision of the kind of America and world he envisions for 1976 and further down the road—the theme of which would be "don't change horses in the middle of this dream."

Of course, the President would envision an America with a realistic and lasting peace abroad secured by a sufficient national security posture; domestic tranquility, based on fairness and justice for all, and firmness in law enforcement; rising prosperity and stable prices; and continued individual freedoms. These aims could be made to contrast with the Demo record of the past and the policies advocated by the opponent, in the right way.

The President should begin campaigning not later than mid-September. Our forces should emphasize our desire for a short campaign in the public interest. We should start this line now to put the Demos on the defensive as having campaigned for the job too long, especially McGovern.

Travel should cover every one of the key eleven states and at least two big rallies in each region so no area should feel written-off or taken for granted. The regional rallies could be in lieu of visits to some of the key states if 19 visits would be deemed too much. However, 19 or 20 visits should be a minimum, unless the polls show a good victory.

The campaigning by the President should not be very partisan and should avoid local ticket entanglements as much as possible without hurting the candidates, especially key prospects, or local party morale. Having the State-wide and/or Congressional slate on the stage might be necessary.

Each regional rally should be regionally televised. At these affairs, the President could be honored with key leader testimonials and in other ways, so that the President has to do little in the way of appearing to be a politician. He should be depicted as the statesman building a better and more stable USA and world.

Appearances in the key states could be varied, depending on the type forums or activities available or which could be created to fit the circumstances of the time and place.

3.   *General thoughts as to strategy for the campaign on issues, timing, points of attack, etc.*

All the attacking should be done by the surrogates and others. Our strategy should be to lay the McGovern statements, policies and record on the line through speakers and advertising. We should lay out a steady stream of McGovernisms to keep the attacks fresh, but also repetitious enough to saturate with the points. He should be shown as the advocate of surrender, weakness, gross welfarism, and appeaser of lawless elements. Moreover, he and his party leaders should be charged with undermining the President's efforts for peace, especially the Senate Demo caucus vote to condemn the President in a time of international crisis (mining). We should contrast peace through strength with peace through surrender. Also, responsibility versus irresponsibility. Much emphasis should be placed on stability, individual and national security, and public saturation in every good detail.

The major concerns in all the polls revolve around personal security—peace, economic security, and law and order. The Nixon record is strong in all of these, but it needs public saturation in every good detail.

Presidential leadership, experience, expertise, and realism should also be stressed. Richard Nixon—the man for these times, based on a solid record of performance under very adverse circumstances and against a stacked deck on Capitol Hill (especially Presidential candidates), the press (care here to except good guys), and as the leader of the minority party (outnumbered 5-3). Many people still don't realize all the obstacles in the President's path.

Timing of the attack strategy will have to depend on developments, but the McGovern record should be aired from the time of his nomination all the way through. Pat Buchanan's compendium on his positions and statements should be helpful in stretching out the attacks.

We must make peace through strength the No. 1 issue—that this determines the success of everything else. The big line of difference should be drawn on this issue.

4. *Thoughts as to what the opposition strategy will be and how we should meet it.*

The opposition strategy will turn on these major points: Vietnam, tax reform, haves vs. have-nots, unemployment, cost of living, credibility, Southern Strategy, insensitivity to the needs of and desires of people (anti-people).

If we do our job offensively on the peace through strength theme, then we will have largely blunted the Vietnam charges. Also, a conclusion there would end the debate and the campaign.

Also, our overall offensive strategy of laying out the President's solid record of achievements could blunt most of the Demo attacks. For instance, on the economy, we have the employment figures (6 million more than in 1968), the CPI index difference, and the surging GNP figures to positively make our case. On unemployment we must do more to show that the higher percentage today is due to the influx of women and youngsters into the job markets and point up the change from a war to a peacetime economy. With war we can get unemployment statistics down but casualties back up (jobs vs. lives).

Southern Strategy when it does come up can be answered with many facts—the leadership to desegregate without bullets, blood and bitterness, full participation administration with all the black, chicano, women, et al, appointmens contrasted with previous, ending of sectionalism and bias against South, etc. Bob Brown and I can put together a paper on this.

Trying to pit the have-nots vs. the haves can be made into a positive issue for us by accusing them of class warfare—also, they have promoted race vs. race and section vs. section, all ended now under RN.

Tax reform can be blunted some by the class warfare attack. Also, we can feed out to outside public conduits information that disproves McGovern's mis-statements about some of the loopholes and make the case that most loopholes are the ones all Americans enjoy. We should not. get ourselves in the position of defending sensitive loopholes. Fortunately, McGovern's extremism with his tax proposals should enable us to discredit many of his tax reform thrusts.

Credibility can be shored up by doing some things, based on opportunities, that further underscore the President's credibility and get them well publicized. The record of withdrawals in VN is a good example of keeping his word. Platform fulfillments as Rhodes lays out can be used. In fact, we should put together a group to work on ferreting out examples to be highlighted and publicized. This means also finding ways to stress the President's personal characteristics. The same applies for the anti-sensitive and anti-people charges. Show he has compassion through anecdotes and publicized public demonstrations. What he did for the new attorney general at the swearing in and how much it meant to his family.

bc: John Mitchell
       Peter Dailey

July 21, 1972

Memorandum for: H.R. Haldeman
From: Harry S. Dent
Subject: *Update on June 16 Campaign Strategy Memo*

I still agree with the basic suggestions contained in my June 16 memo. I add these post-convention suggestions:

1.   A special organization to enlist blue collar workers similar to the proposed Democrats for Nixon organization.

2.   Play up the snubbing of all the groups not given a quota at Miami—like farmers, blue collars, ethnics, senior citizens, veterans, et al. This can be done at our convention.

3.   Establish McGovern's campaign emblem as the white flag—pictures of him with the white flag behind his head.

4.   Devise a PR program for Wallace people showing that RN got "the message." Voter ID programs and polls should reveal potential Wallace votes for us and how to get them.

5.   Set up a realignment operation now to exploit switchover possibilities while the convention is fresh and as campaign heats up. This can be continued after the campaign to encourage and speed switching which should be good between now and 1976. The South is particularly ripe on this. If we don't program and plan on this, we won't reap our potentials.

In August Haldeman was seeking an update on 1972 campaign issues. Here was my response:

August 8, 1972

Memorandum For: H.R. Haldeman
From: Harry S. Dent
Subject: *1972 Campaign Issues*

A.   *RN's four best 1972 issues*

1.   *Peace,* through strength, with honor. Leadership should be pushed here.

2. *Domestic tranquility* (law enforcement; anti-drug abuse progress; riots, burning, looting virtually gone; first family togetherness overall stability).

3. *Balance, fairness, responsibility, and moderation* in appointments, running country, speaking out, etc. End of class, race and sectional warfare fostered by Demos.

4. *Economy moving good.* Take the offensive here and sell our case. (Best defense is a good offense.) We have the statistics to present, and people generally feel times are good. Let's let them know how good.

B. McGovern's four worst 1972 issues

1. *The candidate himself.* Represents radical extremism, poor judgment, indecision, inability to run and control a staff, and lack of confidence abounds in his own party.

2. *Second-class status for America.* Surrender in VN, unilateral disarmament, unrealistic and dangerous defense cuts.

3. *Soak the taxpayer and consumer* with unlimited welfare schemes and other spending programs which would require twice the taxes and cause uncontrollable inflation.

4. *Socialize America,* moving from an enterprising, incentive system of success to a hand-out, socialistic society which produces less at a time when even the USSR is coming to recognize the values of using incentives.

C. *McGovern's four best 1972 issues*

1. *Demos outnumber Republicans*—get unity as fast as possible and address self to fellow Demos and Demo distaste for RN.

2. *Haves v. have nots.* Tax reform in forefront, populism, economics, etc.

3. *Peace in VN.*

4. *Supposed freshness and candor.*

D. *RN's four worst issues*

1. *Lack of trust* Demos can create over ITT, bugging stories, special interests.

2. *War still going on.*

3. *Economic ills,* which are better—thank goodness.

4. *Lack of big domestic legislative achievements.*

On August 30, I became more concerned about the sharp divisions developing between the regular Republican organization across the country and CREEP and its state units.

Realizing that professing Democrats outnumbered professing Republicans almost 2-1 in polls, the Nixon high command decided early in the campaign planning to go with a campaign committee independent of the Republican National Committee. This was absolutely necessary, as it was with Ford in 1976, until after the national convention so the RNC would be neutral in any primary or convention nomination challenge. However, after the 1972 convention, CREEP was to continue with its separate campaign. The plan was to use the RNC operation to get GOP votes and CREEP to get the rest.

Harry Flemming had initial command of the CREEP organizing job. Later, Malek took over. The idea was to organize all citizens groups by categories, such as doctors, lawyers, ethnics, hard hats, farmers, businessmen, and women, as was done in the 1968 campaign. However, this time the CREEP leader in a state would be in charge of the Nixon campaign. Under this leader would come the GOP organization and all the other citizens groups.

This caused many wounded egos, jealousies, overlapping, and duplication of efforts. The main problem was with GOP inferiority feelings. And these feelings exploded at the 1972 national convention when then-GOP national chairman and U.S. Senator Robert Dole revolted against the CREEP leaders and policies. Republican organization leaders were concerned non-Republican types were going to get top campaign slots and attention through the CREEP organization then being established in the states.

I was in-between the two groups. One of the aggravating problems was the arrogant attitude demonstrated on occasion by CREEP officials. They knew they had the real action and the real access . to the real campaign manager—Haldeman. Haldeman never had too much respect for the regular

GOP organization. The RNC was to be used, not listened to or consulted, except when necessary.

In the field and at the RNC I was given the "gripes" to take back to the White House, from whence it was known the campaign was being run. My pleas for the GOP regulars did not help my standing with Haldeman. I was considered too "parochial" on the subject of CREEP-RNC feuds.

I could understand the position of both groups. The regulars were being abused and ignored in some cases, especially where they were weak and Nixon needed strong non-GOP support. All to often this was the case. In Florida, we selected L.E. (Tommy) Thomas, the popular state GOP chairman, as our CREEP chairman. We used Tommy because (1) he was a strong leader; (2) Florida was conservative; (3) the GOP was fairly strong; (4) Florida was a primary battleground, and we needed the GOP chairman; and (5) we were sure to win Florida in the fall.

CREEP represented pragmatic politics, but it also reflected arrogant politics and a lack of political know-how and experience. On the other hand, CREEP had tremendous in-house technical capabilities. And the national political situation called for an independent campaign. Our polls showed the Republican flag was not in the greatest shape, but a broad appeal to the "silent majority," the "forgotten man," the "new Majority" would yield better and bigger dividends. And it did.

However, CREEP's weakness showed in arrogance and "cute" politics— all to the detriment of the president, the Nixon Administration, the GOP, and the USA.

The strain between CREEP and the RNC also produced another problem. What were we going to do about all the GOP candidates grabbing for Nixon coattails in 1972, especially after the McGovern nomination and the soaring Nixon prospects with peace and prosperity in the final months of the campaign.

I addressed myself to Haldeman on this subject in a memo dated August 30, 1972:

> The latest Gallup Poll underscores the importance of making the most of the President's coattails to win more seats in Congress and the State Houses. This will be good for the President for these reasons:
>
> 1) We need more help on Capitol Hill and in the State Houses;
> 2) depending on coattails alone may not prove successful, as

past history shows; 3) GOP leaders and newsmen are now questioning whether we're just doing our own thing; 4) aiding the key candidates and scoring previously unexpected gains will boost the President's stock with the party and increase his grip on their 1976 actions (polls show the GOP and Demo parties have been going downhill, like under Ike, who is remembered by the GOP as not caring and helping).

However, the idea of embracing GOP candidates was generally ignored. This policy was dictated by these considerations: (1) the Nixon determination not to raise a finger against his Vietnam helpers in Congress whether Republican or Democrat; (2) a desire to win as big a mandate for Nixon as possible; (3) a feeling Nixon had done and done for other GOP candidates, now it was time to do for himself; and (4) the Nixon idea of being personally above politics in 1972.

This policy of ignoring some GOP candidates caused real problems also, and the problems came to me. That was my job, keeping up with other races and trying to help as much as possible without direct support from the president.

In Mississippi I came in direct conflict with presidential and CREEP policy when I endorsed Gil Carmichael for the U.S. Senate. * While campaigning as a surrogate candidate in various states, I was doing all I could to help local GOP candidates. My endorsement gave the appearance of a Nixon endorsement.

However, in the case of Carmichael, he was opposing Senator James O. Eastland, the president pro tempore of the U.S. Senate and chairman of the powerful Judiciary Committee into which poured 50 percent of all Senate legislation and all nominations concerning the federal judiciary. "Big Jim" was a powerful ally. He relished demeaning his opponents.

By giving the appearance he had the support of his opponent's party leaders, Attorney General Richard Kleindienst and Vice President Agnew had shown the flag for Eastland in Mississippi and had done nothing for Carmichael. So the Mississippi GOP, my friends and loyal Nixonites, were eyeing me with the "hang dog" look. Would I likewise turn my back on their good candidate in my visit to their state convention and virtually repudiate my good friend Clarke Reed?

No way! Even if it meant repudiation by the president. Fortunately, the only rebuke I got was from Eastland himself.

* In 1975 Charmichael barely missed winning the Mississippi governorship.

While campaigning for the president after the Watergate break-in, we surrogate candidates were constantly faced with the Watergate questions at every news conference. My standard answer was that the break-in was wrong, stupid, and could not have been sanctioned by the president—he was too busy traveling and working for peace with honor.

I never did believe that Nixon ordered the break-in, and no evidence has been brought forward to this effect. However, I did have my concerns about the top of our political operation, and I wondered—like others outside of the White House—how far up the orders and/or knowledge went.

When the break-in occurred, I was in Columbia purchasing a building lot for my new home I planned to construct upon my return home the end of 1972. Watching the initial news account on the 6 P.M. Sunday NBC News telecast, I knew this would not be easily swept under the rug. When the report said a few Cuban-Americans were arrested, I became concerned whether my good friend and frequent visitor Manuèl Giberga was in any way involved. Manuèl, now deceased, was a loyal Republican ethnic leader and a fervent Nixonite who had been much involved in the Bay of Pigs invasion. He had provided Fred Buzhardt and me with much information on the Cuban missile buildup a year before President Kennedy took action against the Soviet missiles. We had used this material in Thurmond speeches warning of the Soviet construction of lengthened plane runways and missile sites—all denied by Defense Secretary McNamara.

So Giberga had built up much credibility with me as a loyalist and as a man of great savvy, knowledge, and daring. The daring is what scared me when I heard the Watergate break-in report.

My family and I drove back to our home in McLean, Virginia, on the Monday following the Saturday evening break-in. We arrived home at midnight. I had just fallen asleep when the phone rang. It was Jack Anderson, the syndicated columnist. He told me he had information indicating Giberga, also a friend of his, was the Watergate mastermind. He recalled Giberga and I were close friends and that I was the political contact man at the White House. To Anderson that morning one Dent plus one Giberga added up to two Watergate masterminds.

Needless to say, I was shocked and stunned. I could not sleep knowing Giberga might well be involved and realizing he would be tied to me even though I knew I was totally uninvolved and unknowledgeable about Watergate.

Finally about 5 A.M. I called one of my assistants, Peter Millspaugh, also a good Giberga friend, and told him to meet me at the office by 6 A.M.

When we got together Millspaugh was likewise concerned Gilberga could be the mastermind. We agreed Millspaugh would carefully seek out Giberga for a chat that day and determine whether he was involved. Much to our relief, Giberga told us he had been tracked down by Anderson that morning and that he had convinced Anderson he had no part in Watergate.

I thus reported all this to the White House Watergate coordinator of investigations, John Dean. The information was passed from Dean to Colson and then to Haldeman, who inquired what Harry Dent was doing talking to Jack Anderson.

After that shock and many more phone calls from inquiring reporters seeking Watergate leads, I determined I did not want to know any more about Watergate than I was reading in the news—and I honestly did not want to know if any of that might be factual.

However, I slipped up late in the campaign and expressed to Jeb Magruder at a dinner at Camp David my concern about the Watergate story ending up at the "Big Man's" door, pointing to the president sitting at the head table. Magruder assured me there need be no fear. He said, "It'll never get past me." After hearing that I was even more convinced I did not want to hear any more because I got the impression my good friend Magruder was subject to being drawn into the fray and might become the ultimate culprit in a valiant ploy to protect the higher-ups.

However, it did not stop with Magruder—he volunteered not to be the hemlock drinker. He decided to tell his story to federal prosecutors. It was a footrace between Magruder and Dean to get to the prosecutors first in the spring of 1973.

Magruder later told me Haldeman sent word to him the president wanted him to talk. Dean gave me a tip-off as to his prospective actions when he told me in early April 1973, "Don't worry about you, Harry, you don't show up anywhere in this Watergate mess. But think of me—they're trying to make me the fall guy. You've got no problems. John Dean has 'em all right now."

The Dean comments of deep personal concern were in response to an uneasy two-week period of concern to me after an ABC-TV News report saying that James McCord, one of the chief plumbers, had linked Colson and me to Watergate activities in his first secret appearance before the Senate

Watergate Committee. I was asking Dean if he knew what could be the basis for such a terribly incorrect report. A week later I finally won a public apology from ABC-TV.

This was about the time Dean was supposed to be writing his version of Watergate at Camp David.

Except for the CREEP Watergate problems and run-ins with the Republican National Committee and local GOP regulars, the campaign was one of the smoothest and most efficient ever run at the national level. The polling was on target, the advertising was most effectively used, free press news coverage was maximized through surrogate news conferences and speeches, use of the president was minimized, the fund collections became the largest in history (and as a result will never be topped again because of new laws), the pro-Nixon issues were properly exploited, the anti-McGovern issues were properly exploited, and the incumbent president—previously not too popular and the leader of a minority party—swept to the biggest popular vote total in history, 47,165,234 votes and 520 electoral votes—everything but the very liberal Massachusetts and the District of Columbia electoral votes.

Nixon was very pleased over his vote. He wanted a big vote for many reasons—among them to establish a record and to go into his second term with a gigantic mandate to reorganize and revamp domestic policies and the government bureaucracy.

The enormity of the victory indicated the beginning of a new coalition tabbed by Nixon as the New Majority. The old Democratic coalition had been routed and shredded by the Nixon strategy. The Democrats had put together a coalition of "in the bag" southern whites, blacks, organized labor, ethnic minorities, Catholics, Jews, and snatches of accommodating businessmen.

Now all that was shattered, and Nixon had forged a new coalition containing many of the elements of the old and previously successful Democratic coalition strategy.

Nixon had the Solid South, most ethnics, most Catholics, more Jews than before, more blacks and browns than in 1968, most businessmen, and he had won the Teamsters Union vote and muted the foremost labor baron, George Meany.

The Grand Old Party was now in grand shape and prepared to weld together this New Majority to last forever—we hoped.

10
Plans for a Successor

A lmost from the moment he was chosen by Richard Nixon to be the GOP vice-presidential nominee, Governor Spiro Theodore Agnew was an asset in the South. He was an asset because he was thought to have been picked by reliable "ole Strom," he was from border state Maryland, he was a symbol of law and order, he was Greek (Greeks are liked down South), and he had an average American background.

As events unfolded in the 1968 campaign and throughout the first Nixon term, Agnew became not only a beloved household name in the South, but to many he became "Spiro, Is My Hero," as the Bo Callaway bumper stickers printed in 1969 attested.

Thus Agnew was a most saleable commodity in the 1968 political campaign in Dixie. He talked right, and he was the man Nixon selected in preference to the liberal choice, and supposedly at Thurmond's demand. This was not exactly so, but the national press carried it that way, and anything the northern newsmen did not like had to be a saleable item down South.

Spiro Agnew came to special national attention on November 13, 1969, when he carried out a Nixon plan to denounce the national news media in a speech at Des Moines, Iowa. The networks carried it on national TV.

From Des Moines on, Agnew was to be the Nixon hatchet man of the media and the left. Haldeman and Ehrlichman did not think too highly of the veep, and evidently the same view was held by the president. So Agnew had to be used to good advantage as a release point for pent-up Nixon emotions and against Nixon's enemies.

No one realized this more than the vice-president, and he chafed under the realization. There have been many unhappy veeps, but Agnew appeared to be the "Most Unhappy Veep." He was my friend. In fact, I felt no one on the White House staff except Harlow, after John Sears was dismissed, was any closer to the vice-president. I liked him and enjoyed his tough speeches, even though I realized the use of Agnew was damaging him for the 1972 reelection campaign and for his own prospects for the presidency in 1976.

The veep blues have seemingly affected all vice-presidents. Woodrow Wilson's running mate, Thomas Marshall, best described the malady this way: "The Vice President is like a man in cataleptic state. He cannot speak; he cannot move; he suffers no pain. And yet he is conscious of all that goes on around him."

This fit perhaps all veeps but Agnew. He could speak—some thought too much, he could move—he traveled more that any, yet he suffered much pain because he was so sensitive to the treatment he received at the White House, in the news media, and on Capitol Hill.

Agnew was a very fortunate man. He had come from virtually nowhere to be elected governor of Maryland and now vice-president of the United States. True, as Haldeman and Ehrlichman saw it, he was a mite on the lazy and lucky side. Every advancement he had made had come as a consequence of being the right man at the right place at the right time. This was true all the way from his lowest and first elective office—that of Baltimore county executive in 1962.

I was living in the Maryland suburbs of Washington when he was elected governor of Maryland over George C. Mahoney, the perennial Democratic statewide runner. Agnew was elected as the lesser evil by the Republicans and liberal Democrats. Mahoney's campaign theme was "Your Home Is Your Castle." This meant Mahoney opposed integrated housing. Agnew took a stance in favor of open housing. In liberal Maryland, he was freakishly elected governor, the same as had occurred in Baltimore County when he won election as county executive and earlier when he was elected to the county council. Each time he had been the beneficiary of a political break, and he was sharp enough to take full advantage of the break. I report all this not in derogation of Agnew, but rather in admiration of one who came from virtually nowhere to the number two job in America and almost to number one in the world.

The vice-president would call me up to his office on the second floor of the old Executive Office Building for a talk every so often—especially when he was feeling down about his Haldeman and Ehrlichman treatment. He wanted to believe they were operating outside the parameters of presidential instructions. I think he realized this was rarely true.

No one in the Nixon Administration was more uncomfortable unless it was William P. Rogers, the secretary of state. Rogers had his competitive problems with Henry Kissinger. And he was a sensitive man and a very fine gentleman. Agnew and Rogers both brooded over their treatment by the White House.

Agnew had no real rival until John B. Connally of Texas splashed on the scene in 1971. I was representing the president at the Republican governors' conference at Sun Valley, Idaho, when the surprise Connally announcement as secretary of the treasury was made in January 1971.

The Texas Republicans vehemently protested. The one Texan Democrat who had thwarted the growth of the Texas GOP was suddenly in a top slot in the Nixon Administration. Since they were my friends and the people I was supposed to keep happy, I got calls immediately at Sun Valley wanting to know "what the hell's going on?" Texas had been betrayed! But I did not see it that way—another smart move by "the Boss" as I saw it, even though I resented the Connally effectiveness in carrying Texas for Humphrey in the closing days of the 1968 campaign, and Connally's success in repelling our 1970 campaign effort in Texas. I had heard that Connally might endorse Nixon in 1968. Then suddenly at the close of the campaign, Connally, LBJ confidant, JFK navy secretary, and former Texas governor, had raised the hand of Vice President Hubert Humphrey at a final Texas rally to deliver close Texas as the only southern state to go to "Triple H." What an act of apostasy! Yet I saw the brilliant pragmatism in the Connally appointment as secretary of the treasury. I could see it, but Texas GOP leaders were up in arms—and I understood their concern and anger.

I later learned from Billy Graham that Connally had come into the Nixon Administration on the coaxing not of the president, but of Graham. My family and I visited the Grahams at their Black Mountain, North Carolina log cabin home in 1971. There we learned of the Graham influence with Connally and Nixon and of Graham's staunch opposition to communism at home and abroad.

Actually, Graham was closer to Connally than Nixon. He almost talked Connally into going with Nixon in the 1968 election. He finally succeeded in 1971. As the late Congressman Mendel Rivers of South Carolina would say, Nixon and Connally mixed together "like grits and gravy."

Bill Safire in his book *Before the Fall* quotes Nixon as saying in 1970 before the Connally appointment (page 148): "Every Cabinet should have at least one potential President in it. Mine doesn't."

Pat Buchanan, the conservative and hard-hitting speech writer, put it to me another way following a Cabinet meeting in 1971. He told me after watching Connally entrance the president with his political savvy and earthy Texas sayings, "John Connally is like a peacock in this Cabinet strutting amongst a bunch of mud hens."

Buchanan meant he was in a class of his own with political charisma and eloquence.

Connally had a few attributes not totally available to any Nixon Administration competitors: (1) Connally was very handsome and charismatic; (2) Connally was full of good Texas humor and personality; (3) Connally fit Nixon's political savvy and philosophy like a glove; and (4) Connally was most articulate and eloquent.

Nixon was intrigued with Connally. Connally was probably the only person in the Nixon Administration deemed by Nixon to be the potential president in the Nixon ranks. He had the blessing and recommendation of Billy Graham, who had plenty of influence on the Nixon mind not only because of his great political savvy, but also because of his being the popular evangelist. This meant something to Nixon, who in my view was a believer in God, but not necessarily a fervent religious believer who looked to God for every decision.

Once in late 1971, Nixon had occasion to display his religious side in a meeting with another evangelist, Oral Roberts. I had set up the meeting through Haldeman. However, I missed the Roberts visit as airline problems made it impossible for me to be present and carry out my assignment to escort Roberts into the Oval Office. In my place, the Reverend Wallace Henley, one of my assistants took Roberts in for the session with Nixon.

Henley told me Roberts convinced the president to get on his knees and lead the trio—Nixon, Roberts, and Henley—in prayer. It was a strange sight, but it showed to the two ordained ministers that Nixon could pray and was not above doing it on his knees, even from his lofty perch.

Soon after Nixon's trip to China, I was told to assemble a group of conservative religious leaders to the White House for a Kissinger briefing on the trip. Among those invited for the Kissinger briefing by Graham was W.A. Criswell, pastor of the First Baptist Church in Dallas, Texas, the largest congregation in the Southern Baptist Convention.

One of those scheduled for the Kissinger briefing on China was Paul Harvey, the popular conservative radio and TV commentator.

While waiting for the briefing scheduled for 5 P.M., I conducted Harvey and his wife Angel, who also was his business manager, on a special tour of the White House. Often, I took many GOP leaders and southern friends on such tours of the West Wing. If the president was in, unusally the Oval Office door was closed. However, sometimes the door was open with the president bidding good-by to his visitors. Knowing I was escorting VIP political visitors, the president would go out of his way to invite me in or to permit me to introduce him to my party. He would give them presidential trinkets, such as autographed golf balls, tie clips, women's pins, or fountain pens. However, if I missed the president, Steve Bull, the staff man under Haldeman who kept the president on schedule, would give me "goodies" to hand out and a special tour of the Oval Office.

I felt it important for the president to see Paul and Angel Harvey, but I neither had the time nor inclination to go through Haldeman's established procedure. Yet I knew the president would want to receive the Harveys. So I checked in with Bull, a dedicated conservative and Nixonite, whose office was next door to the Oval Office. I introduced Bull to the Harveys. He was flattered. Harvey was Bull's hero. And Bull felt he was Nixon's hero, too. So I asked Bull about the possibility of getting me in with the Harveys for an introduction to the president. Bull told me to take them on a tour of the White House residence while he tried to arrange the brief introduction. He told me privately the president was taking a nap in his private office next door to the Oval Office and that he would try to arrange a brief meeting as soon Nixon awoke.

When I got back from the residence tour, Bull caught me in the hall of the West Wing and said the president wanted to see the Harveys. Bull escorted us in for what we expected to be a brief visit. But I was right, the president knew and respected Harvey, and he wanted to talk with Harvey at length. Here was a man who reflected Nixon's personal views on individual freedom and individual responsibility, and Nixon savored the opportunity to talk philosophy with him and his sharp and attractive wife, Angel.

Harvey was impressed, and Nixon was so engrossed that he ran the unscheduled meeting for more than 1 and ½ hours. Haldeman became enraged—and properly so—since he had scheduled several ambassadors that afternoon for presentation of their credentials.

Bull became frantic. He had risked his job to get us in to see the president. Now Haldeman was beating on his door to know why the ambassadors were stacked up outside the president's door.

So Bull repeatedly sent in his briefly typed notes to the president (as he always did) which said in effect, "Get rid of the visitor, you're overtime." I watched Nixon many times crumple such a note and toss it in his trash can, especially when he was conducting a political visit. And Nixon considered this a political visit. Nothing interested Nixon more, unless it was foreign policy, and this visit even got into foreign policy. This was the purpose of the Harvey visit—to be briefed on the president's visit to China.

When we finally left the Oval Office, Bull was sweating with concern. He told me Haldeman would probably have his "Beaver Patrol" head by the morrow. And Harry Dent's would soon follow.

So I started thinking how I could save the two of us. After the Kissinger meeting, as impressive to the group as a presidential briefing, I was told to proceed to the South Lawn for a helicopter trip to the president's yacht, the *Sequoia*. When I got near the presidential helicopter, I accosted Graham as a fellow southern Baptist who had helped establish the White House Staff

Prayer Breakfast Group. I told him of the Harvey episode and the problem created thereby for Bull and me. He told me not to worry, that he would take care of the problem on board the *Sequoia*.

We, meaning Mitchell, Haldeman, Ehrlichman, Kissinger, Graham, and I, flew on the helicopter down to Mount Vernon, where we boarded the *Sequoia* on the Potamac river.

As soon as we got aboard, Graham, in the presence of Nixon and the others, turned to Haldeman and complimented him on his wisdom in permitting me to take the Harveys in to visit with the president. It was a masterful ploy by the preacher—so good that Haldeman's anger vanished, especially after the president made clear his pleasure at the Harvey visit. So there was nothing adverse for Haldeman to say to Bull or me the next day. When I ran into Bull the next day, he called me a "miracle worker." I told Bull not to fret, that miracles were still possible with Billy Graham around. He agreed.

As Agnew declined in presidential favor, carrying out presidential orders, Connally began to rise.

Seemingly every Connally contact with people caused the handsome Texan to exude charm and charisma. Soon after he came aboard, the president had Connally in the East Room to help the president thank a group of GOP congressmen returning from a road show extolling the virtues of the president's New Federalism program. The theme of New Federalism was returning power back to the people—a 1968 promise.

When the president began talking I could see that these GOP loyalists were leery of being in the same room with what some called "LBJ, Jr." A few indicated this to me. When the president finished his remarks he introduced Connally, who got only polite applause. By the time Connally had concluded, the GOP loyalists were wildly applauding, as was the president. Nixon had the most reason to applaud because Connally had effusively praised him in letting the GOP congressmen know how fortunate they were in having such a leader. He told them his only concern was that the president's allies on the Hill were hiding the president's "light under the bushel." He exhorted them to get out and tell the story about the Nixon achievements and aspirations for America and the world. The president could not hide his extreme pleasure at these comments under even several bushels.

Every time I saw Nixon and Connally together, the president seemed to be brimming with confidence. Connally turned Nixon on, and I could see why, especially in the Cabinet meetings. Connally was so confident, so pungent, so eloquent with his comments, and so earthy and humorous with his jokes and illustrations. Nixon would rear back with laughter at his Texas stories, and Connally seemed to have one for every point he would make. Bill Safire says "Nixon was in love" with the secretary of the treasury, which may be saying too much. Nevertheless, Nixon did feel Connally was extra special, even maybe above the other "Big John"—Mitchell. Almost any recommendation by Connally was adopted because he was so persuasive, pragmatic, political, and hard-nosed.

Connally had all the strong Nixon characteristics and more. He was Nixon plus. I think the president realized this. Connally could match the Nixon mind—quick, retentive, and overflowing with savvy. Philosophically, Connally was in the great center with Nixon, and like Nixon his instincts were conservative and hard-nosed. Were they not politicians, they would both be staunch conservatives. Yet they were both pragmatic, based on wisdom and many years of experience in political nitty-gritty.

All of this, plus the Connally confidence, made Nixon feel secure. Prior to Connally, Nixon felt there was not his equal in his Administration. Connally was.

The Nixon respect for Connally showed to the White House staff. And Connally showed it to his own Treasury staff and especially to Haldeman and Ehrlichman. All the other Cabinet members except Mitchell seemed to stand in awe of the "German High Command." They did not like it, but when Haldeman or Ehrlichman called, the Cabinet members came to them.

Connally straightened all this out, right after he rode into town. One of his first actions was to call in his Treasury staff for a meeting, and then get Ehrlichman on the telephone. The salty Texan then castigated Ehrlichman on some point of domestic policy gnawing at the secretary. Needless to say, the staff was impressed. This was indeed "Big John." And Ehrlichman learned where he stood in relation to this Cabinet member. There was no need to press any quarrels about "Big John" with Nixon.

Haldeman came in next for the "Big John" treatment. One day Haldeman called Connally to come over to his office across the street from Treasury in the prestigious West Wing of the White House. But Haldeman was told he would have to be the one to "come over." Shortly thereafter there appeared in the secretary's waiting room the feared German called "the Brush" by some because of his brisk crew cut and personality. Haldeman had to wait and twiddle his thumbs until the secretary could work him in. This had not happened before. Haldeman never left the West Wing except to go home to his family or to go somewhere with Nixon with his movie camera rolling.

To put Haldeman down was the next thing to putting "RN" down. But then that's the kind of clout "Big John" had.

Strangely, one of "Big John's" staunchest boosters after this incident was Haldeman, another indication of the German's loyalty to Nixon.

Agnew realized Connally was rising more and more as his rival to be heir apparent. Thus he grew to dislike Connally and to become resentful of Haldeman, Ehrlichman, and the president himself.

He knew he had been used and abused as the cutting edge against the press and Nixon's enemies on the left. They had sent him sallying forth in the 1970 campaign with Harlow, Safire, and Buchanan in pursuit of the "radic-lib" U.S. Senate candidates, all Democrats except for the GOP's Senator Charlie Goodell of New York. Agnew had faithfully carried out the president's orders to the letter, even as to the timing on labeling Goodell a "radic-lib."

In return Agnew was getting no authority, no power, no respect—only more enemies and an image of being too hardline and too controversial to be elected president in 1976. What he did get was private praise from the president and some public praise. When he would become depressed, he would get a Nixon pat on the back.

The vice-president could feel the thought running through the White House about replacing him on the ticket in 1972. If the president had ever faced Agnew on the subject, Agnew probably would have assented. He was that fed up, and he wanted to get out and make some money. Yet Nixon would never tell Agnew anything. In private meetings Agnew would try to get a signal from Nixon, but Nixon was not prone to deliver bad news. Agnew was a candid man, but not Nixon when it came to bad news.

Nixon had the strength in 1972 to replace Agnew with Connally. He wanted to do it, but he probably remembered only too well the Eisenhower effort to remove Nixon from the ticket in 1956. Mitchell's influence made the key difference in the decision to stay with Agnew.

As much as I liked Agnew personally, I came to see that Connally was a better potential 1976 presidential candidate. He seemed to be meant for the job, and no one was better prepared to be president than Connally. The Office of the Special Watergate Prosecutor did a disservice to Connally and the nation in prosecuting him on such flimsy evidence.

In private conversations with the president, and sometimes Haldeman in 1972, I suggested several times that Connally was the best bet for 1976. The president and Haldeman agreed. I told the president that Connally would be hard to beat because he would be a "sure bet" in the South. My view is that any Republican who can wrap up the South—a total reversal from national politics of previous years—could win the presidency because of inherent GOP strength in the Midwest and Far West. My concern about Agnew was that while he could do well in the South—he always ran behind Nixon in southern polls and did not show up as quite the Dixie vote getter we had thought. Agnew would not be able to get enough electoral votes in the rest of the country because of his controversial image, and the hostility of the news media would make his candidacy impossible.

Yet Connally would have difficulty getting the GOP nomination in 1976 because of the Republican reluctance to take in newcomers. I found in my GOP speaking appearances around the country that Republicans did not "cotton" too well to anyone without long elephantine credentials. This is an inherent GOP weakness, but it is there. So Connally would have to have much good coaching, care, and introduction in order to get into the hearts and minds of GOP regulars.

The president was convinced that with his coaching, care, and introductions Connally could become the 1976 GOP nominee for president. It would have been interesting to watch the Agnew-Connally battle for nomination with the incumbent president trying to finagle for Connally over his vice-president. This was to be the job for people such as I.

Nixon's belief that I would play an important role in positioning Connally for his conversion to Republicanism and his 1976 nomination caused him to ardently request my continuation in his second term while he was accepting resignations from many other Nixon staffers.

The morning following the 1972 election Haldeman called the top White House Staff into the Roosevelt Room for what we thought would be a pat-on-the-back session. We got one pat and then came the back of the hand, after the president retired from the room. Haldeman, in his brusque manner, wanted our resignations by the next day. The president was going to reorganize his Administration. Some few would be kept, but most would go, so start looking.

My plans were already made to return to Columbia and practice law in South Carolina. So I was not shocked like the rest, only chagrined.

After the president got all the resignations in hand and all the ideas for the new administration, he moved up to Camp David in December 1972 to make his decisions. Those whom he desired to be retained would be called up to the mountain for a chat with the president. Agnew and I were the first to be called to the mountain. We went up in the same helicopter on December 8, 1972. I was to meet with the president briefly and then return to the White House with the vice-president.

I waited while the president and vice-president had their private meeting. Then I was called in. The president asked me to stay in his Administration. I assured him I was flattered, but reminded him I had notifed him months before I had to leave. He insisted I stay. He was very complimentary about my services, and I knew he was sincere. He smiled and remarked how we had shown the anti-South folks how much the South was in the American mainstream, unlike the South's critics.

Then the conversation turned to Connally. Nixon asked if I still felt Connally should be his successor. I told him yes, despite my friendship for Agnew. My concern was that Agnew could not win in 1976 with the controversial image he had acquired in taking the fight to Nixon's enemies at Nixon's behest. The president made it clear he thought I could help Connally prepare for succession by staying in the Adminstration and working from within. I agreed I could be helpful and wanted to do so. However, I had already bought a home site in Columbia and had made my pledge to my family to return home.

Then we talked about how I could help on the outside. This later resulted in my being appointed general counsel of the Republican National Committee in early 1973. In this role I was going to do what I could to assist with the Connally plan. I would keep in contact with Haldeman, who was also staunchly in Connally's corner.

The conversation with Nixon then turned to Southerners in the new Administration. I was unexpectedly asked my idea of getting a new Southerner in the Cabinet. Although, unprepared, I blurted out, with apology, the name of Frederick B. Dent, a textile leader from Spartanburg, South Carolina. I said, "I apologize for this name, Mr. President, because he's got my last name and is from my state, but Fred Dent is a top flight man with credentials to be in your Cabinet. And if we're kin, it's some far distant kin." He replied, "Don't worry, Harry, we can make room for two Dents in the Nixon Administration." Then I went on to suggest Howard "Bo" Callaway of Pine Mountain, Georgia, for a Cabinet post or at least secretary of the army, since he was a graduate of West Point and had wanted the army spot the whole first term. (Both won appointments, Dent as Commerce secretary and Callaway as Army secretary.)

Then I got very candid with the president. I explained how impressed I had been with the first term and with Nixon as my boss and leader. We had made history in national politics by winning all of the South for the first time by a GOP candidate, and we had done it easily with an average vote of 70 percent. I told him that he had performed magnificently in splitting the Communist giants at a time when this was vital to the freedom and future of the world. And he had done it all in "the name of peace, peace with honor, and peace through strength, determination, and resolve." What was worrying me now, I said, was what could happen to this great leader of mine. Watergate could be his downfall. Something had to be done. The infection of Watergate could not come to the president's door.

I told him that fortunately my speaking intinerary as a surrogate candidate in the 1972 campaign had left me uninformed on Watergate, except for what I had read or heard in the news. Nevertheless, I did believe it would become unraveled. It was too big, too hot. The cap could not stay on that bottle. I told him I had no idea what part, if any, he had in or even knew of Watergate, but I did know that the press and the prosecution believed the infection would lead right back to some of the president's men. So as long as he was turning over the Nixon Administration, the president could not get rid of most everyone except the men under suspicion. This would be the signal that Nixon was protecting his bad boys. The trail would lead inevitably and inexorably into the Oval Office.

Next I pictured for him what would happen to his place in history, which I painted in glowing terms provided he could handle Watergate properly. But Watergate could ruin it all—not only the place in history, but also all the great good the president had done in foreign policy and was preparing to do in domestic affairs in the next four years.

I shook "the Boss," no question about that. I was pouring out my heart of concern to a man who had done about everything I wanted to see him do for my country. I did not want to see him hurt, much less ruined. Nor did I want to see his programs and policies drowned with Watergate. And I could feel that was coming. He had to act and act now!

As the first step, I suggested he remove anyone under any suspicion immediately. He could do it by throwing them in with the staff shuffle, and that meant anyone—all the way to the top. I told him I was against no one on the staff, that I made it my business to get along with them all. But the presidency had to be saved from contamination.

Our meeting went on for more than 1 and ½ hours—far beyond the scheduled time. We were holding up the veep and his helicopter. Haldeman was waiting on the helicopter also. So the president sent a message to let the helicopter go and to hold Haldeman back because he wanted to talk with him as soon as this meeting was concluded.

At the close of the meeting the president implored me to stay in the Administration. He wanted my suggestions as to what spot I wanted. He insisted that I rethink the matter and get back to him with an answer in two weeks. Again, he said, "We'll make room for two Dents."

With that I departed, sad and also glad. I was sad thinking about our conversation on Watergate. And I was glad I had had the nerve to pour out my concern. I knew I had upset him, but maybe it would cause him to do what he needed to do to face up to Watergate. I was glad; too; that he cared enough to want me in the second term. But I was sad that there was no way I would reverse my decision. As much as I wanted to stay, I also wanted to go.

I've often wondered what the president said to Haldeman after our meeting. One thing that happened within a few weeks was the unexpected exit of Charles Colson, the man at whom the fingers of strongest suspicion were pointing.

After I left the White House, I had a few calls from Haldeman about Connally. I also had a visit with the president in February 1973, when he learned I was in Washington. We were still working on the Connally plan. The president had just addressed the South Carolina General Assembly the previous day, thanking the South for its support of his Vietnam policies. He made a sensational hit, even better than Agnew before the same body a year earlier when selling revenue sharing. With his feet propped on the desk, Nixon wanted to know how good it really was.

Haldeman called me in 1973 to let me know Connally had to be brought over into the GOP ranks soon. I agreed and went to work trying to convince Connally to do so. It was not easy with Watergate coming apart at the seams. In one of my telephone conversations with Connally, I suggested he try to find some way to get the White House to face up to Watergate while he was serving the president on a special short tour of duty as a White House assistant. He gave me the same report GOP National Chairman George Bush had told me: "Haldeman says there's no way to face up to it; there are too many other holes that could break loose in the dam." I talked to Harlow, just as he was being reimpressed into duty at the White House to assist the faltering president in early 1973. I suggested to Harlow that whoever was responsible—I did not know—had to drink the hemlock. Harlow agreed. I got the impression he was working in that direction in his input to the top. But evidently the other holes would permit nothing to be done except to try to ride out the storm.

Connally changed parties in May 1973. No man had ever made the jump under more adverse circumstances. I respected him even more for that tough decision.

A week before the Agnew resignation was announced, I got a call from President Nixon at my law office. I had not talked with him since the White House meeting in February 1973. He told me Agnew would have to resign because of possible prosecution charges involving illegal payments while a public officeholder. Now the question was who Nixon would nominate to be Agnew's successor. He asked the same question again, "Do you still feel the same about Connally?" I responded, "Yes, sir, even though the Democrats are threatening to carve him up in the congressional nomination hearings. He's the man, Mr. President, and the reason the Democrats are yelling so loud is because they fear him as the one man they wouldn't be about to defeat in 1976. Also they're peeved because he switched to our party."

I got the impression Connally would be selected. However, the next day Ford was named by Nixon. The president preferred Connally up to the final decision. The president left it to General Al Haig, the staff chief, to give the news to Connally.

Ford was a good overall selection and seemingly a popular one, particularly where it mattered most—Capitol Hill. His confirmation vote was relatively easy, and his reputation for integrity was just what the country needed at that time of doubt and confusion.

Nixon did not submit the Connally name because of the tremendous controversy the Democrats had promised for the "party switcher." Such a fight would have been bad for Nixon, Connally, and the country. Also, the Ford selection was good impeachment politics, since Democrats and Republicans were lobbying hard for their friend Jerry Ford.

Ironically for me, the president may have been more influenced by my old political comrade from South Carolina, Fred Buzhardt, his Watergate counsel. Buzhardt warned Nixon as he was making the decision that Connally might have some prosecutor problems himself. Evidently, this was the most decisive factor with Nixon.

When Nixon signed the paper nominating Ford, he gave the pen he used to Steve Bull and ordered him to give it to Buzhardt with a message.

Bull went directly to Buzhardt's office in the old Executive Office Building next door. He threw the presidential pen on Buzhardt's desk. Astonished,

Buzhardt asked, "What's this for?" Bull responded: "It's from the President. He said to tell you 'Dammit, I hope you're satisfied now!' "

The president was expressing his disappointment that the Connally plan had been thwarted even though he had no more loyal friend than Jerry Ford, his second choice to be his successor.

Even during the 1976 election period the former president, while trying to remain neutral publicily in the Republican nomination battle yearned for what might have been had he been able to go with the choice of his heart as against the choice of his head. He pushed Connally at me in three conversations. Like we Southerners at the 1968 convention, in 1974 he had placed his head above his heart. However, in 1976 he was in political exile and thus in no postion to do anything but hurt his secret candidate. His old realistic nature had returned so that he knew he could only campaign in secret for Connally.

11
W (h) ither GOP?

T he question of the future potential of the Republican party in the South and across the country is one of the most crucial questions facing Americans, but few realize this. It is not so much what happens to the Republican party, but rather to the competitive two-party system. Since there are only two major parties now, the fate of either one affects the viability of the two-party system.

Twice in recent years we have been, in effect, operating the national government with a virtual one-party monopoly. President Lyndon Johnson's term from January 1965 to January 1969 saw a strong-willed Democrat in charge of an executive branch top-heavy with Democratic appointees; a Congress with Democrats controlling approximately two-thirds of the membership of both houses; and a good majority of Democratic judges, governors, state legislators, and local officers. Ironically, only a divisive war saved the country from eight instead of four years of one-party rule.

In President Carter's first term we have much the same one-sided political control. However, the balance on the Supreme Court has been altered by the four Nixon and one Ford appointments between 1969 and 1976.

It is too early to know whether there will be only four years of one-party domination under the Democrats or eight or more years. More than anyone else, Carter holds the answer to this question. The Republican party, as the minority and out-party, will determine the answer to a lesser but important extent.

So the potential for the demise or extinction of competitive politics in the United States is a real possibility. We could find ourselves in the same position as Sweden was for many years with one dominant party of socialistic predilections. The important check and balance of competitive power is vital to the maintenance of democratic government. Today, there is no competitive veto power or investigative power. A Democratic Watergate may never be uncovered, or fully prosecuted, as was Watergate. A spendthrift Congress may have no bounds, only a Federal Reserve Board with some power to control the supply of money and thereby have an impact on inflation. However, President Carter wants the board subject to more control by the president, such as the authority for the president to appoint a new board chairman concurrent with presidential assumption of power.

The South has only recently moved from one-party politics to a competitive two-party system. The increase in political competition has been largely responsible for the South's new position of importance in national politics. This has come at the same time the southern states have been moving to the fore in national economic and population power. Thus a return to one-party rule in Dixie would undermine a vital ingredient in the prodigal South's return to national power, prestige, and prominence.

The major problem for the southern Republicans is their lack of a political relationship with the increasingly large black voting population. Also, the blue-collar white voter is slipping away to the lures of Jimmy Carter's Baptist religion and populist appeal and brother Billy's red-neckism. The Republicans have shown they can more than hold their own with the white-collar and upper-level white voting population. It has been estimated Ford won 55 percent of the white vote against the regional and populist appeal of Carter in his successful 1976 campaign, compared with a 51-49 split nationally. The problem is not that the blacks are voting in increasing numbers. It is rather that, generally, they cast their votes as a bloc for Democrats in increasing numbers. In some southern states, they vote in better proportion to their registered numbers than do the whites.

The particular problem now confronting the southern Republicans is the fact that the Democrats showed in the Carter election they can put together enough of the blue-collar white voters with the black voters to win in the South. This is a powerful voting combination, as attested to by the Carter sweep of all southern states except Virginia, enabling him to win a close national election.

The Carter coalition may have been a once-only phenomenon. However, the Democrats now have the potential to weld the coalition together indefinitely. They can unionize the South; and through use of union political influence and powers, the Democrats may be able to keep the South solid for the Democratic party. In recent years the South has been determining the outcome of presidential elections.

If the South's electoral votes are denied to a Republican party continuing to shrink in vote potential in its former northeastern bastion and in parts of its previous stronghold, the Midwest, then the party would be largely dependent on the West. Their swing state California has most of the electoral votes of that area. And the 'big casino," as Reagan calls California, should be more apt to vote Democratic than Republican with its 3-2 Democratic majority in voter registration.

Thus the national Republican party is in a precarious position, as is the two-party system.

How can the Democrats bring about the unionization of the hitherto stubborn South? First, by repealing the state right to work laws in 20 states, mostly in the South and in other states that are pro-Republican. The platform adopted at the 1976 Democratic National Convention calls for the repeal of Section 14 (b) of the Taft-Hartley Act. This section of the law authorizes the individual states to have right to work laws. Candidate Carter pledged to sign into law a bill repealing 14 (b).

Right to work laws simply prevent a labor union from organizing a closed or union shop at a plant. That is, a union may win a vote to organize the workers at a southern plant, but they may not require dissenting workers to be members of the union. While the law does not prohibit unionization, it does make union organizing efforts more difficult than in union shop states where a union victory forces all workers at the plant to join the union in order to maintain their jobs.

The January 10, 1977, issue of *U.S. News and World Report* shows union strength in the 11 southern states as follows:

Union Strength in the South

	Union Membership at Latest Count	Percent of State's Nonfarm Jobs
Tennessee	295,000	19%
Alabama	223,000	19%
Arkansas	108,000	17%
Louisiana	194,000	16%
Georgia	264,000	15%
Virginia	247,000	14%
Texas	567,000	13%
Florida	354,000	13%
Mississippi	84,000	12%
South Carolina	82,000	8%
North Carolina	140,000	7%

Source: U.S. Dept. of Labor

The national average for union membership of nonfarm workers is 26 percent as contrasted with the South's range of from 19 percent in Tennessee and Alabama to eight percent in South Carolina and seven percent in North Carolina.

Research work by the National Right to Work Committee, the pro-14(b) organization, shows that during the period from 1964 to 1974, manufacturing jobs increased in the 19 states then having right to work laws by 1,587,900 jobs to 1,165,600 in the 31 nonright to work states.

Expectedly, work stoppages in 1975 averaged 52 for right to work states with 357,600 man-days lost, while nonright to work states averaged 138.8 work stoppages with 787,400 man-days lost.

Since 1975 two states—Arkansas and Louisiana—have tested the right to work sentiment. Louisiana enacted a right to work law effective July 9, 1976, after having dropped such a law previously. The voters in Arkansas rejected by a vote of 67-33 percent a union proposal to repeal its right to work law. This now makes the national count of right to work states 20 as against 30 nonright to work states.

Also important to the labor union efforts to organize southern industries is the proposed law to authorize secondary boycotts through a device known as "common situs picketing."

Common situs picketing is the boycotting by workers of an entire construction site because of grievances with a particular contractor or subcontractor working at the site. The proposed legislation would overturn a 1951 Supreme Court decision that found secondary boycotts to constitute an unfair labor practice.

Common situs picketing was passed by the Congress in 1976, but President Ford vetoed the legislation under Reagan's competitive pressures. With two-thirds control in Congress and a lock on the veto power, the Democrats are now in a position to repeal state right to work laws in the South and to enact common situs picketing to speed the process of unionization in Dixie. This is yet likely despite the 1977 close loss sustained by cocky union leaders in a congressional vote on common situs picketing.

In addition to unionization of industrial workers, there is also the possibility of organizing farm workers through the efforts of Caesar Chavez and his United Farm Workers Union. However, this proposal has further to go in view of the overwhelming setback the voters in California dealt the Chavez forces on November 2, 1976. They rejected his Proposition 14, which would have permitted organization of farm workers on the private property of the farm owners.

The power to accomplish any or all of the aims of the labor unions lies primarily with President Carter. Thus far he has shown a reluctance to give full support to all union aims, except speeding National Labor Relations Board procedures for determining union organization elections at plants. In the past, the Congress has shown its readiness to act for the unions. In 1965 the House approved the repeal of Section 14(b) by a vote of 221 to 203. The Senate effort was thwarted by a filibuster led by Senator Thurmond and the late Senate minority leader, Senator Everett Dirksen of Illinois. Since then, the South has sent to Congress more representatives and senators willing to vote with union wishes. This will especially be so when the party leadership explains the potential for its new Democratic Southern Strategy. My experience as an aide in the U.S. Senate for 11 years convinced me most solons will accede to the party line either overtly or covertly. The pressures of conformity to party positions are strong and usually effective.

Aside from the positive actions Carter can take to consolidate The Democrats' revival in the South, he could also continue to play a negative role on his liberal campaign commitments and retain the confidence of enough southern whites to keep Democratic fortunes alive. This is being accomplished currently by reverting to the more conservative stances he showed in the presidential primary season. Also, a firmer-than-expected hand on inflation and government spending, illustrating that he is more moderate than liberal, has strengthened his position with southern blue-collar workers and has served to dispel the doubts he created with the southern business community in the 1976 general election. Business leaders are very susceptible to accommodation with Democratic leaders. They realize the 2-1 majority Democrats have in numbers and evident national and local power.

President Carter has thus far played a shrewd and successful political hand in using Billy Carter, U.N. Ambassador Andrew Young, and Budget Director Bert Lance. Brother Billy keeps the blue-collar whites happy. Young's strident pro-black statements pacify the blacks. Lance's economic conservatism, until his resignation, served to satisfy the chamber of commerce crowd.

How Carter continues to perform is outside the control of southern Republicans. The Dixie GOP has a most formidable task aside from Carter's successful strategies. The problem is how to find more black votes and also more white votes. This will not be easy for several reasons.

First, most active southern Republicans are very conservative. By nature, they are not nearly as practical as necessary. Few blacks fit into this ideological mold. Nor do many blue-collar whites. Business and white-collar types are usually too practical to be ultraconservatives.

The southern party was "born again" in 1964 with the Goldwater presidential campaign. Its meager ranks were added to by conservative southern whites who saw an opportunity to win control of one of the two major political parties and ultimately a much stronger voice in national power. Generally, the leaders developed in 1964 at the local level continue in control today, especially in the rural areas. In the metropolitan areas, the leadership is more moderate conservative, but hardly ever moderate liberal or liberal.

The rural and small counties have equal representation on state GOP committees that run party affairs and policies between biennial state conventions. At the state conventions the representation is generally based on a more proportional representation of the population in the counties. Thus while the convention may be more moderate, the state committee is exercising power year-round while the convention establishes basic policy once every two years.

One answer to the problem of ultraconservative state committees would be reapportionment on a population basis. This would correct the over-representation problem that exists in favor of a rural county, such as my native county of Calhoun in South Carolina, and against my home county of Richland, which contains the state's capital city of Columbia. The population differential between Calhoun and Richland is 20-1. Yet the state committee representation is 1-1.

By South Carolina law the state political committees in all political parties are held to one vote for each county regardless of size. Since this constitutes state action and not just a purely political act by a political party, the landmark U.S. Supreme Court case of *Baker v. Carr* should apply. This historic case ordered reapportionment of state legislatures on a population basis. It does not apply to the Republican National Committee since there is no state action involved, only convention political action.

Some southern Republican leaders are so ideologically motivated they cannot be practical enough to either nominate a moderate conservative for public office or adapt to some moderate positions on issues in seeking mainstream votes. Some almost seem bent on losing rather than winning. These are dedicated ideologues who are earnestly concerned about free enterprise principles and the threat of Communist domination of the world. Some few are members of the John Birch Society. Others are influenced by the aggressiveness of their secret Birch friends. The Birch members are uncompromising and spend much of their time fighting moderate conservatives in their own party. The moderates are considered to be "expedient." The Birchers study the extremist Birch books ordered from their society president and founder, Robert Welch, at Birch headquarters in Belmont, Massachusetts. These Birch members exert an undue influence within the Republican party, particularly in the South.

By and large, these are well-meaning people who have pledged themselves to a free and conservative America. The problem is their acceptance, almost without question, of the impractical and inaccurate line produced by Welch.

I found when I was in the White House that the society depended primarily on one person, Reed Benson, for its liaison and information on Washington happenings. Birch members believed he was better informed than all the leading figures in Washington. Yet he actually had direct access to very little information other than published information and the few contacts he had on Capitol Hill and elsewhere in Washington.

Birchers are correct in their view of Soviet Communist aims to dominate the world by any means. However, they have drawn some wrong assumptions and conclusions, particularly about who are Communists and tools of communism. I have a loose-leaf book Welch autographed to me in 1961. It absurdly paints the late President Eisenhower as a Communist.

Welch takes a series of events and draws false conclusions based on a paranoia about one of America's most patriotic leaders ever.

People who know no compromise in the political game of give and take and who conclude people such as Eisenhower to be Communist cannot be very effective. They may even have a negative impact on their main goal of fighting communism—and indeed, the Birchers do. However, they work for their convictions while others are playing or sleeping. They fill vacuums in politics, and there are many. Thus their limited effectiveness comes in outworking their competitors.

There needs to be less Birch influence in the Republican party, but more grass-root work in turning out the vote, as the Birchers do. The secret society members need to be brought out in the open so their influence can be realized by their GOP associates and evaluated as such.

The ideological pap test requirement in both parties—liberal in the Democratic party and conservative in the Republican party—was addressed by the late President Kennedy in 1946 in his first campaign for office. He quoted the late presidential contender John W. Davis in speaking to a group of mostly Republicans:

> First, then make choice of your political party, on grounds that satisfy your reason if you can, by tradition or by environment or sentiment or impulse if you have not the wit to do better. In any event, make choice. Do not wait until you find an aggregation of demigods or angels; they are scarce—some people think they are

even scarcer than they used to be. Perhaps even you might not be comfortable in their midst. And do not expect to find a party that has always been right, or wise, or even consistent; that would be scarcer still. Independent judgment and opinion is a glorious thing, on no account to be surrendered by any man, but when one seeks companionship on a large scale he must be content to join with those who agree with him in most things and not to hope to find a company that will agree with him in all things.

The question of racism in the southern GOP is less of a problem. Most who are concerned with this point are active in other political splinter parties or organizations. The great majority of southern Republicans welcome black participation and black votes.

In the Goldwater days concern about racial integration was clearly a motivation. Today any opposition to black participation would be on the basis of political philosophy—the fear by some Republicans that the party may become more liberal by the influx of black and white moderates and liberals.

Being in a minority position throughout the South, too many active southern Republicans are intolerant of any deviations from party loyalty. Yet many southern Republicans are former rebels from the Democratic party ranks. They were repelled by liberalism and also party loyalty pressures.

In the South the average voter is antipartyism. Today, he proudly proclaims that he votes for the man—and some now say—or the woman—not the party. Thus demonstrations of party loyalty and partisan statements by party leaders usually serve to turn off the average southern voter.

Retired General William C. Westmoreland, the anti-Communist Vietnam War commander, was inundated in a South Carolina Republican primary in 1974. He was encouraged to seek the GOP gubernatorial nomination by polls showing him to be the party's only hope for a general election victory. However, he had no previous party loyalty and was an unwitting member of the Council on Foreign Relations, the organization considered by the Birch Society as a more dangerous enemy then the Communist party. He lost 15-1 in ultraconservative Charleston, which cast almost half the primary vote and which also was where he had chosen to make his retirement home. His primary opponent, Governor James B. Edwards, was popular in the Republican party and in Charleston.

I understand all these problems because I have been a party to most all these problems except for Birch membership. I rejected a membership invitation directly from Welch himself in 1963 when he was trying to convince Thurmond to join the society.

My views have mellowed as I have matured through years of political experiences. My basic philosophy is much the same—the desire to be free above the desire to be secure or equal. However, I have come to realize that many people do not share my confidence about facing and winning over life's many challenges and opportunities. Therefore, while less confident people like their freedom, they will accept infringements in exchange for government security. Or in many cases we may desire the best of both worlds— individual freedom and also individual security from want and fear.

This point was well made in the October 1977 issue of *Fortune* magazine in the second of three articles by Everett Carll Ladd Jr. of the University of Connecticut on the state of the U.S. political party system. Ladd sought to answer the mystifying question of why polls show conservatives predominate over liberals 2-1 in the country, yet the more liberal party, the Democrats, outnumber Republicans 2-1?

Ladd answers the political riddle this way (pages 214 and 215) (see also the illustration on pp. 292-293):

> As a result of public satisfaction with the New Deal state, the Democrats have emerged almost everywhere outside the presidential arena as the "Everyone party." The depiction is not intended literally, of course. Rather, it is meant to describe an essentially unprecedented situation in which one party shows more strength than its opposition across virtually the entire range of major social groupings. The Republicans do better among some groups than others, but almost no part of the populace regularly gives them pluralities.

> The Democrats are, for example, well ahead of the G.O.P. in every age group, from the youngest segment of the electorate to the oldest, and their margin is remarkably uniform. Wage workers are more Democratic than businessmen and executives, but a majority of even the latter now identify with the Democrats and vote for Democratic congressional candidates. All educational groups show a Democratic margin. So do all income levels, including the very prosperous. People who come from wealthy family backgrounds prefer the Democrats by a two-to-one margin. The Democrats lead the Republicans in every region, among all religious groupings, among virtually all ethnic groups.

> Perhaps most striking of all, the Democrats lead not only among voters who think of themselves as liberals and moderates, *but even*

among self-described conservatives. A majority of such conservatives voted for Democratic congressional candidates in 1976, and more of them identify with the Democrats than with the G.O.P.

But that isn't so surprising when you stop to consider that a majority of self-described conservatives—1970's style—strongly endorse the New Deal state. . . . overwhelming majorities of self- proclaimed conservativies want either to *increase* government spending in most of the principal policy arenas, or at least to *maintain* existing programs. There may indeed be a conservative majority "out there," as the Republican right has insisted from Taft to Goldwater to Reagan, but evidently one of the things these conservatives want to preserve the most is the New Deal state.

Nearly Everyone
Loves Big Government

The following pie charts show the remarkable breadth of public support for the New Deal tradition of government activism. Americans by overwhelming majorities want to increase or at least maintain present rates of public spending for just about everything. These data come from a 1976 national survey conducted by Gallup for Potomac Associates, a Washington, D.C.-based think tank. Respondents were instructed: "As I mention each program, tell me whether you think the amount of our tax money now being spent for that purpose should be increased, kept at the present level, reduced, or ended altogether." (Reproduced from *Fortune,* Oct., 1977)

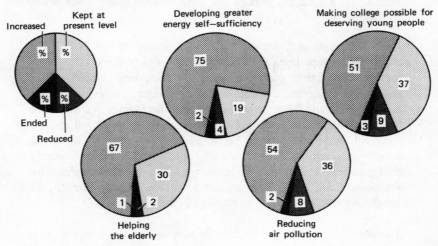

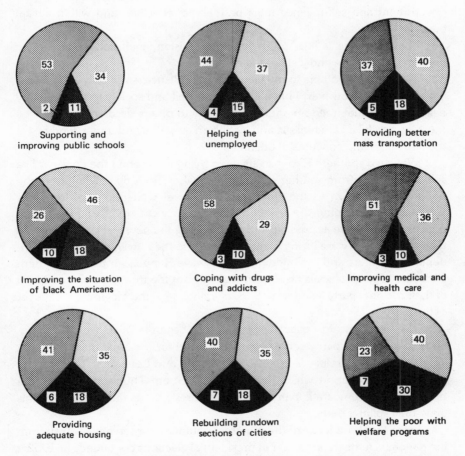

Supporting and improving public schools	Helping the unemployed	Providing better mass transportation
53, 34, 2, 11	44, 37, 4, 15	37, 40, 5, 18

Supporting and
improving public schools

Helping the
unemployed

Providing better
mass transportation

Improving the situation
of black Americans

Coping with drugs
and addicts

Improving medical and
health care

Providing
adequate housing

Rebuilding rundown
sections of cities

Helping the poor with
welfare programs

The rugged individualist wonders why others cannot make their own way in the world as he or she can. In recent years, I have come to understand that while God did create all people equally in His own sight, He did not necessarily bless all people equally with talents so they could all stand equally on their own feet.

My current view of government is that it must seek to guarantee equal opportunity for all without itself becoming oppressive in enforcing equal opportunity. The government must assist less fortunate people in a limited fashion—not to the point of encouraging indolence or to the point of creating undue burdens on the government and the rest of society.

Experience has taught me that the means of achieving my ideals of self-government and self-reliance must be realistic, effective, and within ethical bounds.

For me, there is little room for tunnel vision, inefficiency, or the rationalization that the end justifies the means.

To try to hold others to my views on self-reliance is not only impossible, but also unfair. However, I have a duty to myself and society to try to sell my belief in individual freedom and responsibility to others. In doing so, I will be more successful if I am realistic and exhibit an empathy and understanding for the disabilities and concerns of others.

While we southern Republicans were trying to preempt the conservative side of the road from southern Democrats in the 1960s by building from the national level down to the state and local level with drippings from our Goldwater philosophy, the southern Democrats were smart enough to appear as conservative as possible and yet integrate the new black bloc vote into their ranks. They were losing many adherents to the newly forming sea of independent voters and the budding conservative Republican party. Southern Democratic party officials first began reeling from the more liberal movement of their national party leaders in 1948, culminating in the McGovern takeover of the party in 1972.

The trend toward political independence began in 1948 when both national parties were perceived as being too liberal for the great majority of the voters in South Carolina, Alabama, Mississippi, and Louisiana. This was the presidential election in which then-Governor Strom Thurmond formed the State's Rights Democratic party and ran for president as the nominee of this once-only splinter party.

From that time forward the march of southern conservatives away from the national Democratic banner in presidential elections continued. In 1952 it was Citizens for Eisenhower in some states because some southern conservative leaders still could not bring themselves to use the name Republican. Eisenhower won a respectable southern electoral vote in 1952, carrying Texas, Florida, Tennessee, and Virginia.

In 1956 there was some disillusionment with Eisenhower. Several southern states fielded independent tickets, one with the reluctant Senator Harry Byrd Sr. of Virginia and another for ex-IRS Commissioner T. Coleman Andrews, also of Virginia. This time Eisenhower won more electoral votes in the South, showing there was more willingness to vote directly for the Republican label. For the first time, the Democratic presidential candidate fell below 50 percent in the South.

Then in 1960 the Kennedy-Nixon race left most southern conservatives with little alternative but to choose the Democratic or Republican label nationally. This time the southern vote almost split evenly. Even Thurmond, as a Democratic senator cast a secret Republican ballot in keeping with the style of the late Senator Byrd's practice of "golden silence" in presidential elections.

When the Goldwater candidacy emerged in 1964 there was by that time in place a new party skeleton structure being developed by economic conservatives. To this was added the old southern conservatives who came out in the open to vote and work for the Goldwater Republican candidacy. This brought the Thurmond switch to becoming a "Goldwater Republican."

After 1964 the "Goldwater" half of the label was dropped, and Thurmond and his followers became "Republicans."

The growth factor was more intense at the presidential level, and the differences in philosophy were minimal at the local level. Thus the southern GOP grew rapidly, but more as a presidential party.

As more blacks began voting from the late 1950s forward, the local Democratic leaders and officeholders became more liberal in their statements and actions. As this change occurred, Republicans met with more success in winning state and local elections. This was especially true in presidential election years or when a statewide powerhouse such as Thurmond would spread his coattails.

Some Democratic leaders, seeing the black vote as their answer to the new Republican challenges, began black voter registration efforts and the black vote turnout programs. One key lesson they preached to blacks was to vote for the "Big D." If it were a paper ballot, just mark an "X" in the block by the party column that said Democrat and thus vote a straight-party ballot. If a voting machine were used, the blacks were told to pull the Democratic master lever and vote the straight ticket. This would minimize the potential of ballots being voided because of voting mistakes. It would also insure the salvation of local Democratic officeholders threatened by their first general election competition.

In South Carolina the local Republican candidates benefited from the pull at the top of the ticket in presidential and/or Thurmond elections. So the Democrats would put the statewide offices on one line to let those favoring national Republican candidates to vote Republican and then a straight or mixed ballot for local offices. However, in 1976, the Democrats, with Carter at the top, had South Carolina offices, national and local, all on one line to encourage the straight-party voting with one stroke of the pencil or one pull of the master lever.

Master-lever voting is clearly a problem for the southern Republicans. Since Democrats control all the state legislatures in the South, the Republicans have little hope that the Democrats will give up their master-lever advantage. This is especially so when they believe they have built a new coalition of the black and blue-collar voters, both of which can be expected to use the master lever substantially.

The agruments in favor of outlawing the master-lever voting are most compelling and democratic. Selection of candidates in each race insures a more informed vote and more directly represents the will of the people.

Thus Republicans must hammer away at the undemocratic nature of this pro-Democratic device. If continued, it will maintain Democratic strength in state and local offices and serve to liberalize the records of the officeholders in reaction to the master- lever constituency.

President Carter has proposed four laws that could increase Democratic voting power in elections—North and South. The first is the instant voter registration plan. Its progress has been slowed because of vote fraud expectations and public opinion polls and Capitol Hill comments. The easier it is to vote, the more the lower socioeconomic population will participate and more likely vote Democratic, as in the past.

Public financing of congressional elections, another Carter proposal, will tend to benefit Democratic candidates. So will his idea to liberalize Hatch Act restrictions on federal bureaucrats. The government employee vote is substantially Democratic.

The Carter plan to grant citizenship status—and thus voting rights—to approximately six million illegal aliens in the United States would likewise be a boon to Democratic voter totals. They also may be expected to vote largely Democratic.

Unfortunately for Republican candidates, all these proposals will serve to further dilute GOP electoral strength. Because Republicans generally support the concept of limited government, the party is cast in the light of being negative, anti-people, against progress, and pro-rich. The Democrats try to pit the "have-nots," versus the "haves," the poor versus the rich; race against race, and class against class. McGovern tried this in 1972. However, his campaign backfired against Nixon's moderate conservative and propatriotic positions. Primarily, McGovern's national security and foreign policy stands made him appear almost unpatriotic. He was painted far left, just as Goldwater was cast as far right in 1964. What the people showed in 1964 and 1972 was that they will buy neither extreme—far right nor far left. Carter realized this. He wisely began his campaign as an anti-Washington conservative and then, shifted, with his "good ole southern boy" image intact, to the usual liberal Democratic positions. However, he hedged enough on the Democratic platform to preserve an impression of being a moderate. Thus he averted the extremist image created by McGovern.

At the same time, Carter adroitly pitted the people who consider themselves the "have-nots" against those considered to be the "haves." Ford and the Republicans were pictured as the servants of the rich and privileged, while Carter and the Democrats were projected as the friends—moderately so—of the average man and woman and all who believe they do not have enough of this country's bounty.

Despite Carter's appeal to many whites, the potential for growth among white voters is good for the southern GOP. Many blue- and white-collar white voters have become accustomed to splitting their tickets and voting for Republican presidential and congressional candidates.

Carter's pollster, Pat Caddell, has expressed major concern over another area of potential growth for the Grand Old Party. This is the better-educated portion of the electorate. In his postelection memo to Carter on how to run the government for purposes of winning reelection in 1980, Caddell wrote:

> . . . this group (better educated, white-collar people) is growing so large that simply doing slightly better than the past (speaking of Carter's showing in 1976 over previous Democratic candidates) is not sufficient to guarantee election. If there is a "future" in politics, it is in this massive demographic change. We now have almost half the voting population with some college education, a growing percentage of white-collar workers, and an essentially "middle-class" electorate.

GOP appeals to this group of voters must follow a strategy carefully designed to reflect reason, tolerance and maturity. Simplistic slogans and answers to the major questions will not suffice. Extremism will forfeit the opportunities available here. Winning 55 to 60 percent of the middle-class vote as it continues to grow can be the ultimate salvation for the Republican party.

Unfortunately, the image of the Republican party has become one of "not caring," as put by House Republican leader John Rhodes of Arizona in his book *The Futile System*. Rhodes is a moderate conservative who realizes that people form perceptions and that parties project images. And the Republican image and public perception Republicans must confront is that Republicans are not compassionate—that they do not care about people and their problems. This false impression is far more prevalent than it is true. Republicans especially care about the freedoms of people. But evidently, the materialist concerns appear to be of more concern to others.

Following the 1976 election, Jerry terHorst, the syndicated columnist of the *Detroit Daily News*, wrote a commentary on the GOP image problem:

> Other Republicans talk bravely of broadening the base of the party. Such Republicans, including many who are economic conservatives, rightly perceive that the majority of Americans are middle-roaders and that elections are won by whatever party, Democratic or Republican, that stays in the mainstream.
>
> But broadening the base will never come to the Republican party until it proves to the voters that it is capable of enlarging its heart.
>
> The Republican party must twin its concern for economic conservatism with a concern for equal rights, civil rights, women's rights—yes, even blue-collar rights to a decent job at a decent wage in a decent place.
>
> That's fine, somebody says, but Republicans can't outshout the Democrats in spending money on such things. Well, money isn't everything, especially when it's in short supply. Jimmy Carter understands that, which is why he will proceed more cautiously than a lot of Democrats would like. And voters understand it too. Poor families, after all, can be more caring than the rich.
>
> It is concern and compassion that we are talking about, not cold cash. And it is in this capacity that the Republican party has been weighed and found wanting.
>
> Show me a Republican, conservative or progressive, who demonstrates that he truly cares about the little guy, white and black, in the big city or on the farm, and I'll show you a Republican who can get elected.

May their tribe increase.

Even conservative columnist James J. Kilpatrick appealed for reason among Republican rightists in a February 17, 1977, column (The State, Columbia, South Carolina).

> You wonder, sometimes, if the conservatives really want to win, truly want to organize a government and govern. I don't know.
>
> I do know this: whether they work within the Republican party or seek to establish their own party, the conservative activists will have to develop a tolerance for dissent, a willingness to reach out, an acceptance of political realities. Until they appeal to a broad range of fallible human beings, they will stay in exterior darkness. And speaking simply as one true believer, I am getting awfully tired of the cold.

To accomplish what terHorst and Kilpatrick are advocating does not require a "me-too" GOP. Much can be done by projecting a more reasoned and realistic approach to politics and government. That is, Republicans can show a willingness to offer alternative programs that have the private and public sectors working together to solve people's problems. For instance, the best antidote to the threat of union control is for enlightened management to meet the needs of their workers without having unions force management's hand. The way to avoid government dictation on civil rights for all segments of the population is to insure there is truly an equal opportunity for all Americans.

In addition to a strong program to better organize the party at the grassroots level, Republican National Chairman William Brock of Tennessee has offered Republicans a new direction. He proposes to meet the needs of the average American of all races without bankrupting America or centralizing too much power in Washington. This is the challenge the Republican party faces today—compassionate conservatism through realistic policies or unbridled socialism through Democratic successes. The public generally wants and will support national leaders who can meet basic human needs and desires and yet maintain a government of limited powers.

The majority of Americans expect compassionate concern about jobs, personal and family security through stability in employment, reasonable opportunity for education of their children, home ownership, health care, and a "piece of the action"—as Nixon proposed—in the free enterprise system.

They also desire—first of all—peace, but peace in freedom, not in subjugation—that is, realistic foreign policy and national security positions which recognize basic human rights and enough military deterrent power to insure individual freedom at home.

Brock is one of the most effective pioneers of the Republican revival in Dixie, as is another Tennessee Republican with national prominence and influence, Senate minority leader Howard Baker. They are both moderate conservative Republican leaders who understand the path to GOP success lies in the direction of realistic and compassionate policy positions which recognize that human desires include personal and family security concerns, together with personal freedoms.

Brock's aim is to develop through research, study, and discussion policy proposals that will change the unfavorable Republican image of selfishness expounded by Democratic leaders who have demonstrated their generous hearts by giving away not their wealth but the public treasury of today and tomorrow.

If he can lead the influential party powers, such as Ford, Reagan, and Connally to give united support to such an approach, then there is considerable hope for the party and the two-party system. The prime determinant of this outcome is Reagan, who is beginning to show positive signs of moderation.

The Caddell picture of a Republican party "in deep trouble," with a "restrictive" ideology, with a bent for "self-destruction" is true today. However, the same was true of the Democratic party in 1972. And a wise and moderate national chairman, Robert Strauss of Texas, led the Democrats out of the wilderness of extremism to a successful recovery.

In politics, there is no substitute for a sense of realism—perceiving a situation or problem as it is and addressing the problem with reasoned approaches and solutions.

The greatest lesson in modern politics about the costs inherent in rose-colored perceptions or ostrich (head in the sand) reactions to unpleasant situations can be found in the Nixon administration's handling of the Watergate revelations. This utter lack of realism can most be attributed to Haldeman's usual tunnel vision affliction. Subsequently Nixon, the most realistic person I have ever known, evidently lost all sense of reality in failing to face up to the facts of Watergate while trapped in his White House bunker under media and Democratic seige.

The Bert Lance affair is another bad example of unrealistic reactions to unpleasant events. Supposedly, President Carter and everyone else had learned the lessons of Watergate from the sad Nixon administration performances and resultant punishments. Yet Carter, Lance, and their White House comrades committed the same misjudgments as the Nixon crowd on a lesser scale. Friendships and cover-ups were at the root of the faulty decisions in both the Watergate and Lance affairs, from the first revelation to the last.

In addition to the adoption of this pragmatic middle course for the Republican party, the party leaders and members must intensify efforts to merchandise the basic values of a system of government rooted in individual freedom and individual responsibility. The public needs to better understand how a free system provides not only more freedom of thought, choice, and actions, but also translates into more material goods and comforts for all people as demonstrated by the American standard of living compared to the remainder of the world.

An educational program aimed at the youth and the working people is vital in the battle to keep our country from following the mother country in its steady descent to becoming "Little" Britain with minimal influence on world affairs and maximum attention to robotizing its citizens, industries, and institutions in the once most powerful empire of its day.

Republicans predominate in the business and professional life of America and likewise with material resources. Thus the means to cultivate these fertile and open young minds—also the masses of middle Americans—are available. Instead, the basic means of communications and education is tilted toward a more socialist approach to government. To this point, the forces bent on emphasizing equality or security over freedom are in the ascendancy because they are in control of the vital areas of influence. The average American is more convinced today that big government is his Santa Claus rather than the absorber of his freedoms. He needs to better understand, as President Ford emphasized, that a government big enough to give you anything you want can take or control everything you have, including your freedom.

This is the crux of the problem for the Republican party—how to contain the socialist tide with realistic answers to human concerns while re-educating Americans on the "Blessings of Liberty" embodied in our "R"epublican form of government.

Cracking this "political nut" will not be easy for a party whose basic shock troops are rugged individualists who resist the calls to compromise. Yet the nut must be cracked if the Republican party is to rebound in the South and across the country—and it cannot rebound without southern success.

Realism and compassion in pursuit of freedom is not only a political ideal for Republican partisans, but it is also an imperative for Republican survival and the hope for the maintenance of the libertarian concept of government.

I am both hopeful and optimistic about the outcome, despite the canny course Carter and Caddell have set for a Democratic southern strategy designed to return Dixie to a one-party system and thus lead the nation to a new era of Carter-style benevolent democratism. Carter may well have serious problems surviving in the 1980 Democratic convention. The same type convention split which doomed Ford in 1976 could open the door to the recapture of Dixie in 1980 by the Republican Party, especially if Carter is dumped, and the reinstallation of the day of the Elephant at 1600 Pennsylvania Avenue.

To paraphrase Mark Twain, the reports of the passing of the Grand Old Party are greatly exaggerated despite her current image ailments.

Name Index

303